CONFEDERATION OF TOURISM AND HOSPITALITY

Front Office Operations

Study Guide

THIS STUDY GUIDE

BPP Learning Media is the **official publisher** for the CTH Diplomas in Hotel Management and Tourism Management.

IN THIS JULY 2009 FIRST EDITION

- The CTH 2009 syllabus, cross-referenced to the chapters
- Comprehensive syllabus coverage, reviewed and approved by CTH
- Plenty of activities, examples and discussion topics to demonstrate and practise technique
- Full index
- A full CTH past exam for exam practice

LEARNING MEDIA

First edition July 2009

ISBN 9780 7517 7795 6

British Library Cataloguing-in-Publication Data
A catalogue record for this book
is available from the British Library

Published by

BPP Learning Media Ltd
BPP House, Aldine Place
London W12 8AA

www.bpp.com/learningmedia

Printed in the United Kingdom

Your learning materials, published by BPP Learning
Media Ltd, are printed on paper sourced from
sustainable, managed forests.

We are grateful to the Confederation of Tourism and
Hospitality for permission to reproduce the syllabus and
past examination questions and answers.

©
BPP Learning Media
2009

CONTENTS

How to use this study guide

This is the first edition of BPP Learning Media's ground-breaking study guide for the *Front Office Operations* paper of the CTH Diploma in Hotel Management. It has been specifically written to cover the Syllabus, and has been fully reviewed by CTH.

To pass the examination you need a thorough understanding in all areas covered by the syllabus.

Recommended approach

(a)   To pass you need to be able to answer questions on **everything** specified by the syllabus. Read the study guide very carefully and do not skip any of it.

(b)   Learning is an **active** process. Do **all** the activities as you work through the study guide so you can be sure you really understand what you have read.

(c)   After you have covered the material in the study guide, work through the questions in the practice exam at the back.

(d)   Before you take the real exam, check that you still remember the material using the following quick revision plan.

   (i)   Read through the chapter learning objectives. Are there any gaps in your knowledge? If so, study the section again.

   (ii)   Read and learn the key terms.

   (iii)   Read and try to memorise the summary at the end of each chapter.

   (iv)   Do the self-test questions again. If you know what you're doing, they shouldn't take long.

This approach is only a suggestion. You or your college may well adapt it to suit your needs.

Remember this is a **practical** course.

(a)   Try to relate the material to your experience in the workplace or any other work experience you may have had.

(b)   Try to make as many links as you can to other CTH papers that you may be studying at the moment.

Help yourself study for your CTH exams

Exams for professional bodies such as CTH are very different from those you may have taken at school or college. You will be under **greater time pressure** before the exam – as you may be combining your study with work. There are many different ways of learning and so the BPP Learning Media study guide offers you a number of different tools to help you through. Here are some hints and tips: they are not plucked out of the air, but **based on research and experience**. (You don't need to know that long-term memory is in the same part of the brain as emotions and feelings - but it's a fact anyway.)

The right approach

1   **The right attitude**

   Believe in yourself

   Yes, there is a lot to learn. Yes, it is a challenge. But thousands have succeeded before and you can too.

   Remember why you're doing it

   Studying might seem a grind at times, but you are doing it for a reason: to advance your career.

2   **The right focus**

Read through the Syllabus and the chapter objectives

These tell you what you are expected to know.

Study the Exam Paper section

It helps to be familiar with the structure of the exam that you are going to take.

3   **The right method**

The whole picture

You need to grasp the detail - but keeping in mind how everything fits into the whole picture will help you understand better.

- The **objectives and topic list** of each chapter put the material in context.

- The **syllabus content** shows you what you need to **grasp**.

In your own words

To absorb the information (and to practise your written communication skills), it helps to **put it into your own words**.

- **Take notes.**

- Answer the **questions** in each chapter. You will practise your written communication skills, which become increasingly important as you progress through your CTH exams.

- Draw **mindmaps**. The chapter summaries can be a good starting point for this.

- Try **'teaching' a subject** to a colleague or friend.

Give yourself cues to jog your memory

The BPP study guide uses **bold** to **highlight key points**.

- Try **colour coding** with a highlighter pen.
- Write **key points** on cards.

4   **The right review**

Review, review, review

It is a **fact** that regularly reviewing a topic in summary form can **fix it in your memory**. Because **review** is so important, the BPP study guide helps you to do so in many ways.

- **Chapter summaries** draw together the key points in each chapter. Use them to recap each study session.

- The **self-test questions** are another review technique you can use to ensure that you have grasped the essentials.

- Go through the **examples and illustrations** in each chapter a second or third time.

Developing your personal Study Plan

BPP's **Learning to Learn Accountancy** book (which can be successfully used by students studying for any professional qualification) emphasises the need to prepare (and use) a study plan. Planning and sticking to the plan are key elements of learning success.

There are four steps you should work through.

STEP 1   How do you learn?

First you need to be aware of your style of learning. The BPP Learning Media **Learning to Learn Accountancy** book commits a chapter to this **self-discovery**. What types of intelligence do you display when learning? You might be advised to brush up on certain study skills before launching into this study guide.

BPP Learning Media's **Learning to Learn Accountancy** book helps you to identify what intelligences you show more strongly and then details how you can tailor your study process to your preferences. It also includes handy hints on how to develop intelligences you exhibit less strongly, but which might be needed as you study for your professional qualification.

Are you a **theorist** or are you more **practical**? If you would rather get to grips with a theory before trying to apply it in practice, you should follow the study sequence on page (vii). If the reverse is true (you like to know why you are learning theory before you do so), you might be advised to flick through study guide chapters and look at examples, case studies and questions (Steps 8, 9 and 10 in the **suggested study sequence**) before reading through the detailed theory.

STEP 2   How much time do you have?

Work out the time you have available per week, given the following.

- The standard you have set yourself
- The time you need to set aside later for revision work
- The other exam(s) you are sitting
- Very importantly, practical matters such as work, travel, exercise, sleep and social life

	Hours
Note your time available each week in box A. A	

STEP 3   Allocate your time

- Take the time you have available per week for this Study Text shown in box A, multiply it by the number of weeks available and insert the result in box B.   B | |

- Divide the figure in box B by the number of chapters in this text and insert the result in box C.   C | |

Remember that this is only a rough guide. Some of the chapters in this book are longer and more complicated than others, and you will find some subjects easier to understand than others.

STEP 4   Implement

Set about studying each chapter in the time shown in box C, following the key study steps in the order suggested by your particular learning style.

This is your personal **Study Plan**. You should try and combine it with the study sequence outlined below. You may want to modify the sequence a little (as has been suggested above) to adapt it to your **personal style**.

BPP Learning Media's **Learning to Learn Accountancy** gives further guidance on developing a study plan, and deciding where and when to study.

Suggested study sequence

It is likely that the best way to approach this study guide is to tackle the chapters in the order in which you find them. Taking into account your individual learning style, you could follow this sequence.

Key study steps	Activity
Step 1 **Topic list**	Look at the topic list at the start of each chapter. Each topic represents a section in the chapter.
Step 2 **Explanations**	Proceed methodically through the chapter, reading each section thoroughly and making sure you understand.
Step 3 **Definitions**	Definitions can often earn you *easy marks* if you state them clearly and correctly in an appropriate exam answer
Step 4 **Note taking**	Take brief notes, if you wish. Avoid the temptation to copy out too much. Remember that being able to put something into your own words is a sign of being able to understand it. If you find you cannot explain something you have read, read it again before you make the notes.
Step 5 **Examples**	Follow each through to its solution very carefully.
Step 6 **Discussion topics**	Study each one, and try to add flesh to them from your own experience. They are designed to show how the topics you are studying come alive (and often come unstuck) in the real world.
Step 7 **Activities**	Make a very good attempt at each one.
Step 8 **Answers**	Check yours against ours, and make sure you understand any discrepancies.
Step 9 **Chapter summary**	Work through it carefully, to make sure you have grasped the significance of all the key areas.
Step 10 **Self test questions**	When you are happy that you have covered the chapter, use the self-test questions to check how much you have remembered of the topics covered and to practise questions in a variety of formats.
Step 11 **Question practice**	Either at this point, or later when you are thinking about revising, make a full attempt at the practice exam.

Moving on...

However you study, when you are ready to start your revision, you should still refer back to this study guide, both as a source of **reference** (you should find the index particularly helpful for this) and as a way to **review** (the chapter summaries and self-test questions help you here).

And remember to keep careful hold of this study guide – you will find it invaluable in your work.

More advice on study skills can be found in BPP Learning Media's **Learning to Learn Accountancy book.**

Syllabus

CONFEDERATION OF TOURISM & HOSPITALITY

DIPLOMA IN HOTEL MANAGEMENT
MODULE SYLLABUS

DHM 122: Front Office Operations

Description

This module introduces students to the systems and procedures required for Front Office Operations. It provides an overview of the functions and supervisory aspects of the front office department. Students will develop knowledge and skills in departmental procedures as well as understanding the key legislation.

Summary of Learning Outcomes

On completion of this module the students will be able to;

- Demonstrate knowledge of the functional areas of the front office

- Describe the function and activities of the reservations, reception and cashiers departments

- Analyse guest accounting processes

- Review the use of yield management, statistics and reports within the front office operation

- Explain the importance of security and safety within rooms division including key legislation for reception operations

- Describe the key features of the communication services available to guests

- Explain the role front office plays in selling hotel services and facilities.

Syllabus		Chapter
Introduction to front office operations	The organisation structure of rooms division. Front of house departments; reception, advance reservations, cashiering, guest relations, switchboard, concierge, portering. Roles and responsibilities of front of house staff. The guest cycle. Property management systems. Liaison with other departments.	1
Reservation procedures	Recording reservations – the information needed when receiving a request. Manual methods used to record bookings – diaries, conventional charts, density charts. Electronic booking systems which provide hardware and software and support point-of-sale systems. Guaranteeing reservations, advance deposits and pre-payments. International terms for rooms and bed types. Packages offered by hotels. Room allocation (covered in Chapter 3). Confirmation procedures, deposits and guaranteed arrivals. Reservation status, release times. Cancellation procedures. Handling corporate and group reservations. Booking bedrooms for conference and banqueting events.	2

CONFEDERATION OF TOURISM & HOSPITALITY

Syllabus		Chapter
Check-in procedures	Procedures for receiving and checking in guests. Manual and electronic room status systems. Chance arrivals. Group check in. Non-arrivals. Walking a guest. VIP and guests with special requirements. Wake up calls and papers.	3
Check-out procedures	Posting charges. Preparing and presenting guest bills. Payment procedures, accepting different methods of payment. Express check-out. Recording deposits and prepayments. Processing visitors paid outs (VPO's), disbursements, petty cash. Foreign currency exchange. Safe handling of cash and other forms of payment.	4
Guest accounting	Front office accounting systems. Machine billing, computer billing. Banking procedures including documentation. Bank reconciliation. Administering floats. Night audit. Ledger accounts. Operational reports (covered in Chapter 6). Establishing credit worthiness and credit control.	5
Yield management, statistics and reports	Control and manage levels of bookings and reservations. Forecasting and statistical data including length of stay, origin, average expenditure, source of bookings. Maximising occupancy and room revenue. Occupancy rates, average room rate, revenue achieved, REVPAR and GOPPAR. Arrivals list. Departures list. Room list. Function list. Guest history records.	6
Security and safety responsibilities	Security aspects of the hotel. The Data Protection Act and the duty to protect guest's personal information. Manual and electronic keys. Managing safety deposit boxes. Individual room safes.	7
Guest services & communications	Managing the switchboard. Handling incoming and outgoing mail. Communication systems. Guest business centre. Guest internet access and electronic mail. Multi-lingual staff.	8
Selling methods used by front office staff	Skills and techniques required when selling the facilities and services within the hotel. Benefits to organisation, increased occupancy, customer loyalty, new business. Staff training. Selling techniques, product knowledge, up-selling, selling other services, using sales leads, repeat sales, referred sales. Paying commission.	9

Assessment

This module will be assessed via a 2 ½ hour examination, set and marked by CTH. The examination will cover the whole of the assessment criteria in this unit and will take the form of 10 x 2 mark questions and 5 x 4 mark questions in section A (40 marks). Section B will comprise of 5 x 20 mark questions of which candidates must select and answer three (60 marks). CTH is a London based awarding body and the syllabus content will in general reflect this. Any legislation and codes of practice will reflect the international nature of the industry and will not be country specific. International centres may find it advantageous to add local legislation or practice to their teaching but they should be aware that the CTH examination will not assess this local knowledge.

Further guidance

Recommended contact hours: 45   **Credits: 10**

Delivery Strategies

This module covers the theory of Front Office Operations but wherever possible this should be related to practical situations to reflect the nature of the commercial work environment. Visits to a range of hotels and businesses that operate a front office are essential to allow students to see the application of the theory into practice. Visiting speakers would also be beneficial. Industry representatives such as Front Office Managers, Rooms Division Managers and employees of Front Office will all assist in contextualising the classroom based learning.

Recommended Prior Learning

There is no required prior learning however students must have completed formal education to 18 years old or equivalent and an interest in Front Office Operations and Customer service is essential.

Resources

Learners need access to library and research facilities which should include some or all of the following;

Key Text

- *Front Office Operations*, CTH Study Guide (2009), BPP Learning Media, ISBN 9780 7517 7795 6

Key Supporting Texts

- Abbott, P., & Lewry, S., (1999), *Front Office Procedures, Social Skills and Management*, Butterworth Heinneman, ISBN 0750642300

- Baker, S., Bradley, P., & Huyton, J., (2000), *Principles of Front Office Operations*, Cassell, ISBN 0826447090

- Boella, M., & Pannett, A., (2000), *Principles of Hospitality Law,* Cassell, ISBN 0826452736

- Braham, B., (1999), *Hotel Front Office,* S. Thornes, ISBN 0748716327

- Dix, C., & Baird C., (1998) *Front Office Operations,* Longman, ISBN 0-582-31931-5

- Bowie, D., & Buttle, F., (2004), *Hospitality Marketing,* Butterworth Heinneman, ISBN 0750652454

Magazines and Journals

- The Caterer and Hotelkeeper
- Hospitality
- Voice of the BHA

CONFEDERATION OF TOURISM & HOSPITALITY

Websites

www.bha-online.co.uk	British Hospitality Association
www.caterer.com	Caterer and Hotelkeeper
www.instituteofhospitality.org	The Institute of Hospitality
www.hospitalitynet.org	Hospitality Net
www.htf.org.uk	Hospitality Training Foundation
www.ico.gov.uk	Office of the Data Protection Registrar
www.instituteofcustomerservice.com	Institute of Customer Service (ICS)

Notes on recommended texts

This module should be based on the syllabus and the supporting BPP Learning Media CTH Study Guide. The lecturer's lesson plans should be based on the module syllabus and supported by the BPP Learning Media CTH Study Guide for the subject.

Lecturers may also use other relevant texts and supplementary material familiar to the lecturer and based on the lecturer's experience. It is not essential to use all the recommended texts and lecturers should use their experience to decide which ones are most appropriate for their students. Where available and appropriate, past module examinations are available to support lecturers.

CTH will always answer any questions from the centre's Head of Department either by email or by phone.

The exam paper

All the CTH examinations for the Diploma in Hotel Management and Diploma in Tourism Management follow the same format.

Exam duration: 2½ hours

Section A:		Marks
10	2 mark questions	20
5	4 mark questions	20
		40

All questions in Section A are compulsory

Section B:		
5	20 mark questions (candidates must choose 3)	60
		100

Other titles in this series

BPP Learning Media publishes the following titles for the CTH Diploma in Hotel Management

- Food and Beverage Operations
- Food Hygiene, Health and Safety
- Front Office Operations
- Housekeeping and Accommodation Operations
- Finance for Tourism and Hospitality *
- Introduction to Business Operations*
- Marketing*
- The Tourism Industry*
- The Global Hospitality Industry

*These titles are also papers within the CTH Diploma in Tourism Management qualification.

In July 2010 BPP Learning Media will publish the remaining titles for the Diploma in Tourism Management:

- Travel Geography
- Travel Agency and Tour Guide Operations
- Introduction to Tourism Economics
- Special Interest Tourism
- Destination Analysis

CHAPTER 1

INTRODUCTION TO FRONT OFFICE OPERATIONS

Chapter objectives

In this chapter you will learn

- The importance of effective front office operations
- The organisation structure of front office operations
- The roles and responsibilities of front-of-house departments and staff
- An overview of the guest cycle: pre-arrival, arrival, occupancy and departure
- The role of property or hotel management systems
- How front-of-house departments liaise and communicate with other departments in the hotel
- How hotels and other accommodation providers differ, in such a way as to require different procedures and systems

Topic list

Front office operations
Front of house organisation
Roles and responsibilities of front of house staff
The guest cycle
Liaising with other departments
Property management systems
Different types of hotels

1 Front office operations

1.1 What is the 'front office'?

When people decide that they want, or might want, to stay in a hotel, they may:

- Check out the hotel's , and e-mail the reservations department to ask about room rates and availability

- **Telephone** the hotel office or **switchboard** and ask to speak to someone (perhaps in the reservations department) about room rates and availability, the facilities and location of the hotel and other information that will help them make the decision to book

- **Walk in** off the street and approach the front desk to ask about room rates and availability (and perhaps test out the friendliness and general 'look' of the hotel).

Someone will give the prospective guest the **information** (s)he requires to make a decision, and may then take a **booking** for a certain type of room for a given number of nights. There may be some follow-up **correspondence** to confirm the booking, give extra information (such as maps on how to get to the hotel) or make adjustments to the booking as the guest's plans change.

When the guest arrives, (s)he will go to a **reception desk** to register, be allocated a room and receive a room key – perhaps along with information about the facilities and services of the hotel. There may be a **porter** to help the guest with **luggage** and/or to show the guest to the room.

During the guest's stay, (s)he may **return periodically** to the reception area for a number of reasons: to collect messages, to leave and pick up keys, to ask for information, to make a complaint or to get problems solved. (Perhaps the air-conditioning isn't working, or more towels are required. Perhaps the room isn't to the guest's satisfaction for some reason.) The hotel may offer additional **guest services**, such as currency exchange facilities; or use of an in-house office facility, restaurant or spa; or an information and reservation/ticketing service for local attractions and activities. Guests will often access

Photo: www.lda.gov.uk

these services by ringing the hotel switchboard, or approaching the front desk.

At the end of a stay, a guest will generally return to reception to hand in the room key and receive and **settle the bill**: help may be required with luggage or onward transport. Even after (s)he has departed, the hotel office will keep the guest's registration details on file for a specified period – in case of queries – and may also use guest contact details to '**stay in touch**' (perhaps with a feedback form, newsletter or special offers), so that the traveller will think of the hotel next time (s)he requires accommodation in the area.

All these important customer contacts, which shape the total experience a guest has of the hotel from first impression onwards, are the job of the 'front office', or what used to be called the '**reception**' of the hotel.

DEFINITION

Front office is the term now often used in hotels to refer to the customer-facing departments dealing with reservations, reception, room allocation, guest information, billing and payments. Strictly speaking, it should only cover staff in direct help-desk contact with guests, with supporting administrative sections known as the 'back office', but the term is now generally used to cover the whole range of 'front of house' activities.

BPP
LEARNING MEDIA

In a small hotel, front office functions may be carried out by a single person at a reception area or front desk: answering the switchboard, taking bookings, welcoming and registering guests, billing and processing payments and so on. In a large hotel, there may be separate departments dividing these responsibilities, including:

- **Switchboard**: taking and routing telephone calls

- **Reservations**: taking bookings

- **Reception (or front desk)**: welcoming and registering guests at the main reception desk

- **Concierge/enquiries**: answering guests' and visitors' questions; handling mail and guest keys; perhaps also handling car hire, tour bookings and entertainment tickets for guests

- **Billing office**: preparing guests' accounts and bills

- **Cashier**: receiving guests' payments and processing other financial transactions (such as foreign currency exchange)

- **Guest relations**: handling guests' problems and complaints, and dealing with VIP guests and guests with special needs

- **Uniformed staff:** luggage porters, lift attendants, doormen, cloakroom attendants, garage attendants or valet parking etc

We will look at the roles and responsibilities of each of these units or departments in more detail later in the chapter.

FOR DISCUSSION

Before you read on, why do you think front office roles are **important** for the functioning and success of a hotel?

1.2 Why are front of house activities important?

Front of house activities are important for several reasons, as you may gather from our rough sketch of their scope.

- Front office may be the **first contact** a guest or prospective guest has with the hotel – whether in writing, by telephone or in person – and is, therefore, the source of crucial **first impressions**, which may:

    - **Help people decide** to whether to choose the hotel (or not!) – winning or losing a prospective customer;

- **Influence** everything else they think about the hotel. Due to what psychologists call the **'halo effect'**, a good first impression may predispose guests to think well of their rooms, the service they are given during their stay and so on. A bad first impression may put them on the alert for other bad 'signals', and incline them to find fault with everything else.

- Front office is the '**service hub**' of the hotel: the area where most guest contacts and transactions take place throughout their stay. Guests' experience of 'hotel service' is, therefore, mainly shaped by front office personnel and procedures. This is important because the quality and style of service is a major factor in:

  - Providing an enjoyable, relaxing, satisfying experience for guests – which is, after all, the hotel's *raison d'être*;

  - Helping the hotel 'stand out' from its competitors, which may have similar rooms and facilities;

  - Ensuring that guests will want to return again – and meanwhile, will give a positive report of the hotel, or recommend it, to other people. Hotels rely on this positive **word of mouth** promotion, and definitely *don't* want guests spreading *negative* reports, especially since the Internet allows them to tell *thousands* of other travellers (in online hotel review sites or travel 'blogs') when they've had a good – or bad – experience.

- Front office has a special responsibility for dealing with guests' **problems and complaints**: the 'critical incidents' which can make all the difference between satisfaction and dissatisfaction.

- Front office is the **communications hub** of the hotel, through which information is exchanged by and with all other departments of the hotel. If reception fails to tell housekeeping to make a room ready for arriving guests; or fails to relay a guest complaint about faulty air conditioning to the maintenance department; or fails to make a booking in the hotel restaurant for the guest – the system breaks down, and the guest is not served. Likewise, if reception fails to heed housekeeping's warning that a room needs repair or redecoration; or fails to add a dinner charge, sent through from the restaurant, to the guest's bill – the system fails.

- Front office is the **administrative hub** of the hotel, where reservations are logged, room allocations are planned, room status is monitored, guest bills are prepared, payments are processed, records are kept, information displays are maintained; and so on. If all these tasks aren't carried out efficiently, the hotel would simply cease to function.

Throughout this Study Guide, we'll be talking about procedures and systems, documents and information flows. But never forget: front office is also the '**face**' of the hotel to guests and visitors. It shapes the whole 'personality' or 'style' of the hotel. Guests coming to a hotel don't just buy a bed for the night: they buy a welcome – hospitality. And it is front office staff who make that crucial difference.

ACTIVITY 1   30 minutes

If you have acces to the Internet, log on to the hotel/destination review site: Trip Advisor.

Link: http://www.tripadvisor.com

Browse through some of the reviews left by travellers about different hotels. Make some notes about the factors that cause hotels to be positive and negatively reviewed – taking particular notice of the comments about customer service. (How important is it for guests to be 'made welcome', or for their questions and complaints to be 'well handled'?) Also note any differences between the factors positively and negatively reviewed by leisure, single, family and business travellers.

What are the implications of your findings for front office staff?

2   Front of house organisation

Front office is, as you should be aware from other modules in your studies, only one of the departments within a hotel (or other accommodation provider).

2.1   Organisation structure

A typical structure for a **small** hotel offering both accommodation and catering might be as shown in Figure 1.1. Staff members are likely to carry out a variety of tasks within their general area: the restaurant staff, for example, will also deliver room service and serve tea and coffee in the lounge; the receptionist will handle reservations, check-in and check-out, billing, mail and switchboard; and so on. The manager and assistant manager will handle a variety of administrative and decision-making tasks: purchasing, book-keeping, marketing and so on.

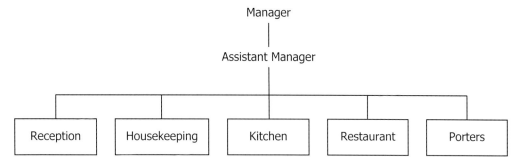

Figure 1.1: A simple small hotel structure

In a **larger hotel**, it is possible to organise staff into more clearly defined departments, each with a supervisor or department head (in a medium-sized hotel) or a manager (in a large hotel). There will also be more specialised staff, because the hotel can afford to employ more people – and there will be more work for each person to do.

The main revenue-earning functions of the hotel are generally split into a **Rooms Division** (responsible for accommodation) and a **Food and Beverages Division** (responsible for catering).

In a medium-sized hotel, there might be a manager and one or more **assistant managers**, who supervise operations (probably on a shift basis, so that there is some managerial supervision seven days per week).

In a large hotel, there will be a **general management team**, responsible for planning and co-ordinating the business and operations of the hotel. Unlike the 'hands on' manager of a small hotel, the manager here is essentially a business manager, responsible for policy, planning and control: (s)he may only rarely encounter guests or intervene in day-to-day hotel decisions. The '**duty manager**' – as assistant managers at this level are often called – is the one with hands-on responsibility for dealing with guests, and resolving problems and queries referred by front office staff. A number of duty managers may be employed to cover a 24-hour roster, so there is always someone available to deal with guest issues.

The organisation structure for a **large hotel** might, therefore, look more as follows: Figure 1.2.

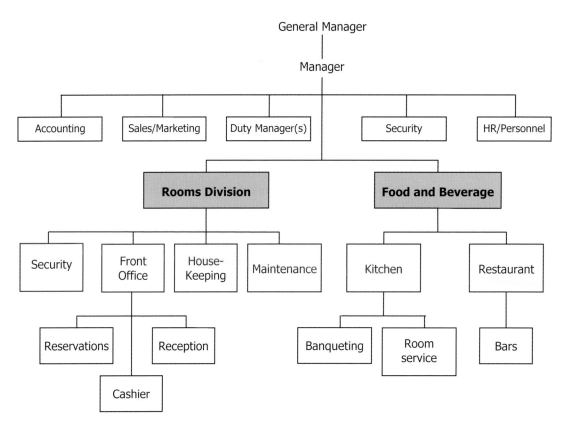

Figure 1.2: A sample organisation chart for a large hotel

The thing to notice about an **organisation chart**, if you ever have to draw one yourself, to depict the organisation structure of a hotel or other hospitality business, is that:

- The 'branches' of the chart show how **roles and responsibilities** are divided up into sections or departments. So, for example, the management of the hotel shown above is divided into two basic divisions: the Rooms Division and Food & Beverage. The **Rooms Division** is, in turn, divided into four basic functions: Front Office, Housekeeping, Maintenance and Security.

- The vertical connecting lines of the chart are also lines of **authority and reporting**. So, for example, reservations staff report to the Front Office Manager, who reports to the Rooms Division Manager – or, to look at it another way, policies and instructions flow *down* from the Rooms Division Manager to front office staff.

- The connecting lines of the chart are also lines of **communication and liaison**. So, for example, it is clear from our chart that staff in the reservations, reception and cashier sections need to communicate with each other: each contributes something to the overall work of the Front Office. At the same time, there is a line connecting reception and maintenance, say: if a guest comes to reception and says that her TV isn't working, or her window doesn't open, reception will have to liaise with maintenance to make sure it gets fixed. We will look at how Front Office liaises with the other departments of the hotel in more detail later.

2.2 The Rooms Division

A typical structure for the Rooms Division in a large hotel – subdividing our organisation chart (Figure 1.2) into more detail, may look as follows: Figure 1.3. There may be additional sections, where required: eg if reception also has retail space for an in-house kiosk or shop, or a separately managed tour/entertainment reservations desk or in-house florists.

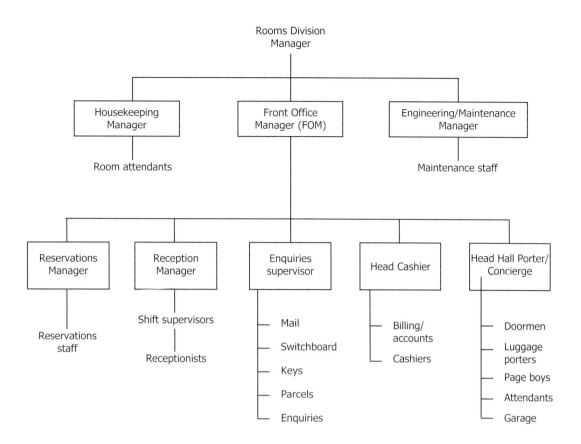

Source: adapted from *Abbott & Lewry* (*Front Office*, p 185).

Figure 1.3: Organisation chart for the Rooms Division in a large hotel

So now let's get some idea of what all these people actually do!

3 Roles and responsibilities of front of house staff

Before we start our description, we must emphasise again that these are not necessarily separate jobs carried out by separate individuals or teams. In a very small establishment, *all* the following roles may be shared by one or two people. In a large hotel, there may well be separate teams, but the hotel may group and allocate tasks in a variety of ways. There are no hard and fast rules.

FOR DISCUSSION

'Why do you need so many people front of house these days? Mobile phones have replaced switchboards. The Internet has replaced reservation clerks. You can do everything with computers: the hotel could be more or less 'self service' for guests, without having all these staff hovering around.'

Do you agree with this argument? If not, why not?

3.1 Reservations

Reservations clerks are responsible for taking enquiries from prospective guests, travel agents, group or conference organisers and other parties who may wish to reserve accommodation.

Their role is to obtain the information required to make a booking; record that information in manual or computerised reservation records; monitor the levels of reservations; issue any documentation to guests to confirm the booking (eg confirmation letters, requests for deposit); and ensure that reception is informed of the confirmed reservation details and expected arrivals for each day.

A **reservations manager** or supervisor will be in control of the section, organise staff duty rosters, and make decisions on whether and which bookings should be accepted (if the hotel is fully booked, or bookings have to be 'juggled' to maximise occupancy).

Advance reservations may be handled by the receptionist in a small hotel, but many hotels will have a separate reservations desk or department – perhaps in a back office near reception, since most reservation requests come in by telephone, mail, e-mail or online, rather than via 'walk ins'.

The reservations department generally operates during business hours (say 8.00 am to 6.00 pm) to cover the peak times for bookings: outside these hours, telephone reservations can be taken by reception.

3.2 Reception (front desk)

'Reception' may be an umbrella term for all front-office functions, but in larger hotels, there is likely to be a special reception desk.

The main roles of **receptionists** (or **front desk agents**) are: taking enquiries and reservation requests from 'walk in' visitors; preparing for the arrival of guests; greeting guests on their arrival; checking guests in (registering them, allocating suitable rooms and checking methods of payment); selling the facilities and services of the hotel; responding to guest problems and queries, or referring them to other departments that can do so; providing information about guests to other front office units and departments of the hotel; and maintaining guest records.

There may be a **senior receptionist** in charge of each team or shift of reception staff, who will take responsibility for staff rosters, and the handling of more challenging tasks such as group arrivals and guest problems, requests and complaints. There will also be a reception or **front desk manager**, with responsibility for the training, supervision and motivation of reception staff; the maximisation of occupancy and revenue (yield management) from the sale of hotel facilities and services; and higher-profile guest duties (eg greeting VIP guests).

The reception desk in a very small hotel may only operate extended **business hours** (say, 7.30 am to 8.30 pm) to cover the main peaks of activity. The hotel will often post an 'after hours' contact number (or operate an intercom system) to allow late-arriving guests, or guests with problems during the night, to contact a designated 'on-call' person (often a resident caretaker or manager). A larger hotel will seek to cover the reception desk on a 24/7 basis, with a permanent night staff or night shift.

EXAMPLE

'A Word from the FOM (Front Office Manager)'

In our hotel (a medium-sized 4 ½ star hotel in Sydney, Australia) we have deliberately given front desk staff the title of 'Guest Service Agents'. We want to emphasise – to the staff, as well as to the guests – that 'reception' is not just there to 'receive' or greet guests on their arrival, but to provide service to them throughout their stay. 'Receptionists' are perceived to have certain tasks that are 'their job' – but 'guest service agents' understand that it's their role to be willing and flexible in trying to meet guests' needs. We think the title also gives the role the importance that it deserves.

3.3 Guest accounting/billing

The **accounting/billing office** is generally a 'back office' role, both because it does not require direct guest contact – and because it requires detailed, methodical (un-distracted) working with numbers, calculations and records! Its main roles are:

- The posting of charges (expenses incurred by the guest for accommodation, meals and other extras) and payments (eg deposits, pre-payments, staged payments and/or the final settling of the bill) to each guest's bill.

- The recording of charges/sales and payments in relevant accounting records, and the 'balancing' of those records (so that amounts owing always equal amounts paid or due to be paid).

- The preparation of relevant accounting records and management reports (eg summaries of sales figures).

3.4 Cashiering and night audit

The **cashier's department** is like the 'bank' of the hotel, with responsibly for handling payments, monies and valuables. Cashiers may report either to the front office manager or to the accounts manager – or both, according to the nature of their work.

Depending on the facilities offered by the hotel, the role of front office cashiers may include:

- The opening and preparation of guest accounts (if not handled by a separate accounting/billing department)

- Accepting and processing payment from guests in settlement of their bills

- Handling foreign currency exchanges for guests (if the hotel is registered to provide this service)

- Accepting and processing takings from other departments of the hotel (eg the restaurant and bar), for account-keeping, reporting, safe storage and banking procedures

- Providing the cash requirements of other departments (eg the cash 'float' held by the restaurant or bar, in order to be able to give change to customers, or the 'petty cash' held at reception for small cash expenses)

- Administering the safe custody system, whereby guests can deposit their valuables for safe-keeping by the hotel

A cashier will usually be on duty during extended business hours, to allow for most guest transactions. However, the 'graveyard shift' (the night hours between 11.00 pm and 8.00 am) is a great time to get some of the detailed record-keeping, checking and report preparation done. This is generally the responsibility of a **night auditor**, whose role is to post the latest batch of charges/expenses to client accounts, balance guest and hotel accounts, prepare revenue reports, and produce statistics and summaries for management.

With computerised hotel management systems, much of the work of accounting, billing and auditing is carried out automatically by the system throughout the day: the night auditor's role, in particular, may be simplified to running off computerised reports, undertaking some manual summaries and checks – and backing up the computer system (making copies of files, in case of system failure).

ACTIVITY 2   10 minutes

What do you think would be the essential attributes and skills required of:

- Reservations staff?
- Reception/front desk staff?
- Cashier or night audit staff?

3.5 Switchboard

In 'the old days' (not so very long ago), basic telephone functions had to be handled by a central **switchboard operator**. However, more sophisticated networks now allow guests to dial out direct from their rooms (to external numbers, other room extensions and selected departments of the hotel), and to receive calls direct from other rooms and departments of the hotel. Such systems may also have added facilities for automatic logging of guest call charges to the billing office; automated wake-up calls; and hotel and guest 'answer machine' or 'voice mail' (message taking) systems. Where such systems are in place, switchboard operators have *much* less to do: mainly, directing in-coming calls to the appropriate guest rooms (consulting a guest directory) or to appropriate departments of the hotel; and dealing with answer machine messages.

In smaller or more old-fashioned hotels, however, the switchboard may be a general communications 'hub': putting internal and external calls through for guests; taking messages for guests; making personal wake-up calls; and perhaps also handling incoming and outgoing mail.

3.6 Concierge and uniformed staff

'*Concierge*' is the French term for 'porter', but the concierge department in a large hotel (which may also be called 'lobby services') may cover a variety of roles, often divided into:

- An **enquiries desk**, which may be responsible for general guest or visitor enquiries and directions; handing out and accepting guest keys; handling incoming and outgoing mail for guests; and organising taxis or valet parking.

- A **bookings desk**, which may handle car hire, flight confirmations, tour bookings and entertainment tickets for guests. (This desk may also be operated by specialist car hire companies and/or booking agencies, who pay for the right to operate on a 'concession' basis within the hotel.)

- A **baggage handling** and storage desk, or 'porterage' desk (although this may also be handled from reception).

- **Security** in the lobby/reception area, if this is not handled by a separate security officer or team.

Traditionally, 'concierge' is the title given to the **Head Porter**, who manages all these services and supervises a range of uniformed staff.

Uniformed staff include:

- Doorpersons (or greeters): who open doors; bring luggage from guests' transport to the hotel (and *vice versa* on departure); and hail or call taxis on request

- **Porters**, 'bell staff' and/or pages, who carry luggage to and from guests' rooms; keep the lobby area clean and tidy; run errands and relay messages

- Lift attendants, parking attendants, cloakroom attendants and so on

3.7 Guest relations

In large hotels, **Guest Relations Officers (GROs)** are sometimes employed to create a more 'personal' relationship with guests – who might otherwise have very little human contact with hotel staff.

Their main role is to make guests feel welcome and provide personalised service, by greeting guests; attending social gatherings held by the hotel (as social 'facilitators'); and perhaps talking to those who are travelling alone.

Guests with special needs, problems or complaints may be referred to GROs by reception. GROs may also be given the task of greeting and liaising with **Very Important Persons (VIPs)**, **Commercially Important Guests (CIGs)** and **Special Attention guests (SPATTs)**.

GROs may support sales staff (eg by escorting potential clients around the hotel, or providing guests with information about the hotel's services and facilities), and provide non-routine guest services when required (eg sending a fax for a guest after the hotel's business centre has closed).

3.8 Job descriptions for front office roles

DEFINITION

A **job description** is a broad statement of the main duties and tasks of a job, its objectives and its place in the structure of an organisation.

Job descriptions are often used in the recruitment of staff, both to prepare job advertisements, and to measure the skills, characteristics and experience of candidates against the requirements of the job. They are also used as a guide to the induction and training of new staff, as the list of duties can be used as a 'checklist' for what recruits need to be able to do to work competently in the job.

If you are asked to prepare a job description for a front office role, the key is to keep it brief and simple. It should generally contain:

- The job title, department and place of work

- A 'job or role summary': a short paragraph describing the major function of the job (perhaps with an organisation chart to show where it 'fits' in the rooms division or front-office structure)

- The person/or position to whom the job-holder is responsible (ie a manager or supervisor)

- Any persons/positions *for* whom the job-holder is responsible, or who report to the job-holder: that is any staff (s)he will have to manage or supervise

- A list of the main duties, tasks or responsibilities entailed by the job

- Where relevant, a note of other departments or roles with which the job-holder must regularly liaise, communicate or co-operate.

The following is an example of a job description for a receptionist in a fairly small hotel.

Hill Town Hotel

JOB DESCRIPTION

Job Title:	**Receptionist**
Division:	Rooms Division
Place of Work:	Hill Town Hotel, Blayney
Job Summary:	The job-holder will carry out general reception duties, as described in the hotel's operating manual, and assist the front office manager in maintaining an efficient, guest-focused and profitable reception department.
Reporting to:	Front Office Manager

Responsible for:	Switchboard operator, porters
Main tasks and duties:	To ensure that all guests are dealt with efficiently, courteously and promptly on check-in, in the event of queries or requests during their stay, and on check-out
	To carry out guest check-in and check-out procedures in accordance with the hotel's policies and operating manual
	To carry out the duties of the reservations clerk or switchboard operator as necessary
	To sell the facilities and services of the hotel to guests in an appropriate manner
	To maintain relevant guest and room status records as laid down by the hotel's operating manual
	To issue information about guests, room status and action requirements to other departments of the hotel, as laid down by the hotel's operating manual
	To maintain a high standard of personal hygiene and appearance at all times
	To ensure that strict security is maintained in respect of all monies, keys, guest property, hotel equipment and guest information
	To be fully conversant with the hotel's fire and emergency evacuation plans, and able to act in accordance with those plans
	To carry out any duty fairly and reasonably as requested by management
Liaison:	Regular communication and collaboration will be required with the Reservations, Guest Accounting/Cashier, Housekeeping, Maintenance and Food/Beverages departments
Prepared by:	The Front Office Manager, May 2009

Figure 1.4: Job description

A C T I V I T Y   3   1 5   m i n u t e s

Choose any one of the front office roles we have described in this chapter, and draft a job description for that role, using the example above as a guide.

If you work in a hotel (or similar) environment, you might try to get hold of your own job description, and (if available) the job description of some other front office roles. (Ask your manager, or the Personnel/HR department.)

3.9 Working in shifts

As we suggested earlier, a small hotel or guest house may shut down its front office over night, leaving an 'Out of Hours' or 'Emergency' contact number (and/or front entrance intercom) for late arrivals or guests with problems during the night.

A large hotel, however, never sleeps: some front office staff will be available to meet guest needs 24 hours per day. Most **back office departments** will operate normal or extended office hours: reservations will tend to be concentrated within business hours, and billing and cashiering activity in the early morning (posting of last-minute charges), middle of the day (lunchtime postings and banking of takings) and evening (opening bills for new arrivals).

However, certain significant **front office roles** (reception, night audit, porter and switchboard, say) will have to be covered overnight.

Work is therefore usually organised on a shift basis.

- Day staff may work an **early shift** (say, 7.00 am to 3.00 pm) or a **late shift** (3.00 pm to 11.00 pm), on a rotating roster system, five days per week (with varying days off). The main peaks of activity at front desk will be check-out time (7.30 – 10.30 am) and arrival time (say, 3.00 – 7.00 pm).

- A separate (generally smaller) **night staff** will usually be employed to cover the night or 'graveyard' shift (11.00pm to 7.00 am), to enable them to establish a routine of night working – rather than rotating between day and night shifts.

- **Shift hours** usually also allow 15–30 minutes for **'hand-over'** between shifts, so that unresolved issues can be notified to the incoming shift, responsibilities for the cash drawer signed over and so on.

Drawing-up and maintaining shift rosters, to ensure that all shifts are adequately covered – while being flexible to the needs of staff members – is a significant challenge for the front office manager!

E X A M P L E

Abbott & Lewry (Front Office) suggest that the general 'flow' of a **hotel day** might look something like the following. Don't worry if some of the activities are unfamiliar: we'll cover them all in future chapters...

07.00 – 09.00	Night shift hands over to early day shift: check cash float, discuss hand-over issues Switchboard/receptionist works through early morning calls, newspapers etc Receptionist/cashier handles departures: check-out, presentation of bills, payments Departed guest records are filed
09.00 – 12.00	Sort and process incoming mail (advance bookings, confirmations etc) Check overnight stays on chart; liaise with housekeeping re room make-up; check guest credit limits Check and update room availability; process reservations Check housekeeper's reports and account for discrepancies (if any)
12.00 –	Post lunch charges to guest accounts Cash-up lunch/bar receipts
15.00	Outgoing shift checks cash/safe, compiles hand-over reports etc
15.00 – 17.00	Early shift hands over to late shift: check cash float, discuss issues etc Check room availability and arrivals list; confirm arrangements for any VIP arrivals Prepare arrivals/departures lists and guest registration cards for following day File correspondence (in quiet periods) Check-in early arrivals
17.00 – 20.00	Check-in normal arrivals Check non-arrivals and release non-guaranteed (6 pm release) rooms for chance arrivals
20.00 – 23.00	Post room charges, plus dinner/bar charges Outgoing shift checks cash/safe, compiles hand-over reports etc
23.00 – 07.00	Late shift hands over to night shift: check cash float, discuss issues etc. Check-in late arrivals/chance guests and update room status Carry out night audit and compile reports Run computer system back-up procedures

4 The guest cycle

Our discussion of the roles and responsibilities of front office staff is like a snapshot of its activity at any given moment: some people are taking reservations, while others are preparing accounts, taking messages and so on – juggling all the activities that make a hotel function. As you may have noticed from our organisation charts, the grouping of tasks into divisions and departments sets up a series of 'vertical' chains or structures, reflecting the separation of specialised activities.

But looked at from the point of view of a guest coming into a hotel, the 'flow' of activity doesn't look like this at all. A guest experiences the hotel less as a vertical structure than as a **horizontal process**. (S)he makes a booking, has it confirmed, arrives at the hotel on the due day, checks-in, requests various services as the stay unfolds, then turns up to check-out, receives the bill, pays it – and departs. For the guest, the experience is **chronological**: unfolding as a series of events, activities and services received over time.

In a sense, the guest doesn't need to know – and ideally, shouldn't feel – that (s)he is having to cross over from one separate department to another at each stage: (s)he should be able to progress more or less **seamlessly** from booking (reservations) to check-in (reception) to occupancy (housekeeping, food and beverage and various other departments as required) to check-out (billing, cashier). In order to create this seamless service, it is useful to think of the role of front office, not in terms of departmental roles and responsibilities, but in terms of the guest cycle.

DEFINITION

The **guest cycle** refers to the various stages of a guest's experience of a hotel, and the activities and processes that are carried out at each stage: pre-arrival (eg reservation), arrival at the hotel (eg check-in), occupancy (the period during which the guest stays at the hotel) and departure (eg check-out and payment).

At each stage of this cycle, there are certain types of interaction or transaction that will take place between the guest and the hotel.

Baker, Bradley & Huyton (*Principles of Hotel Front Office Operations*) helpfully depict the guest cycle as shown in Figure 1.5. The central part of the diagram depicts the four basic stages of the guest cycle, while the outer ring shows the various transactions and services typically carried out at each stage.

A C T I V I T Y   4   1 0   m i n u t e s

Outside the outer ring of the diagram in Figure 1.5, write down the department or section that would be mainly responsible for *each* of the activities shown (with an arrow, if necessary, to indicate which department/section is responsible for which activity).

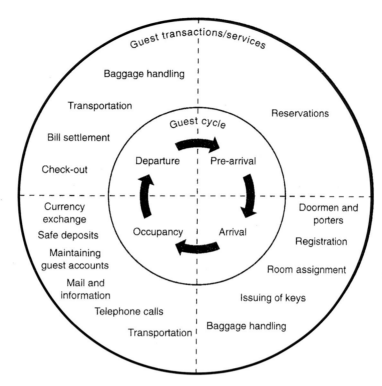

Source: Baker, Bradley & Huyton *(Principles of Hotel Front Office Operations*, p. 44)

Figure 1.5: The guest cycle

The chapters of this Study Guide follow syllabus, rather than guest cycle order – but by the end, you will be knowledgeable about all these transactions and services!

5 Liaising with other departments

5.1 Other departments in the hotel

We saw from our discussion of hotel organisation structure that there are a number of **departments** in a large hotel.

- Some of them will be concerned with **raising revenue**, or earning money for the hotel: the rooms division and food and beverage divisions are the main ones – but the hotel may also earn revenue through recreational facilities, guest laundry/dry cleaning, a business centre and so on.

- Other departments may fulfil the **management and support functions** of the hotel: for example, sales and marketing, accounting/finance, security, engineering/maintenance, premises management, information technology (IT) and HR/personnel.

Since front office will have to liaise with various other departments in the hotel, let's look briefly at what the main ones do, and why **liaison** is required.

Department	Main responsibilities	Liaison with front office
Food and beverage (F & B)	Purchasing, preparation and provision of food, drink and catering services to guests: via banqueting (function catering); restaurant; bar; perhaps coffee shops; 'floor service' (refreshments delivered to the lounge or pool area, say); and room service.	▪ F & B needs occupancy forecasts to estimate provisions requirements ▪ F & B needs confirmed arrival/ departure info to control guest credit ▪ FO needs info on food/drinks charges to add to guest bills ▪ FO may take or refer restaurant bookings ▪ F & B takings will be 'paid in' to the cashier for accounting and banking
Housekeeping	The management of guest rooms and cleanliness of all public areas of the hotel; cleaning, making-up and supplying of rooms (eg with soap, towels, mini-bar stocks); preparing housekeeping/room status reports.	▪ Housekeeping needs arrival/departure info to plan its staff rosters and room-cleaning schedules ▪ Housekeeping needs info about special requests, complaints or urgent room preparation requirements ▪ FO needs up-to-date info on rooms (occupied, vacant but not ready, out of order, ready to let) to update room status/availability records: the housekeeper's report
Maintenance	The maintenance and operation of all machinery and equipment (eg lighting, heating, air conditioning); carrying out minor repairs and works (carpentry, upholstery, plumbing, electrics).	▪ Maintenance needs info about repair/ replacement requirements ▪ FO needs confirmation that guest repair requests have been seen to ▪ FO needs up-to-date info on out of order rooms (closed for maintenance) to update room availability records
Accounts	Monitoring, recording, checking and reporting of all financial activities of the hotel: processing and banking takings; processing of payrolls; preparing internal reports, audits and financial statements; compiling statistics.	▪ Accounts needs front office takings paid in, with relevant records ▪ Accounts needs guest billing info, for credit control, entry in main hotel accounts, revenue reporting etc ▪ FO needs clear policies, procedures and authorisations for handling and recording of transactions; and lists of credit-approved guests

Department	Main responsibilities	Liaison with front office
Security	The safety and security of guests, visitors and employees: patrolling premises; monitoring surveillance equipment; handling security incidents; liaising with police if required.	■ Security needs to be alerted to suspicious persons or activities, reports of security breach etc ■ FO needs warnings (eg to evacuate premises) and incident reports (for future planning) ■ Security helps with special needs guests ■ May administer first aid ■ Deals with problems with guest safes, guests locked out of rooms and opening of inter-connecting doors ■ Deals with lost property
Sales and marketing	Generating new business and increased sales for the hotel: sales of rooms, facilities and services; advertising; promotions; PR and publicity; winning corporate, tour operator, and agency business; designing the web site; etc.	■ Sales needs info on room availability to know what rooms to sell ■ Sales needs info on guest types/origins to develop marketing strategy and target key guest segments ■ Sales needs FO support in selling rooms, facilities and services ■ FO needs info on special promotions (eg special rates and inclusions); campaigns (to anticipate increased demand); etc
Human resources (HR)	Recruitment and selection of staff; staff induction and training; performance appraisal; rewards and career planning; employee relations; compliance with employment law	■ HR needs info on FO job requirements (for recruitment planning); FO staff performance and training needs; FO staff problems and concerns ■ FO staff need info on all HR policies and rules; training/career opportunities etc

5.2 The flow of information within a hotel

In the following chapters of this Study Guide, we will identify a number of routine reports and notifications that will need to flow **from front office to other departments**. Examples include:

■ A list of guests currently in residence – or guest index – in alphabetical order, so that any member of staff can look up a guest or locate their room number when necessary

■ A list of anticipated arrivals (based on reservations), group arrivals and VIP/special needs arrivals, so that departments can prepare for them

■ A list of amendments to the arrivals list (eg last-minute bookings and chance walk-in guests)

■ A list of guest amendments: changes of room number, number of guests, terms and so on, so that departments can adjust accordingly

- A list of anticipated departures (based on booked departure dates), so that departments can plan to prepare rooms for re-letting, prepare bills for departing guests and so on.

- A list of amendments to the departures list (eg guests extending their stay)

- A list of guests who have left the hotel, so that telephone calls and messages can handled accordingly, and rooms prepared for re-letting.

In return, of course, front office will **receive reports and notifications** from other departments: about amounts guests have charged to their accounts in the hotel restaurant or bar (for inclusion in their bill); about the status of rooms as confirmed by housekeeping (vacant, vacant but not yet ready, out of order, ready for letting); and so on.

And, of course, there will also be a flow of information **within front office sections**.

- **Concierge/enquiries** will need arrivals, departures and current guest lists, in order to sort incoming guest mail, take messages, give the right keys to the right guests, and take the right baggage to the right rooms.

- **Switchboard** will need the current guest list and checked-out guest list, in order to handle incoming phone calls and charge guests calls to the right rooms.

- **Reception** will need all the information collected by the reservation section, in order to prepare for and verify the bookings of arriving guests, maintain room availability records and so on.

- **Reservations** will need information on returning guests, compiled by reception, in order to offer a personalised service.

- **Cashier** will need guests' reservation and check-in information in order to open a guest bill, charge the correct rate agreed with the guest, confirm the guest's payment details, check corporate accounts and so on. They may also need access to guest history records, in order to check that guests have paid their bills in the past, or to identify guests who are entitled to special discounts.

The picture – even greatly simplified – thus looks somewhat like the following: Figure 1.6.

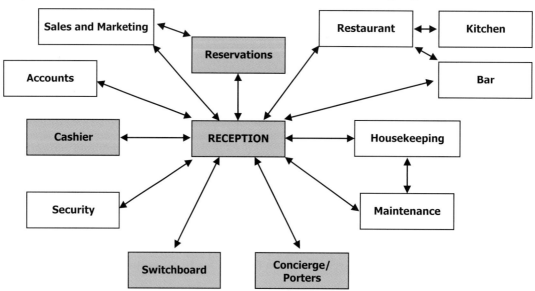

Figure 1.6: The flow of information within a hotel

The reception department is really the '**communication** hub' of the hotel.

E X A M P L E

'A Word from the FOM (Front Office Manager)'

Communicate, communicate, communicate. This is the most important thing for front office personnel to bear in mind. Communication is what most often breaks down and causes problems.

Pass on information to other departments – and follow up: if you've asked someone to do something, check that it's been done.

Communicate from shift to shift: there's nothing worse for a guest waiting for action on a problem or request than finding that 'the person who was dealing with that is no longer here, and we know nothing about it'. Use shift hand-over reports, daily 'running sheets' or department diaries: keep a running log of what's happened; what issues have been resolved and what haven't; what the next shift needs to keep an eye on; what you've learned about a guest. Note down every interaction with a guest, and every action you take on a guest's behalf: you don't know what may later turn into a complaint or query – or something to learn from!

6 Property management systems

6.1 Hotel, property or premises management systems

DEFINITION

A **Hotel Management System, Premises Management System** or **Property Management System** is a specialised **computer** software package which automates many of the routine tasks of letting accommodation, throughout the guest cycle: from room availability and room status records, to reservations, check-in and check-out systems, billing and payment, guest accounting and guest records. The system may also include a range of premises management functions, such as energy management (controlling the automatic switching on and off of heating and lighting) and telephone call management.

A total Hotel Management System may include a wide range of systems, applications and features. We will explain the main ones as we encounter them at each stage of the guest cycle, in future chapters but, just to give you an idea, a computerised hotel may offer:

- Database for recording **enquiries** (and converting enquiries to confirmed reservations and guests records as appropriate), with up-to-date records of enquiry status

- **Reservations** and group booking applications, with up-to-date records of the status of all reservations

- Computer-aided '**yield management**' functions: helping reservation staff to make decisions about which reservations to accept, and at what rate, in order to maximise revenue

- The generation of **arrival and departure lists** and amendment notifications (from the most up-to-date reservation, check-in and check-out records)

- Up-to-date records of **room status and availability** (automatically up-datable as rooms are reported vacant, reading to re-let, allocated to arriving guests and so on)

- **Guest records** (containing information about each guest's reservation, stay, charges etc), which can be used with applications for reservation handling, registration (check-in), guest billing, check-out and so on

- **Electronic Point of Sale (EPOS)** links from the restaurant, bar and reception through to guest billing, so that sales are automatically charged to accounts as they are processed

- Itemised **guest accounts** (posting all deposits, pre-payments, room charges and extra charges for inclusion in the final bill), automatic generation of bills, paying processing, and automatic links through to general accounts functions

- Automatic **night audit** functions (checking and balancing all reports and accounts)

Source: http://i.d.com.com/i/dl/media/dlimage

- Computer-aided **housekeeping and maintenance scheduling** (from centrally logged requests and arrival/departure information), and logging of housekeeping and maintenance reports to the main room status system

- **Management information system** – compiling forecasts, graphs, charts and statistical reports and analyses from all the other data stored in the system

- **Calendar**, diary and message facilities

- Internal and external **telephone call handling** (switchboard), call logging, allocation of call charges to guests' accounts and automated early morning calls

- Integration with **word processing packages**, in order to personalise correspondence with guests' contact details

- **Building management** applications, such as energy monitoring and management systems (minimising unnecessary use of electric power); the use of electronic key coding for guest room doors; fire/intruder/theft alarm sensing systems; and so on

- **Marketing applications**, linking the reservation system to tourist information centres, hotel booking agencies and other group hotels, for example

Obviously, a book like this can't teach you to *use* such systems in practice – particularly since there are so many different programmes available! Hopefully, your college will be able to give you access to a computerised system so you can try one out, but in any case you will have to learn whatever system is used in your workplace. What we can do, here, is give you a very broad outline of what to look for – and an appreciation of the advantages and disadvantages of computerised systems in general.

The 'screen-shots' we show in this Study Guide, for illustration purposes, are mostly drawn from a hotel management system package called **Hotel Perfect**. This package has been designed for establishments with under 150 rooms, and is compatible with Microsoft Windows and fully integrates with MS Word.

Another well-known system is the **MICROS-Fidelio** property management system (PMS) – also known as **Fidelio**. Designed to meet the varied requirements of any size hotel or hotel chain, the Fidelio (OPERA) PMS provides a range of tools for the day-to-day tasks of front office: handling reservations, checking guests in and out, assigning rooms and managing room inventory, accommodating in-house guest needs, and handling accounting and billing.

E X A M P L E

The key features of the **Fidelio** system, as advertised by MICROS-Fidelio, are as follows.

Reservations: integrated with other applications such as profiles, cashiering, and deposits. The module offers a complete set of features for making and updating individual, group, and business block reservations, including deposit handling, cancellations, confirmations, wait-listing, room blocking, and sharing.

Front desk: serving arrivals and in-house guests. This module handles individual guests, groups, and walk-ins, and has features for room blocking, managing guest messages and wakeup calls, and creating and following up on inter-department advisories.

Rooms management: handling all facets of room supervision including availability, housekeeping, maintenance, and facility management. The 'Queue Rooms' feature co-ordinates Front Office and Housekeeping efforts when guests are waiting for rooms not immediately available for assignment.

Cashiering: posting guest and visitor charges, making posting adjustments, managing advance deposits, settlements, checkout and bill/folio printing. Cashiering accommodates multiple payment methods per reservation including cash, cheque, credit cards, and direct billing.

Accounts receivable (credit accounts): for direct billing, invoicing, bill payments, reminder and statement generation, and account research.

Commissions: calculating, processing, and following up on travel agent and other types of commission payments.

Reporting: over 360 separate standard reports, which can be customised for each hotel.

Security: user permissions determine which features may be accessed by each user and user group.

Global perspective: supports multi-currency and multi-language features to meet the requirements of global operations. Rates and revenues can be converted from the local currency to any other currency. The appropriate language for guest correspondence can be automatically determined by the guest's profile language.

Hospitality system interfaces: can be linked to other hospitality systems including yield management, telephone and electronic switchboard, TV and video entertainment, electronic key locking, restaurant point of sale systems, activities scheduling, mini-bar charges, and wakeup call systems.

If you want to find out more about Fidelio, see:

Link: http://www.micros.com/Products

For a very accessible summary of Front Office Management systems (by a provider called WinFoms), see:

Link: http://www.pcscholl.ch/EN/index.htm

6.2   General advantages and disadvantages of 'computerising' the hotel

We will evaluate the use of computers for particular applications in the relevant sections of this Study Guide. However, the general advantages and disadvantages can be summarised as follows.

Advantages of computerised systems	Disadvantages of computerised systems
▪ Reduction in entries required, due to automatic updating of related records: multiple records and reports can be compiled from the same data	▪ Initial set-up cost
▪ Automation of routine processes for speed and accuracy	▪ Time and cost of staff training in use of the system (which can be considerable)
▪ Reduction in duplications and messages for inter-departmental data sharing	▪ Limitation in memory/speed, for older computers
▪ Reduced time and cost of data handling	▪ Limitation in speed eg to find relevant fields and key in data (compared to writing entries into the right spaces on a form), to answer security questions ('Are you sure you want to...?')
▪ Reduced human error in copying across data and making calculations	
▪ Streamlined procedures (saving staff time and improving guest service)	▪ Lack of compatibility, if the hotel has built up a number of different applications separately: may not interface or integrate with each other
▪ Storage of data without physical space	
▪ Ease of access to data through 'search by' fields: no need to leaf through files	▪ Vulnerability to human error (eg inputting data)
▪ Updating of records without separate entries, erasures, crossing out etc	▪ Need for paper documents in any case (eg for 'audit trail', written confirmations, back-up copies): may not save on paper/filing space!
▪ Speed of data searches, updates, calculations, report/document preparation	▪ Extra 'housekeeping' tasks for night audit staff (eg backing-up the system, archiving old files)
▪ Presentation of reports and guest documentation in a variety of formats, with professional (printed presentation)	▪ Potential security risks if the system is misused
▪ Decision support applications: modelling of different 'what if' scenarios to help planning	▪ Potential security risks to data from hacking and computer viruses
▪ Automatic checking and reconciliation of data, and reporting on discrepancies	▪ Vulnerability to technology problems and failures: loss of data (if not properly 'backed-up') and inability to maintain procedures
▪ Enhanced security through password protected access	▪ Dependency on suppliers for serving, IT support, training etc (which may be a problem if a small software or hardware supplier goes out of business or is busy)
	▪ Loss of staff knowledge and experience of underlying procedures and manual processes, in case of systems failure

'A Word from the FOM (Front Office Manager)'

A computerised system is definitely your friend – but you need to (a) learn how to use it well – and (b) learn how *not* to use it, because it will invariably break down when you least want it to. We always print out 'shift reports' from the system: room availability, departure and arrival lists, guest lists, guest accounts and so on – all the basic records we need to keep the hotel running for 24 hours without power, or with a 'crashed' computer system. We print out updated versions at *least* once per shift.

7 Different types of hotels

As we proceed through this Study Guide, we will be looking at general, and typical, ways of doing things, to give you a good basic grounding in the principles. However, you need to be aware that no two hotels are exactly alike. Each has its systems and procedures, and its unique 'character' and house style. If or when you are employed in a hotel (or other hospitality establishment) you will hopefully receive further training in exactly how that particularly organisation goes about things, and the particular systems and technologies it uses.

For the moment, however, just be aware that different types and sizes of establishment may require different systems and procedures, and may organise their front office functions differently.

7.1 Different types of establishment

In addition to hotels (and variants such as **motels**, **serviced apartments** and **conference centres**), there are a number of other types of organisations letting accommodation, including:

- **Camp sites** may let accommodation in the form of cabins or caravans, or may let space for guests to provide their own accommodation (eg tents or caravans). Either way, there are reservations, registrations and billing to be processed, and facilities and services to be provided and maintained (eg on-site shops, washrooms, utilities).

- **Ships and boats** may also offer accommodation. Cruise liners are often called 'floating hotels', and have much in common with their land-based equivalents. Smaller boats (eg a yacht or canal boat) may also be chartered by customers. This is a slightly different scenario, because the accommodation and services move off site: nevertheless, reservations, registrations and payments (and boat cleaning and maintenance between trips) are still administered from a front office.

You might also think of **time-share apartment** complexes, student **halls of residence**, health spas and hospitals as establishments providing accommodation and catering for a fluctuating group of temporary residents and, therefore, having to pay attention to space planning, bookings, billing, information and service provision, housekeeping and maintenance, and so on. The processes and terminology used in such contexts may not be exactly the same as in a hotel but the basic requirements, activities and challenges will be broadly recognisable.

7.2 Different hotel types

There is also, as we will see, a wide variety even among hotels and their direct equivalents. Hotels may differ according to factors such as:

- **Size**, or capacity. In the UK: a small hotel would be classed as one with 25 bedrooms or fewer; a medium-sized hotel, one with 25-99 bedrooms; a large hotel as one with more than 100 bedrooms; and a 'major' hotel as one with more than 300 bedrooms. Small hotels might also include bed and breakfast (B&B) establishments, public house and farm-stay accommodation.

- **Location**, which tends to influence the type of clientele and style of the hotel. (Business travellers, for example, tend to be attracted to hotels close to transport, central business districts and conference facilities, with good communications infrastructure. Leisure travellers may be attracted to more remote or exotic locations.) Hotels may be classed by location as: city centre, main road (motel), airport, suburban, resort or country hotels.

- **Grade**. Depending on a hotel's location, facilities/amenities and service standards, the price of accommodation may vary widely, from budget to luxury. There are a number of schemes to classify hotels by grade, so that would-be guests know what facilities and standards to expect. Most schemes award an increasing number of **stars** on the basis of assessed quality.

The following examples are the classifications set out by the **English Tourism Council (ETC)**, **Automobile Association (AA)** and **Royal Automobile Club (RAC)**.

★   A hotel with:

- Practical accommodation with a limited range of facilities and services (75% of bedrooms with en-suite or private bathroom facilities), but a high standard of cleanliness throughout.

- Friendly and courteous staff to give guests help and information needed to enjoy their stay.

- A restaurant/eating area open to residents and their guests for breakfast and dinner.

★★   A hotel with all one-star facilities PLUS:

- Good overnight accommodation with more comfortable bedrooms, better equipped: all with en-suite or private bathroom facilities and colour TV.

- A relatively straightforward range of services, including food and drink and a personal style of service.

- A restaurant/dining room for breakfast and dinner.

★★★   A hotel with all two-star facilities PLUS:

- Possibly larger establishments, but all offering significantly greater quality and range of facilities and services, and usually more spacious public areas and bedrooms.

- A more formal style of service, with a receptionist on duty and staff responding well to guests' needs and requests.

- A restaurant/dining room for breakfast and dinner.

- Room service of continental breakfast, and a wide selection of drinks, light lunch and snacks served in a bar or lounge.

- Laundry service available.

★★★★   A hotel with all three-star facilities PLUS:

- Accommodation offering superior comfort and quality; all bedrooms with en-suite bath, fitted overhead shower and WC.

- Spacious and very well appointed public areas, with a strong emphasis on food and drink.

- Staff with very good technical and social skills, anticipating and responding to guests' needs and requests.

- Room service of all meals and 24-hour drinks, refreshments and snacks.

- Dry cleaning service available.

★ ★ ★ ★ ★   A hotel with all four-star facilities PLUS:

- A spacious, luxurious establishment offering the highest international quality of accommodation, facilities, services and cuisine.

- Striking accommodation throughout, with a range of extra facilities.

- Professional, attentive staff providing flawless guest services.

- A hotel that fits the highest international standards for the industry, with an air of luxury, exceptional comfort and a sophisticated ambience.

FOR DISCUSSION

Looking through the attributes of the differently star-rated hotels listed above, what implications can you see for the organisation and role of Front Office in each of the star ratings?

If you would like more information on hotel classifications, the English Tourism Council, AA and RAC ratings are explained – for hotels, guest accommodation (diamond ratings), caravan parks and self-catering establishments – together with accessibility categories (for disabled travellers) at:

Link: http://www.fweb.org.uk/dean/visitor/accom/symbols.html

7.3 Different guest types

Different types of guest may travel at different times of year or week. They may have different needs and preferences in regard to the rooms, services and facilities offered by the hotel. They may have different budgets available to spend on their stay.

It will, therefore, be important for hotels to be aware of who their guests are, and to classify them as distinct **'market segments'**, when: planning the facilities and services to be offered by the hotel; selling the facilities and services of the hotel to prospective guests; anticipating and meeting the needs and wants of guests during their stay; and determining pricing policies that will attract the kind of guests the hotel wants (or gets).

Leisure or pleasure travellers

Leisure travellers (or tourists) travel for sightseeing, relaxation or entertainment. They are often highly seasonal: travelling during school holidays, best-weather periods or attracted by special events in an area. Because they are self-funding, they are price-sensitive and attracted by value for money. Their main requirements from a hotel may be comfort, entertainment, budget accommodation, convenient location (for tourism and transport), foreign currency exchange facilities – and helpful front office staff! Leisure travellers may be classified in any way that is helpful for the hotel, but you may hear the following terms:

- **Domestic tourists** are local people who stay at a hotel for weekend breaks or special functions.

- **Foreign independent travellers (FITs)** are international tourists who have made their own travel arrangements.

- **Group inclusive tours (GITs)** are groups of tourists travelling together on a 'package' tour, with accommodation and meals often booked in advance by the tour operator. Budget is often a consideration on such tours, because they may have limited 'spending money' on top of inclusions.

- **Special interest tours (SITs)** are smaller groups who are visiting an area with a special interest eg eco-tours, adventure tours or cultural tours, seeking particular locations, experiences or activities.

Business travellers

Business travellers are those who travel for the sole purpose of undertaking business: sales representatives, people attending meetings and conferences (or on their way to them), and so on. Business travellers are the largest year-round source of demand for hotel accommodation.

- **Individual business travellers** travel independently and alone.

- **Corporate business travellers** represent companies which may make regular bookings. They may be sub-divided into 'negotiated contract' travellers (who have negotiated a special discounted rate and terms with the hotel, based on a guaranteed volume of business) and 'non-negotiated' travellers (who may be eligible for a standard discounted corporate rate, on the understanding that there may be repeat business available).

- **Conference** delegates may have accommodation booked in the hotel where (or near to where) a conference is being held, perhaps reserved by their company, or by the conference organiser.

In general, business travellers tend to require accommodation at short notice: they often seek to develop special relationships with hotels, so that rooms are made available – and perhaps even 'held' for their company on a standing basis. They are generally less price sensitive than pleasure travellers (because their expenses are paid for by a company), but they are generally offered discounted and credit terms in return for volume business. They may have a different range of requirements from leisure travellers: eg for ease of reservation, efficient/speedy check-in and check-out (perhaps with early breakfast, if they have to be 'on the road' early), the use of meetings rooms, client entertainment facilities, and access to communication/office services.

Groups

A 'group' generally means five or more people travelling together, or ten or more rooms being booked together: the rooms being booked at the same time, the members paying the same rate, and generally arriving and departing at broadly the same time. Groups can range from five or six people on a small tour to hundreds of people attending a conference at the hotel.

Groups create certain challenges for hotels, over and above those presented by independent travellers. For a start, there are more people to deal with – generally all at once, which can put pressure on reception at check-in and check-out time! Groups may also have fixed timetables for their meals, activities, arrival and departure times, and this reduces their flexibility, and that of the hotel.

We will look separately at the issues of groups, at each stage of the guest cycle.

7.4 The point being...

You need to be aware, as you read on, that the kind of Front Office organisation, procedures and systems that suit one type of hotel may not suit another. For example:

- A small hotel or other accommodation provider may have a simple Front Office structure, perhaps with only one or two people performing all the tasks, while a large hotel may have a complex structure of inter-related departments and specialist service units, to which different types of guest needs will be referred.

- While larger hotels are likely to operate computerised reservation, check-in and billing systems, a small or medium-sized country hotel, inn or bed and breakfast may not (yet) have moved to such a system, and may use manual systems. (We will cover both in this Study Guide, because manual systems are still in use – and because if computer systems crash, it helps to know how to do the same tasks using a pen and paper!)

- Hotels catering for business travellers (city or airport hotels or motels) are likely to offer a different range of guest services (eg internet access, e-mail facilities, perhaps an executive lounge, meeting rooms, office services), administered from and promoted by Front Office, than hotels catering for leisure or special interest travellers.

- A four- or five-star hotel will require higher standards of social skills and customer service training for its Front Office staff, in order to respond positively and professionally to a range of guest needs and wants, than a one-, two- or three-star hotel.

These are the kinds of things you will need to bear in mind if asked to contextualise assignments or exam answers.

SUMMARY

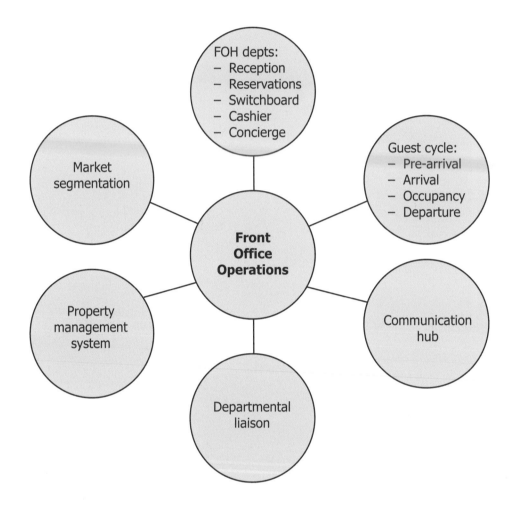

SELF-TEST QUESTIONS

1 List eight separate roles which may make up 'front office'.

2 Identify the two main revenue-earning divisions of a hotel.

3 List the main roles of a receptionist or front desk person.

4 What is (a) a 'GRO' and (b) a 'concierge'?

5 What are the peak times at front desk?

6 List the four stages of the guest cycle, in chronological order.

7 The .... department is responsible for processing staff payroll, while the .... department is responsible for PR and publicity for the hotel.

8 What do the acronyms PMS and EFTPOS stand for?

9 How many rooms would a medium-sized hotel have?

10 What are FITs and GITs?

SELF-TEST ANSWERS

1 Switchboard, reservations, reception, concierge, billing, cashiering, guest relations, uniformed staff.

2 Rooms Division and Food & Beverage

3 Taking enquiries from walk ins; preparing for arrivals; greeting guests; checking-in guests; selling; dealing with guest problems and queries; providing information to other departments; and keeping guest records.

4 Guest Relations Officer; Head Porter

5 Check-outs (7.30 – 10.30 am) and arrivals (3.00 – 7.00 pm)

6 Pre-arrival; arrival; occupancy; and departure

7 The **Accounts** department is responsible for processing staff payroll, while the **Sales and Marketing** department is responsible for PR and publicity for the hotel.

8 Property (or Premises) Management System; Electronic Point of Sale

9 25 to 99

10 Foreign Independent Travellers; Group Inclusive Travellers

ANSWERS TO ACTIVITIES

1   No answer is given for this activity, because it requires your own research and reflection.

2   A reservation clerk should have good telephone skills, because many reservations will come in this way: a clear speaking voice, the ability to ask questions and elicit information and so on. In addition, (s)he will have to have good administrative skills to process the reservation efficiently.

A front desk receptionist will have to have excellent social and hospitality skills, because of the need to welcome guests and deal with a range of problems and queries. (S)he will have to be flexible and resilient (eg not taking complaints and awkward situations personally). (S)he will also have to pay attention to personal grooming and hygiene, because of the amount of personal contact with guests, and the importance of first impressions.

A cashier or night auditor will need a number of specialised skills and attributes: good numerical abilities; confidence in handling large sums of money; methodical and careful working; tolerance for working at night (in the case of night audit); and, above all, honesty and integrity.

3   No answer is given for this activity, because you were asked to choose whichever role you were most interested in. However, material for an answer was given in section 3 of the chapter, with guidance on format in the example job description given.

4   Your answer might be something like the following (drawn from *Baker et al*, p 48).

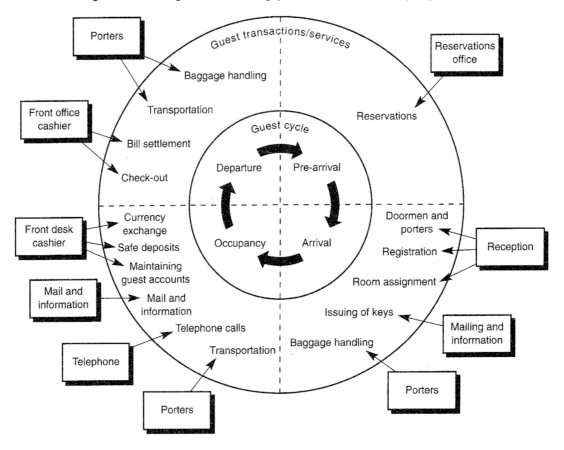

CHAPTER 2

RESERVATION PROCEDURES

Chapter objectives

In this chapter you will learn

- How to handle initial enquiries
- How to receive and record reservation requests
- How to use manual and electronic systems for recording bookings
- How to guarantee reservations, using deposits and pre-payments
- The international terminology for rooms and bed types
- The different packages and rates offered by hotels
- How rooms are allocated
- How to confirm reservations
- How to monitor the status of reservations
- How to cancel reservations if required

Topic list

Handling enquiries
Handling advance reservations
Computerised reservations
Understanding rooms and rates
Confirmations and guarantees
Group and conference reservations
Reservations from other sources

1 Handling enquiries

The process of making a hotel booking or reservation usually begins with an **enquiry** from prospective guests, who contact the hotel to ask for a brochure, or to ask specific questions about the price and availability of rooms for the period they are interested in. First of all, such a request is an opportunity to give a **good first impression** of the hotel: a prompt, positive and courteous response will reassure prospective guests that they will receive good service if they book into this establishment.

1.1 How do enquiries come in?

Guests may make enquiries in various ways.

- **In person**. People may come in 'on the off chance' of immediate accommodation, often because they are travelling unexpectedly, or touring (usually in the off season) without making advance plans. A local person may also 'drop in' in person, since it is convenient to do so, to make a booking on behalf of others: an out-of-town friend, say – or a tour group or conference (eg if the local person is the organiser). Enquiries which come in 'off the street' like this are often known as '**walk ins**'. Face-to-face enquiries offer the advantage of interactivity: enquirers and reservations staff can both gather information and get their questions answered in real time – and written confirmation of the details can also be prepared and handed over on the spot.

DEFINITION

Walk-ins are people who turn up in person at reception, enquiring about the availability of accommodation, either immediately (eg if they are travelling unexpectedly or touring without advance plans) or to make an advance booking for a later visit.

- **In writing**. People may send a written request for a booking, in the form of a letter or booking form (from a hotel brochure, say), by mail, facsimile transfer (fax) or e-mail. Written enquiries are useful for the hotel, as they may set out clearly the details of the guest's requirements (room types, number of guests, arrival and departure dates), and contact details for the hotel to gather additional information and/or confirm the booking. Letters, e-mails and forms can also be used to *confirm* bookings made by telephone, so that both parties have written evidence of what was discussed and agreed, which they can refer to later if they need to. The particular advantage of e-mail and fax, compared to the postal system, is that they can be used to send and receive bookings and confirmations almost instantly (via telecommunication links) from one side of the world to the other, regardless of distance, time zones and so on.

- **By telephone**. The phone is a fast, convenient and cost-effective way of making an enquiry. Its interactive nature allows the prospective guest and the hotel to ask questions and exchange information in real time – without written to-ing and fro-ing – for quick, accurate agreement on details. Because guests can *know* that their enquiry has been received and answered, on the spot, the phone is often used to make last-minute bookings: no risk of turning up at the hotel to find that no-one has checked the e-mail or fax machine lately! The disadvantage of phone enquiry is that it doesn't get the details of the conversation down in black and white: some form of note-taking and/or written confirmation (if there is time) is often required to ensure that everyone is on the same 'page'.

- **Online**. Increasingly, guests and travel agencies gather information about hotel rates and room availability via the **web sites** of individual hotels, centralised booking sites for hotel chains, and agency booking sites (some specialising in particular types of travel, or in last-minute discounted packages, say). On many sites, bookings can be made online and processed directly by the hotel's or agency's computerised booking system: leaving an electronic record for the hotel, and generating an electronic confirmation for the guest – without human intervention or involvement. This can be extremely cost effective for a hotel with the relevant systems set up, so many such hotels offer incentives for people to book online (eg by passing on some of the cost savings in the form of online booking discounts).

BPP
LEARNING MEDIA

EXAMPLE

'A Word from the FOM (Front Office Manager)'

When training our staff to take enquiries and making reservations, we use the acronym: QQI.

Qualify: get details of the customer's requirement, plus any discount vouchers or loyalty cards they hold, and any discounted or negotiated rates they are entitled to. Check room availability.

Quote: you can then make a suitable offer to the customer: what room type you have, what the facilities and inclusions are, and what the best available room rate you can offer is.

Invite: ask the customer whether (s)he would like to make a reservation on that basis.

We might also add another 'C' on the end, because it is always advisable, once the customer has said 'yes' and made the reservation, to **confirm** all the details that have been agreed: repeat them back to the customer and ask for confirmation that they are correct.

1.2 What information will be exchanged?

In order to handle an enquiry – and turn it into a **reservation** – certain **information** will have to be exchanged between the prospective guest and the reservation clerk or enquiry handler.

Questions the prospective guest may ask	Questions the reservation clerk must ask
■ Is there are room of a particular type available on a particular date?	■ What type of room is required?
■ What types of room are available?	■ When (on what dates) is the room required?
■ How many people does a room sleep?	■ For how long (nights) is the room required?
■ What facilities are offered in the room?	■ How many people will be staying in the room?
■ What facilities and services does the hotel offer?	■ The room rate is x (per person or per night): is this acceptable?
■ Does the hotel have particular facilities (eg parking, childcare, business services)?	■ What is the name of the guest (and how is it spelled)?
■ What is the cost of the room (per person or per night)?	■ What is the title of the guest (eg Mr, Mrs, Ms, Doctor, Professor)?
■ What is included in the cost/tariff (eg breakfast, access to the hotel facilities)?	■ What is the guest's address, phone number and/or e-mail address?
■ What is the star rating of the hotel?	■ How would the guest prefer to settle the bill?
■ Where is the hotel located (and/or how can the guest get there)?	■ May the hotel take the credit card number of the guest (and if so, what is it)?
■ Is the hotel close to transport/attractions?	■ How will the guest be arriving at the hotel (eg by car, or by what train or flight)?
	■ What is the guest's anticipated time of arrival at the hotel?
	■ Has the guest stayed at the hotel before?
	■ Is the guest a member of the hotel's loyalty programme (or 'frequent guests club')?
	■ What is the guest's nationality?

EXAMPLE

Consider the following telephone reservation request.

Reservations clerk (RC):   Good morning. Hill Town Hotel: Reservations. Jo speaking.

Customer (C):   Good morning, I'd like to book a room for next Wednesday the 18th, if possible.

RC: Certainly, madam. For how many nights did you want the room?

C: Three nights.

RC: Three nights... And what type of room were you interested in?

C: A double room, please.

RC: I can offer you a standard double for £79 per night, or a deluxe queen-bedded room at the special rate of £99 per night, plus VAT. The deluxe is more spacious, with a queen bed, and has a fine view over either the gardens or the city.

C: I'll take the deluxe, please.

RC: Thank you. May I have your surname and first initial, please?

C: Yes, my name is Mrs D Chapman.

RC: Is the room for yourself, Mrs Chapman?

C: No, I'm booking for some friends.

RC: May I have the names of the guests, please?

C: Yes, its Mr and Mrs L Cavalleri. That's C-A–V-A-L-L-E-R-I.

RC: Thank you. Do you know how they will be arriving at the hotel?

C: By air.

RC: Do you know their flight details, or approximate time of arrival?

C: I believe their flight is due in at about 4.30 pm. Can I request a city view for them, if possible?

RC: I'm afraid I can't guarantee that, Mrs Chapman, but I'll certainly note it down as a request, and we'll do our best. And may I take a contact telephone number for you, please, Mrs Chapman?

C: Yes, it's 208 740 2222.

RC: Thank you. And can I also take your address, so that I can send you a letter of confirmation?

C: Certainly. It's 5 Bannerman Street, Guildford, Surrey, SL3 6AR.

RC: Thank you. Let me just confirm the details with you, Mrs Chapman. You have reserved one deluxe queen room, in the names of Mr and Mrs L Cavalleri: arriving on Wednesday 18th June and departing on Saturday 21st June: that's three nights. The room rate will be £99 per night plus VAT. The room will be held until 6 pm on the evening of Mr and Mrs Cavalleri's arrival – unless you would like to guarantee the reservation by paying a deposit?

C: No, that's fine, thank you. The Cavelleri's will pay for the room themselves, by credit card.

RC: That's fine, Mrs Chapman. I will send a confirmation letter out to you this afternoon. Is there anything else I can help you with today?

C: No, thank you. Goodbye.

RC: Thank you for your reservation, Mrs Chapman. Goodbye.

2 Handling advance reservations

Dealing with **advance reservations** is one of the most important and tricky tasks of the hotel Front Office team. Reservation clerks routinely have to sort out multiple requests for accommodation to ensure that every request is dealt with, individual requirements are catered for, the hotel's interests are served – *and* a positive impression of the hotel is conveyed at every step.

Reservations constitute a 'promise' to guests: that the rooms they have booked will be available when agreed, on the terms agreed, and with special requirements catered for. A mishandled reservation – where these promises are not met when the guest arrives – can be a major source of customer dissatisfaction and complaint. Reservations are also a first step in building-up a 'picture' of guests and their needs and wants, which helps the front office and hotel management to provide individualised, satisfying service when guests arrive.

In addition, reservations may be received many months in advance, and are therefore (as we will see in Chapter 6) a useful tool for forecasting future levels of business. These forecasts can help managers to plan advertising and special offers to stimulate occupancy in 'slow' periods – and to plan the deployment of staff and resources to cover busy periods.

FOR DISCUSSION

Thinking through a basic reservation enquiry, such as the example given above, what are the basic requirements for a reservations 'system'? What kinds of information will the reservation clerk need access to, in order to take the reservation? And what kinds of information will reception staff need, in order to prepare to welcome the booked-in guests?

2.1 Reservation form

DEFINITION

A **reservation form** records the information about a booking enquiry, setting out the prospective guest's needs and contact details, and an on-going record of the progress of the handling of the request (whether the booking has been confirmed and so on).

A standard **reservation form** may look similar to Figure 2.1 below.

Such a form:

- Provides a hard copy record of the details of the booking request

- Summarises and records the information in a standardised, easy-to-use format

- Acts as a checklist of the information a reservations clerk needs to get from the prospective guest

- Identifies the person who took the booking, in case of queries or errors which need to be followed-up later

- Provides a quick check on the progress of the reservation: has it been processed, has it been confirmed to the guest, has the booking been guaranteed?

- Captures information which may be useful for marketing and/or improving services in future: for example, the source of the booking and how the booking was made.

In a manual system, a completed reservation form becomes the top sheet of an on-going **guest file,** in which will be placed correspondence, registration documents and so on. It allows quick reference to what has been agreed with the guest, to prepare for their arrival at the hotel.

A C T I V I T Y   1   5   m i n u t e s

Work through our earlier example of a telephone reservation, and fill the details into the specimen Reservation Form overleaf, as far as you are able to.

Hill Town Hotel

RESERVATION FORM

Arrival date: .... Est. arrival time: .... Nights stay:...........................

Room type: .... No of persons:............................... Rate/terms: ....

Guest contact details:

Name: ....

Address: ....

....

E-mail:.. Phone: (...................................)

Booking placed by:

Name: ....

Address: ....

....

E-mail:.. Phone: (...................................)

Special instructions/requirements

....

....

....

Request made: In person ❑   By phone ❑   Letter ❑   E-mail ❑   Fax ❑   Online ❑

Guaranteed: ❑   Guaranteed to:...   at 6pm ❑

To be confirmed: ❑   Confirmed ❑ by:.......................................   Wait list ❑

Clerk: ....   Date: ....

Figure 2.1: Reservation form

If the hotel uses a **computerised reservation system**, the details can be input immediately (from the enquiry letter, e-mail or phone call) into an on-screen electronic reservation form. This has the advantage that the information can be automatically linked to other electronic records and documents, as part of the 'history' of the dealings with the guest. However, *Abbott & Lewry* (*Front Office*) suggest that there is *still* an argument for using a paper-based reservation form to take the initial enquiry, before *transferring* the details to the computerised system later (during a quiet period).

- It may be quicker and easier to use a paper form, which allows you to 'skip' to relevant fields as required (without complex on-screen navigation) – especially if you are on the phone with the enquirer and do not have a 'hands-free' telephone headset.

- Using a paper form may enable you to give your full attention to the enquirer – rather than to the computer system!

Transferring the details from the form to the computerised system later may leave the booking records temporarily incomplete: if advance bookings look as if they are nearly full, availability should be checked carefully, and the details transferred immediately to the computerised system.

2.2 Will you accept the booking request?

Of course, the whole point of a hotel is to take guests – and most of the Front Office role will be concerned with ensuring that the hotel gets as many bookings as possible. However, there may be circumstances in which hotel will want to **turn down a reservation**.

Some guests are more welcome than others...

DEFINITION

A **black list** is a record of individuals or corporations whom the hotel does not wish to accept as guests, for various reasons, for use by reservations staff when handling booking requests.

The **Hotel Proprietors Act 1956** provides that a hotel has a legal obligation to accept *bona fide* (genuine) travellers who 'appear able and willing to pay a reasonable sum for the services and facilities provided, and who are in a fit state to be received', if rooms are available. In the UK, various equal opportunities legislation also imposes a duty *not* to discriminate unfairly against prospective guests on the grounds of sex, age, race, religion or disability, in the provision of goods, facilities or services.

However, as the Hotel Proprietors Act suggests, a person may legitimately be blacklisted – or refused the services of the hotel – if:

- (S)he has previously stayed at the hotel and failed or been unable to pay the bill.

- (S)he has previously stayed at the hotel and behaved in an undesirable way: causing damage, disturbing other guests, or being abusive towards staff – perhaps while under the influence of alcohol or drugs.

- (S)he has been suspected of illegal behaviour while in the hotel (eg drug dealing, prostitution, theft from the hotel or guests).

- (S)he turns up at the hotel in a state, or behaving in such a way, as to suggest the likelihood of the above problems – even if there is a confirmed booking: such behaviour may be interpreted as breaking the implied terms of the contract with the hotel, entitling it to require the guest to leave.

- The bill will be paid on account by a company which owes the hotel large sums of money, routinely pays late, or is otherwise not credit-worthy (eg at risk of insolvency, so that the hotel would not be able to recover money owing to it).

- The individual or company has been reported to the hotel – on any of the above grounds – by *other* hotels who have found them undesirable in the past. Hotels often exchange this kind of information.

The list of 'undesirables' may be kept in any format that is easy for front office staff to consult – without being visible or accessible to the general public! Blacklists and refusals are very sensitive, with the

BPP LEARNING MEDIA

potential to offend people and cause awkward conflict situations (especially if the hotel has suspicion rather than proof of undesirable behaviour). If a reservation clerk recognises the name of a blacklisted individual on a booking request, the best response is probably simply to say that no rooms are available.

Some bookings are more desirable than others...

All things being equal, a hotel would prefer to take longer bookings (less costs of guest turnover and room preparation), from known guests (less risk), at the best possible room rate (ie not at discounted rates). Some bookings are, therefore, 'better' for the hotel than others.

The discipline of **yield management**, which we will discuss in detail in Chapter 6, helps the hotel to:

- Forecast how full the hotel is likely to be on a given date in the future (based on previous occupancy and booking patterns, projected into the future).

- Determine how reservations can be 'juggled' to get the fullest possible occupancy at the best possible rate. On a Sunday evening, for example, a discounted rate may have to be offered to fill a room. However, if the room can be let from the Friday night to the Sunday night at full rate, this same room will generate more revenue.

The hotel may, therefore, turn down a reservation, stating that no rooms are available, because it anticipates being able to let the room at a higher rate, or on more beneficial terms, at a later date. (Don't worry if this seems complicated now: we'll work through the logic in Chapter 6.)

2.3 Can you fulfil the booking request?

The next step is to check whether the hotel has a suitable room free on the dates requested by the prospective guest. **Availability information** should be readily visible, using various diary, chart and/or computerised reservations records – making it easy to see at a glance what rooms are available when – which we will discuss below.

- If a **suitable room is free** on the dates requested, the reservations clerk may offer it to the enquirer, quoting any rates and conditions (eg arrival or check-out times) that may influence the decision. If the enquirer accepts, the booking can be logged and confirmed.

- If a **suitable room is not, currently, free** on the dates requested, a number of different options may be available.

    - The enquirer may be offered a different room type for the same dates.

    - The enquirer may be asked whether (s)he is flexible on dates, stating the dates on which the requested room type are available.

If the prospective guest accepts either of these options, the booking can be logged and confirmed. If *neither* of the options fits the enquirer's plans, further options may (depending on the circumstances) be proposed.

    - The enquirer may be offered the option of going on a **waiting list** for the room, to be confirmed by a certain date, subject to availability (for example, in the event of a cancellation, or change in room allocations).

    - The enquirer may be offered the option of **accommodation at another hotel**: often a sister hotel with whom the first hotel has reciprocal referral arrangements – or another hotel of similar quality nearby. If the enquirer accepts this option, the clerk may make an initial availability enquiry (by telephone) on his or her behalf, and transfer the enquirer to the other hotel's reservation desk (or arrange to have the other hotel contact the enquirer).

If the enquirer says no to all the available options, the enquiry is terminated. However, it has hopefully been dealt with in such a helpful and positive way that the prospective guest will consider the hotel next time (s)he is in the area.

Once a prospective guest has accepted the offer of a room for specified nights on specified terms, a **confirmed reservation** can be made and recorded. There are various ways of doing this, both manual and computerised, as we will see below. But first...

2.4 Planned overbooking

We have just said that the reservation clerk will check whether rooms are available before offering a room to a prospective guest – but in practice, that is not always the case! Hotels – like airlines and other services – routinely **over-book** their accommodation: that is, they take more bookings than they have rooms available.

DEFINITION

Planned overbooking is the practice, often pursued by large hotels, of intentionally taking more bookings than there are rooms available, by a pre-determined (limited) number or percentage. This means that the hotel can maximise its forward occupancy, by taking into account the likelihood of a certain percentage of 'no shows' (non-arrivals), cancellations and early departures.

Why on earth would you want to over-book your accommodation: risking having to tell a guest that you've double booked his room? The economic arguments – and the underlying mathematics – are quite simple. Many hotels suffer considerable loss from reserving rooms for people who book and then don't turn up ('**no shows**') or who cancel or shorten their stays at the last minute: it is generally too late to expect replacement bookings, and unless the rooms have been paid for in advance, the hotel loses out. No-shows are particularly common for hotels which cater to business travellers. Based on their own past, and industry, experience (occupancy, no show and cancellation statistics), the hotel can estimate what proportion of bookings will be cancelled or cut short, and attempt to minimise their losses by overbooking to this percentage. The aim is *not* to have double-bookings, but for the over-bookings and no-shows to **cancel each other out**.

The **permitted overbooking rate** may therefore vary from hotel to hotel – since hotels with a high proportion of transient trade will have a higher no-show proportion than a long-stay resort, say. The rate may also vary from week to week, and should be clearly stated on the reservation charts for any given period. In a computerised system, the software will automatically monitor the ratio of reservations to actual arrivals, and adjust the overbooking parameters for different periods, room types and types of bookings.

As you can imagine – especially if you've ever been on the receiving end of overbooking – there is a good side to this policy, and a bad side.

Advantages of planned overbooking	Disadvantages of planned overbooking
■ Minimises financial losses from cancellations, no-shows and shortened stays	■ Based on past statistical trends: may not be reliable, and cause double-bookings
■ Minimises unnecessary refusals, which may send prospective customers to competitors	■ Double-bookings and relocations may alienate prospective guests: lost opportunity of lifetime revenue
■ Based on past statistical trends: should not result in excessive double-bookings	■ Double-bookings and/or confusions over bookings can cause unpleasant and stressful conflict for front office staff
■ Planned re-locations, in the event of double-bookings, can help 'juggle' bookings for better yield management	

As an alternative to overbooking, the hotel may accept bookings on a waiting list, if guests are able to be flexible about taking rooms on short-notice when cancellations occur.

Re-locating guests in the event of double-booking

So what if the allowed-for 'no shows' or cancellations don't, in fact, happen – and you end up with double-booked accommodations? The hotel needs to have a contingency plan to **re-locate** or **book out** some of its guests, so that their dissatisfaction is minimised by having satisfactory alternative arrangements made for them. We will discuss this in Chapter 3.

FOR DISCUSSION

What is your opinion of the practices of (a) planned overbooking and (b) black-listing? You might like to pair up with a fellow-student or colleague and debate the 'pros' (arguments for) and 'cons' (arguments against) for both the guest and the hotel.

2.5 The bookings diary

The main purpose of any diary system, such as you might use to organise your personal life or studies, is to record what is due to happen on any given day: your appointments, tasks, events to remember and so on.

A hotel **bookings diary** is a record of expected arrivals due to stay at the hotel on each day of the year.

DEFINITION

A manual bookings diary system can take a variety of forms.

A traditional bookings diary

A traditional diary format allows reservations staff to list all the arrivals due on a particular date, often on pages in loose-leaf folder (so that pages can be taken out when no longer relevant, leaving today's date always at the front). Diary entries are made in chronological order, as they are booked, see Figure 2.2.

DATE OF ARRIVAL: 28 May 2009							
Date booked	Name	Stay	No of persons	Room type	Room allocated	Terms	Notes
23/1/09	Greene, Mr & Mrs AB	2N	2	+B	12	Room only	Wheelchair access
19/3/09	Blew, Ms D	1N	1	−S	11	B & B	Bill to Azure Ltd
20/3/09	Pincke, Dr ML	2N	2	=B	13	Early booking discount	Arriving late

Figure 2.2: A traditional bookings diary page

We have used some of the standard 'shorthand' symbols for different room types here:

−	Single room
+	Double room
=	Twin room (N or Nt is often used as shorthand for 'nights')
B	With bath
S	With shower

Note that entries are only made for the **date of arrival**: the full length of stay (and therefore the status of the room) would be separately recorded on some form of **room availability record** (covered below).

Whitney system card racks

For a large hotel, it might be more efficient – instead of making fresh entries in a bookings diary – to simply file reservation forms in batches, according to date of arrival (and then in alphabetical order): all you have to do then is consult the file for a particular day. A streamlined at-a-glance form of this approach, pioneered by the Whitney Corporation, is the **Whitney system** – which you can still see in some large hotels as a manual 'back-up' system to computerised reservation systems.

Reservation details are entered on standard-sized index cards, which are designed to fit into **wall-mounted racks**: the cards overlap, just showing the top line (arrival date, name, and room type, say, for ease of reference). Sections of the rack are labelled (using moveable header slips) with each of the days of the current month, plus each of the next twelve months, plus a section for bookings beyond that.

As new bookings come in, the card can simply be slipped into place under the month, week or day concerned, and sorted as required. Cards can be inserted in alphabetical order, making it easy to locate particular bookings. They can also be colour-coded, to identify VIP arrivals, group bookings and so on. If the reservations are changed, slips can simply be amended and slotted into another arrival date, as required – without messing up the record in any way (as with a diary). As each arrival date comes, the relevant rack can be taken out, the others moved along, and emptied racks slotted in on the end.

A card-rack system thus offers a constantly up-to-date, at-a-glance look at expected arrivals for any given period.

2.6 Room availability records

Room **availability** records enable front office staff to assess at a glance whether (and which) rooms are available for booking and/or allocation.

There are three basic manual systems currently in use:

- A **bedroom book** or **reservations journal** (very small hotels)
- A **conventional chart** (small to medium-sized hotels)
- A **density chart** (medium to large hotels).

Bedroom book (reservations journal)

This is much like a bookings diary, except that the entries are made against room numbers, and guests names are entered against their allocated room number for each night of their stay.

Date: 28 May 2009		
Room	Name	Notes
11(S)	Blew	(x 1)
12(D)	Greene	(x 2)
13(T)	Pincke	(x 2) Arriving late
14 (T)		

Date: 29 May 2009		
Room	Name	Notes
11(S)		
12(D)	Greene	
13(T)	Pincke	
14(T)		

Figure 2.3: Bedroom book

ACTIVITY 2   **5 minutes**

What do you think would be the disadvantages or limitations of a bedroom book system? (Think about different lengths of stay, and different sized hotels...)

What do you think are its advantages?

Conventional chart

A **conventional chart** is a simple **bookings control chart** that allows front office staff to see at a glance the overall booking position of the hotel. It is a form of Gantt chart (such as is also used to plan staff holidays and project work). At the same time as an entry is put into the bookings diary, another entry is put onto the chart: blocking out reserved rooms with a line from the arrival date to the departure date of each guest. This can be shown as follows at Figure 2.4.

Month:	June 2009														
Room no	Room type	1	2	3	4	5	6	7	8	9	10	11	12	13	14	15
11	–S			←------Emerald-----→							←-----Whyte Ltd-----→				
12	+B						←Dunne→				←-----Whyte Ltd-----→				
13	=B	←BN→	←----Redde----→							←-----Whyte Ltd-----→				
14	=B										<A>				

Figure 2.4: A conventional bookings control chart

The system works best for smaller resort hotels, where reservations tend to be for longer periods such as a week, as one night stays are fiddly to insert: by convention, each date column represents the night of the guest's stay, so a guest arriving on the 28th and leaving on the 29th would be blocked against the 28th only.

Entries are usually made in **pencil**, to allow for cancellations and room changes, including stay reductions or extensions, or the 'juggling' of bookings to fit everyone in. It is essential to record these, and also on-the-spot lettings (not booked in advance), because the chart must at all times show which rooms are booked on a given night.

The chart offers a simple and easy to use system. However, it suffers a few limitations:

- In order for the system to work, you have to **allocate a particular room** to guests at the time of booking. Many hotels prefer rather to reserve a room *type* at the time of booking, and allocate particular rooms when guests arrive, according to the guest's preferences, whether the room is ready for occupation (prepared by housekeeping), how room requests need to be 'juggled' to maximise occupancy and so on.

- It is difficult to operate **planned overbooking**, because there are no spaces to allow for it: the system only suits hotels with low 'no show' rates (and therefore little need to overbook).

- It is not easy to find an immediate **tally of free rooms** on any given night – and this may be a limitation if a hotel needs to take short-notice group bookings.

- **Space** is limited, and the chart can swiftly get cramped and messy, especially if there are a lot of short stays and reservation changes. The system really only suits hotels with fewer than 60 rooms.

Density chart

Density charts are designed to overcome some of the limitations of conventional charts: in particular, a hotel's reluctance to allocate specific rooms at the time of reservation.

DEFINITION

A **density chart** is a chart recording the number of rooms of a particular type which have been booked for each night. Individual reservations are not linked to particular room numbers until the date of arrival, when guests are allocated rooms on check-in.

This system suits **large hotels** with **standardised rooms**, because prospective guests probably don't have preferences about which particular room they get: they merely request a particular *type* of room on reservation, and wait to be allocated a room when they arrive at the hotel.

A density chart looks similar to a conventional chart, but instead of room numbers, the horizontal rows represent the total number of rooms of a specified type. Rooms may be classified as follows, with the total number of rooms of each type shown in brackets:

- Twin with bath (15)
- Twin with shower (12)
- Double with bath (30)
- Double with shower (15)
- Single with shower (6)

A chart is then drawn up for each room type for a given period (say, a month), with spaces (or circles or icons or whatever) corresponding to the number of available rooms. When a booking is received, a stroke (/) is used to 'block out' a room in the appropriate date column. As more bookings are received for that room type, for that date, the strokes progress down the column, forming an instant 'tally' of how many rooms are booked (and free, reading down the left-hand tally column) for that date as illustrated in Figure 2.5.

Single with shower																			JUNE 2009
No of rooms	1	2	3	4	5	6	7	8	9	10	11	12	13	14	15	16	17	18	19
6	/		/	/	/	/	/	/	/	/	/	/	/	/	/	/	/	/	/
5	/		/	/	/	/	/	/		/	/	/	/	/	/		/	/	/
4	/		/		/	/	/	/		/	/	/	/	/	/		/	/	/
3		/		/	/	/					/	/	/	/	/		/	/	/
2				/	/	/					/	/	/	/	/			/	
1				/	/	/					/							/	
−1				/	/														
−2																			

Figure 2.5: Density chart

In our example, the reservations clerk can instantly see that there are no more single rooms with shower available on the 5th of June (unless the minus rows are used for planned overbooking). However, there are three such rooms available for a group booking on the 8th to the 10th of the month. (If a booking is made for three days, three scores are made – one in each date column – but they probably won't be in the same row, because of the different tallies already notched up for the different days.)

Group bookings can be indicated by drawing a line around the strokes represented by the booking (as shown in our example), perhaps with the booking or file number added to identify the group.

Density charts appeal to large (usually modern) hotels with standardised accommodation, which cater for a lot of block bookings, and need to operate over-booking to compensate for no-shows. (Even if such hotels are likely to have computerised reservations systems, these days, room availability data is often displayed on the same principles as the density chart, but on the computer screen...)

Advantages of density charts	Disadvantages of density charts
▪ Less work, with less data to be recorded	▪ Difficult to check accuracy, as strokes aren't related to particular bookings
▪ Space for more rooms (larger hotels)	
▪ Allows at-a-glance tally of the number of rooms left on a given night (eg for group bookings)	▪ Only suitable for standard rooms: can't satisfy guest preference for particular rooms
▪ Allows for overbooking (by using minus rows) to maximise occupancy	

ACTIVITY 3   5 minutes

(a) A caller has asked for two single rooms on the 10th. Are they available? If so, mark them on the density chart above.

(b) An e-mail asks about availability for a group, which requires three single rooms on the 4th and 5th. As a second-choice alternative, the group could switch to the 16th and 17th. Which option will be available? Assuming you take the reservation, mark it on the density chart.

(c) The front desk is asking how many single rooms are available on the 8th. What will you tell them?

(d) A reservation request has come in for a single room for the 16th, 17th and 18th. Assuming that you are allowed to overbook to the maximum shown on the chart, is a room available? If so, mark it on the density chart.

(e) What do you notice about bookings on the 2nd, 9th and 16th? What might this tell you, and what might you recommend to the hotel's management?

Stop-go (space availability) charts

DEFINITION

A **stop-go (or space availability) chart** summarises the information on the main chart in visual form, so that the reservation clerk doesn't have to refer to the detailed booking chart every time a reservation request is received. The chart indicates whether a particular room type is available, fully booked or close-to-fully booked for a given night.

A stop-go chart is basically a calendar for the year, with symbols inserted (in pencil) on a given day if there are no rooms left of a particular type (no singles, no twins); or if the hotel is completely full (S/O or Sold Out) or nearing capacity (G/S or 'Go Slow') and so on.

- If a date is clear, the clerk could 'safely' go ahead and take a booking: rooms are **available**.

- If there is a symbol indicating a particular room type, but there is **no availability** of that type of room: the clerk will have to offer alternative options to the enquirer.

- If there is a '**Go Slow**' marking, the clerk will have to check the more detailed reservation records to check on up-to-date availability, or might be able to sell individual rooms but check if a group booking is received.

- The stop-go chart can be used by the reservations manager to **block further reservations** on particular room types at particular periods, or at reduced rates, in order to 'save' the rooms for longer-stay or higher-rate bookings: the process of yield management, mentioned earlier. This may be annotated on the chart as R (Refer): the clerk would refer the reservation request to the Reservations Manager, who would decide whether to release the room – or whether a more advantageous option might become available. (Again, we'll discuss this in detail in Chapter 6.)

Like all the other charts, the markings will have to be **kept up-to-date**, as particular room types reach capacity, or as rooms become available again through cancellations and so on. Like all the other charts, too, this is much more efficiently displayed on a computerised system!

2.7 Guest histories

Handling reservations starts the process of providing efficient, satisfying service to guests. For those hotels wishing to provide a more personalised service for guests on subsequent visits, a **guest history card or file** is an important *aide memoire* (or memory prompter) for staff, so that the hotel appears to recognise each returning guest and recall his or her needs and preferences.

We will discuss this in detail in Chapter 6, as part of the reporting function of Front Office. However, it is worth noting that building guest history files starts with the **initial enquiry and reservations**, during which the staff member can find out a great deal of information about the requirements and preferences of prospective guests. During occupancy, the guest history can be added to with information on dates and purposes of visit, likes and dislikes, preferred methods of payment, feedback and so on. Gathering and recording this information is part of the daily work of the customer-facing staff at front office. (Note that this kind of information may also contribute to the black list, discussed earlier...)

3 Computerised reservations

As we noted earlier, advance reservations can be a complex planning exercise, juggling the needs of guests with the needs of the business: a jigsaw puzzle fitting together people, dates and rooms. In recent decades, computer software programmes have increasingly been used to carry out the complex calculations, maintain up-dated running totals and so on that would be time-consuming and messy to do with a manual system.

Computerised advance reservation systems are now widespread in large hotels – and even, as prices come down and computers are in widespread use, in small ones. There are many software packages available for reservations – generally linked to a suite of other functions including room availability records, check-in and check-out systems, billing and payment systems, guest database systems and all sorts of other processes, records and reports. These suites of functions are often called Hotel Management Systems (HMS) or Premises Management Systems (PMS), as we saw in Chapter 1.

3.1 How computerised reservations work

Fortunately, **computerised reservations** work much in the same way as the manual systems discussed above. The same kinds of information need to be recorded, and the same kinds of displays and records need to be available, for the same reasons. Mostly, however, the displays will *look* different on screen – and you will have to learn to navigate within a system to 'find' the pages/records/functions you want to use at any given time.

If you get a room enquiry, you will need to:

- Access the **Advance Reservations** or Reservations part of the programme. There will usually be a 'main menu' or 'home' screen, giving you options as to which type of programme you want to enter.

- Access the **Room Availability** display, and type in the dates you are interested in. The screen will show room availability data, usually in the form of a table displaying the numbers of each room type available. This is a bit like a density chart, except that instead of adding 'scores', the computer software simply updates the running total for you as new reservations are made as shown in Figure 2.6.

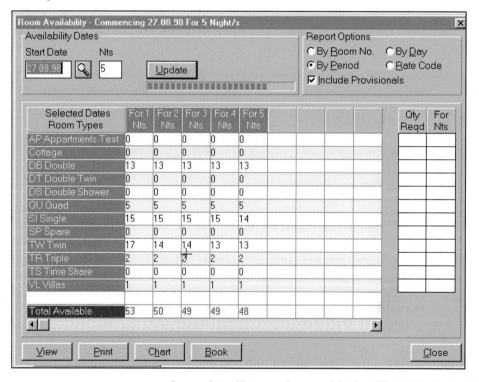

Source: http://intranet.bpc.ac.uk/widecoll/hotel/HotPerAv.html

Figure 2.6: Room availability display (in Hotel Perfect)

- Having established room availability for the enquiry, you can access the **Bookings** section of the programme, which is like an on-screen version of the Reservation Form. You can therefore add the guest details and a tariff code or terms. You can usually add a range of other information: a reference identifying a group booking (so that the rooms can be checked-in and checked-out together); the company (if any) paying for the booking, so that it can be billed direct; special requests and pre-booked extras; how the booking has been made, whether it has been guaranteed and confirmed and so on. You may also, at this point, allocate a particular room to the booking, if this is the hotel's policy.

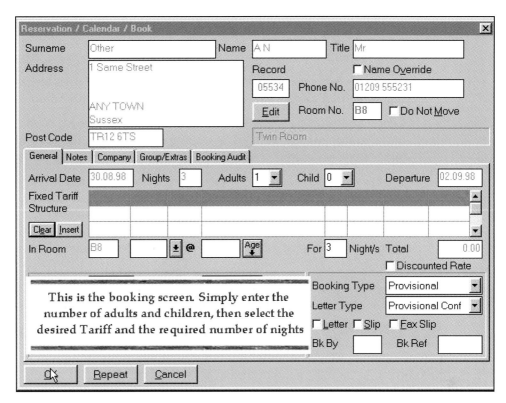

Figure 2.7: The reservations screen (in Hotel Perfect)

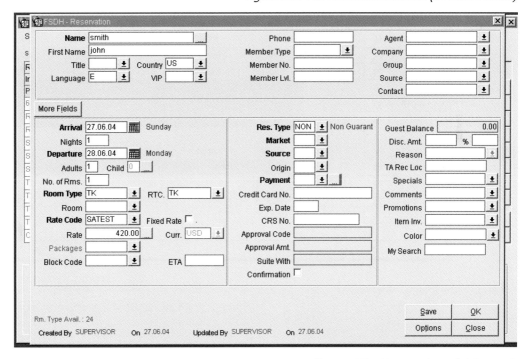

Source: http://www.micros-fidelio.co.uk

Figure 2.8: The reservation screen (in Fidelio's OPERA Reservation System)

Once the booking has been entered into the system, the software can use the data to process a wide range of linked reports, updates and displays.

- The **room availability data** is adjusted to take account of the newly booked room, and if a specific room has been allocated, it is 'blocked' so that it does not show up as available for anyone else (ie the software acts as both a density chart *and* a conventional chart): Figure 2.9.

- A **room control chart** can be produced, for an at-a-glance display of the status of each room: not just in terms of bookings, but availability for guest arrival/allocation (eg if a room is currently being cleaned), as a trigger for further action (eg room moves, billing, departures) and so on.

- An **arrivals list**, group arrivals list and VIP/Special Attention Guests list can be prepared (and kept up-to-date) for each day, allowing front office staff to plan for check-ins.

- **Cancellations** can be processed in one operation – simultaneously deleting all records related to the reservation (without the need for crossing out or Tippex in the diary, conventional chart, guest record and so on).

- The **guest details** can be used in various ways: linked to word-processing programmes (to input all the bookings details on a confirmation form or letter, say); searched by name (eg if someone enquires about a guest who has not yet arrived); searched by group (eg if you want a list of group members for other purposes eg restaurant bookings); searched by type or status (eg if you want to compile a list of expected VIPs – or 'black listed' individuals); and so on.

- The bookings details will be automatically **linked to other programmes**, which carry out the tasks we will cover in later chapters: check-in, check-out, billing and payment, guest history records, yield management (maximising occupancy and revenue) and so on.

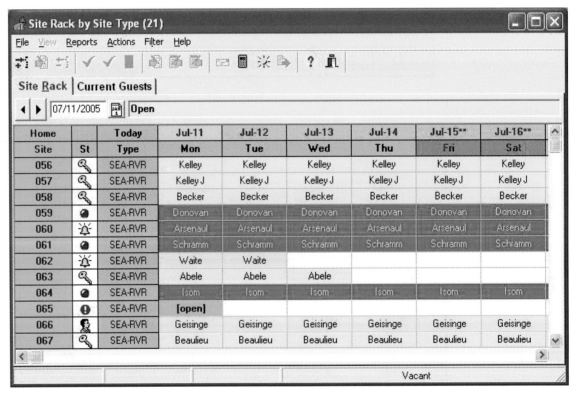

Source: www.mkmware.com/roomrack

Figure 2.9: An availability/room chart or 'room rack' (in MotelMax)

ACTIVITY 4   1 5   m i n u t e s

From what we've said above, and from our discussion of Hotel Management Systems in Chapter 1, compile a simple table showing the advantages and disadvantages of computerised reservation systems.

4 Understanding rooms and rates

Before we go any further, perhaps we'd better take a step back and look at what exactly it is that front office is reserving or 'selling' – as terminology varies from country to country and in different hotels. What exactly is the product offered by a hotel, and on what terms is it sold?

4.1 Room and bed types

Hotel accommodation varies in different ways:

- By **grade or standard**, depending on size, décor and furniture, location/view and in-room facilities. A hotel may classify its rooms as standard, superior and deluxe, for example – or have its own special terminology to describe different grades. Customers are unlikely to know what these descriptors mean, so reservations staff will have to be able to describe the amenities provided by each grade of room – and the value added at each higher grade: superior rooms are larger, say, or have ensuite bathrooms, or mini-bar facilities.

- By **number and size of beds per room**. This is the main way in which prospective guests will enquire about rooms.

Type of room	Number of beds per room	Size/width of bed	Occupants per room
Single	1 (single bed)	3 feet	1
Twin	2 (single beds)	3 feet	2 – but may be let for single occupancy
Double	1 (double bed)	4 ft 6 inches	2 – but may be let for single occupancy
Queen	1 (queen size)	5 feet	2 – but may be let for single occupancy
King	1 (king size)	6 feet	2 – but may be let for single occupancy
Family	3+ (double plus singles or bunks)		3+

In addition, the hotel may offer '**suites**', which may have separate lounge or dining areas in addition to one or more bedrooms.

- By **target customer**. Some hotels offer special types of accommodation for particular types of customer.

   - There may also be '**presidential suites**' or 'penthouses' for VIP and wealthy guests: usually a suite of rooms, which are spacious and decorated to a very high standard.

   - There may be areas of the hotel designated for **female travellers** only (to enhance their comfort and security), or for **smokers** (to avoid placing non-smokers in rooms which have absorbed tobacco smells).

   - A hotel with a high proportion of business trade may set aside '**executive floors**', with room types and facilities specially catering to the needs of business travellers: meeting rooms, communication facilities, lounge and bar for client entertaining and so on.

Room 2, Twin, private shower room

*Photo:*http://www.windsorgardensbedandbreakfast.co.uk   *Photo:* http://www.gokarna.com

FOR DISCUSSION

The photos above might both, technically, be classed as 'twin' rooms: one in a high quality bed and breakfast hotel, and one in a luxury resort hotel. Supposing for a moment that these rooms were both available in the same establishment (one as a 'superior twin' and one as a 'luxury twin'), how might you describe them to a guest who has called to enquire about a twin room?

4.2   Room rates or tariffs

DEFINITION

Room rate or **tariff** refers to the price at which a hotel sells or lets its rooms. Each room type or grade – and perhaps each different room in a small hotel – may command a different rate, according to the amenities it offers to guests: the size of the room/bed, the décor, location, view, extras provided etc.

The rate for any given room may also vary, according to:

- The **day of the week**. Occupancies may be higher from Monday to Thursday for hotels with a high proportion of business guests, so it may set a lower 'weekend rate' to attract guests on the weekends. For tourist hotels, conversely, a lower 'weekday' or 'mid-week' rate may be set to attract business during the week.

- The **season and seasonal demand**. Similarly, discounted seasonal rates may be set to increase occupancy in 'out of season' months; while higher 'peak season' rates get the maximum revenue from high demand.

- The **customer**: the hotel may offer discounted rates to attract corporate/business travellers (who may bring in high volume business), tour groups or travel agency business, for example.

It is, obviously, important for front office staff to be aware of the different room rates – and who is eligible for discounted rates – in order to quote accurate and attractive rates to guests (while also seeking to maximise the revenue earned by the hotel, an issue we will return to in detail in Chapter 6).

EXAMPLE

'A Word from the FOM (Front Office Manager)'

'Best available rate' is a highly fashionable concept at the moment, particularly with the flexibility of room rates due to the practice of yield management.

It sounds much better, and much more competitive, to customers – who will often in any case ask if any discounts are available – to say: 'The best rate I can offer you for a room on that day is...' – regardless of whether the rate is high (because there is high demand for that period and the hotel can afford to charge more) or low (because the hotel is having to discount the room to try and fill it).

Different terminology is used for different types of room tariffs. The most common ones are:

Rate	Comment
Rack rate	The standard 'full' rate for the room, without inclusions (eg meals), discounts or reductions
Corporate rate	The standard rate charged to corporate (business) customers
Commercial rate	A rate negotiated between the hotel and a business customer, for all its individual room reservations
Children's rate	The rate at which children will be charged if they share the same room as their parents (up to a specified age limit): often free or at a nominal rate
Loyalty rate	The discounted rate for members of the hotel's loyalty scheme, intended to increase repeat business for the hotel
Flat or group rate	The flat rate per room agreed in advance by the hotel and a tour or conference group, regardless of variations in rack rates for different rooms
Airline/agency rate	The rate negotiated between an airline, travel agency or tour operator and the hotel, based on the volume of business the hotel gets or anticipates
Online rate	The standard rate for a room reserved via the Internet, usually at a discount on rack rate, because of the money the hotel saves on administration, which can be passed on to the guest
Packaged rate	A discounted rate offered to individual guests or groups with the inclusion of some meals, as an incentive to boost occupancy in periods of low demand.
Advance purchase rate	A discounted rate offered for booking a minimum of 28 days in advance of arrival (with no amendments or cancellations allowed).
Best available rate	The lowest rate that can be offered to a customer on the day, usually on a room-only basis. This may fluctuate with demand, according to the hotel's yield management policies.

Inclusive and non-inclusive tariffs

Four main types of tariffs are generally available to take account of the inclusions of meals and other extras, and the terminology used varies. It is worth your knowing the different terms, to avoid confusion.

UK terminology	US term.	French term.	Inclusions
Room only	European Plan		None: the rate quoted is for the room only, whether on a per person or per room basis.
Bed & breakfast (B&B)	Continental Plan		The rate includes room plus breakfast. (May specify inclusion of a cold or continental breakfast only, with a cooked or English breakfast at extra charge.)
Half board or semi-inclusive	Modified American Plan (MAP)	*Demi-pension*	The rate includes room, breakfast and one main meal (in the UK, usually dinner).
Full board or fully-inclusive	Full American Plan (FAP)	*En pension*	The rate includes room and all main meals (and sometimes also afternoon tea).

Price display

Regardless of which rate or package has been negotiated with individual guests, the Tourism (Sleeping Accommodation Price List Display) Order 1977 requires all hotels and guest houses to clearly display, at the reception desk, the standard tariff for rooms of each type, together with taxes (such as VAT), service charges and inclusions. This presents a hotel from opportunistically charging *more* than its rack rate for a room, taking advantage of chance guests.

Value added tax (VAT)

Accommodation, along with other goods and services, is subject to Value Added Tax (VAT) in the UK – and a goods and services tax (GST) in many other countries – collected by business on behalf of the government (in the UK, HM Customs and Excise). Room and package rates will be quoted inclusive of VAT – and many other goods and services (with some exceptions, such as newspapers) will also have VAT added to them.

TERMS AND CONDITIONS

Daily rates are expressed in US dollars, European Plan (room only), and are subject to change without notice. Either one king or two double beds may be requested for Deluxe Oceanfront, Deluxe Mountainview and Deluxe Oceanside rooms. There is no charge for children under 18 years staying in their parents' room. Add $90 per night for a third adult staying in the same room.

MEAL PLAN OPTIONS

Several attractively priced meal plans, for your choice of meal times, are available for your convenience and to assist you in planning your vacation.

Modified American Plan (MAP):
Breakfast and Dinner $105 per person per day
Full American Plan (FAP):
Breakfast, Lunch and Dinner $130 per person per day

Children under five accompanied by a parent eat free in our restaurants (not applicable to In-Room Dining, poolside meals or informal outlets).

Guest room rates at the Resort are subject to 9% government tax and a 10% service charge. Guest food & beverage charges at the Resort are subject to 9% government tax and a 15% service charge. A $10 per day Coastal Protection Levy will be applied to room charges only. There are no supplemental gratuities levied during your stay, nor is additional tipping expected.

Airport and water transfers to the Resort are additional ($50 per room round trip for Nevis airport transfers and $100 per person round trip for St. Kitts airport).

Source: http://www.fsestatesnevis.com

---

5   Confirmations and guarantees

5.1   Confirming reservations

In order to make a booking 'firm', it is usual for:

- The hotel to send a **Booking Confirmation letter or e-mail** to the prospective guest, confirming the details of a booking made online or by phone. This gives the prospective guest a written copy of the details discussed and agreed, both as an itinerary (a reminder of where they have to be and when) and as a confirmation record (which can be produced if there is any problem on check-in or billing). This confirmation may also include a request for deposit, or a receipt for any deposit paid, or an invoice showing any deposit paid and the balance of the amount payable (eg for payments in advance). It is also an opportunity to give the guest information on the **terms and conditions** of booking, such as:

- **Cancellation periods** (within which the guest must cancel the booking, in order to avoid being liable for a cancellation fee)

- **Release times** (the time, on the target day of arrival, at which the room will be made available for re-let if the guest has not arrived, unless late arrival has been notified or a deposit or guarantee has been paid).

- The prospective guest to send some kind of **confirmation letter or form** to the hotel, in order to confirm their intention to stay at the hotel; to ensure that the hotel has the details right; and perhaps also to 'secure' the booking by paying a deposit.

5.2 Guaranteed reservations

DEFINITION

A **guaranteed reservation** is one for which the hotel is guaranteed to receive payment, whether or not the guest actually arrives to take up the accommodation. In return, the hotel promises to hold the room until the check-out time of the following day.

Guaranteed (or **guaranteed arrival**) bookings are desirable for the hotel, because it does not lose out in the event of a 'no show', and therefore need not worry about late arrivals, or having to re-let a no-show's room (perhaps at a reduced rate).

Guarantees also protect guests, because the room is held for them, regardless of what time they arrive for the night. They can arrive late – or even early in the morning – if their transport plans require it, or if they are subject to unforeseen delays, without fearing that the room will have been given away to someone else.

There are various ways in which a booking can be guaranteed by a prospective guest:

- **Pre-payment**: the guest pays for the room charges in advance, whether direct to the hotel by cheque or credit card at the time of booking, or to a travel agent (often as part of a package of travel and accommodation bookings). In the latter case, the travel agent will guarantee payment to the hotel and supply the traveller with a voucher (or confirmation letter) indicating that this is the case. Pre-payment is also advantageous for the hotel, because it eliminates the risk of guests' 'skipping out' without paying, or having insufficient funds or credit to pay the bill.

- **Partial pre-payment** or **deposit**. A hotel might typically ask for a deposit of one night's payment for each room reserved, so that the room can be held all night – in the event of a late arrival or no-show – without losing revenue. This deposit will be credited to the guest's account against their stay. If the guest fails to show or cancels the booking on the day of arrival, the hotel may retain the deposit as compensation (or return it to the guest, if the hotel is able to re-let the room, depending on hotel policy). If a guest booking is cancelled within an acceptable cancellation period, any deposit will usually be fully refunded.

- **Credit card bookings**: these are generally guaranteed, under the terms of sale (and prospective guests are often warned that this is the case). If the guest has given a credit card number at the time of booking, and does not cancel the booking within the allowed period before the scheduled arrival date, the hotel is entitled to process the credit card payment, up to an agreed amount.

- **Special agreements**: a company client or airline, for example, may pay for rooms to be 'held' for its use, regardless of whether or not the rooms are actually taken up.

5.3 Non-guaranteed reservations

DEFINITION

A **non-guaranteed reservation** is one for which the guest has agreed and 'confirmed' that (s)he will arrive, but has made no guarantee of payment to the hotel if (s)he does not do so. In return, the hotel does not guarantee to have a room available for the guest, or to hold a room available past a specified time (known as the 'release time').

There are two basic types of non-guaranteed reservation, with different degrees of certainty for guests about whether they will have a room when they arrive.

- A **6 pm release** reservation means that the room is held for the guest until 6 pm on the evening of their arrival. If (s)he arrives after this time, she will have to take a chance on a room still being available: from 6 pm onwards, the hotel has the option of re-letting the room. This arrangement absolves a late-arriving or no-show guest from cancellation fees, while allowing the hotel to re-let the accommodation to maintain occupancy.

- A **take or place (T or P)** booking is a kind of 'waiting list' facility offered by chain hotels, especially to regular customers if they reserve at short notice and the hotel is full. The hotel is assuring the guest that it will *either* take them (if there has been a cancellation or no-show) *or* find a place for them in a comparable hotel, ideally a sister hotel in the same chain, which has vacancies. This helps to satisfy loyal customers, while maximising occupancy for individual hotels (eg through planned overbooking) and 'smoothing out' overbookings and vacancies within hotel chains or groups.

DEFINITION

A **release date** is the date on which a booking will be cancelled if a booking confirmation and/or deposit has not been received. A **release time** (often 6 pm) is the time at which a non-guaranteed booking will be cancelled, and the room made available for waiting list or walk-in guests, if the guest has not arrived and checked-in as expected; in other words, the time at which the guest will be considered a 'no show'.

5.4 Cancellation procedures

If a guest cancels a reservation, then the whole reservation procedure will have to be '**reversed**': the diary entry will be deleted; various chart entries erased; and the notice of cancellation appended to the guest reservation record (in case the guest actually turns up!). Cancellations will also be entered in the **guest history card** (if any). If a pattern of persistent cancellations occurs by an individual or company, the hotel may wish to pursue compensation or black-list the guest. Over time, **cancellation statistics** will also be kept, to support the calculations for planned overbooking (as explained earlier).

In a **computerised system**, the 'reversal' of the reservation procedure will be automatic by marking the reservation as cancelled: all related records and charts will be amended. (We promise you'll grow to love the new technology!) The reservation can also be retained in the system, marked as cancelled, in case of query.

Most hotels set a **cancellation period** (eg 36 hours of the reserved arrival date) before which reservations must be cancelled: beyond this point, the prospective guest will incur a specified short-notice cancellation penalty (which may be deducted from any deposit paid). Some reasons for cancellation are genuinely unavoidable, however, and hotels will often use their discretion to waive penalties – especially for repeat or potentially profitable guests, and *especially* if (as in the case of city centre hotels) there is a reasonable chance of re-letting the room, even so, the stated penalty may act as a disincentive to 'frivolous' bookings and no-shows.

If a tour group cancels at very short notice, however, the hotel may suffer substantial losses and this eventuality is normally covered by the terms of the contract between the hotel and tour operators, in which the tour company 'indemnifies' the hotel against any such losses, ie guarantees to make them good.

The hotel will in any case strive to re-let cancelled accommodation, and can only claim against guests (if it chooses to do so) for losses actually incurred. If a guest cancels a five-day booking at short notice and the hotel manages to re-let the accommodation for three of those days, it can only claim compensation for two days. (It is not allowed to let the same room twice, which is what it would effectively be doing if it got paid by the new guest *and* by the guest who cancelled.)

BPP
LEARNING MEDIA

6 Group and conference reservations

6.1 Group reservations

Group reservations, whether of tourist groups or corporate groups, are often very attractive because they represent 'volume' business for the hotel.

- A sizeable number of rooms may be booked, increasing occupancy.

- Groups are often booked in well in advance, which helps the hotel manage its occupancy, and gives it a measure of security.

- Groups may be booked on the same flat room rate – which may increase the average room rate.

- Groups tend to be booked in and paid for in single transactions conducted by the tour organiser, operator or agent (rather than requiring individual transactions for each member of the group), which cuts down on administrative time, effort and cost.

- Groups will tend to have uniform arrangements: the hotel can anticipate their arrival, departure and having meals at broadly the same time.

- Groups tend to be accompanied by a leader or organiser, who can liaise and help organise some of the administrative tasks of the guest cycle.

- Groups generate added revenue through their spending in other departments of the hotel (eg in the restaurant).

- Groups often offer the potential for repeat business, through the company, travel agent or tour operator.

On the other hand, however, large groups can be challenging – especially in terms of finding space and handling mass simultaneous check-ins and check-outs.

In addition, **groups** change the 'atmosphere' of the hotel – and may alienate independent travellers (particularly if the group is paying a discounted 'package' rate for the same rooms and facilities). A hotel will usually have worked out a desirable ratio of FIT:GIT (that is, independent-to-group) guests, to use as its 'sales mix', depending on the type of hotel, the most common type of business, the most profitable type of business, and patterns of weekly or seasonal demand. Groups often represent higher occupancy – but lower average revenue per room (because of discounted group rates).

F O R   D I S C U S S I O N

'Group bookings: you can't live without them – and you can't live with them!'

Discuss what you see as the advantages and disadvantages for different types of hotels of taking large group bookings.

Group package negotiation

A group or conference organiser is often in a strong bargaining position, compared to an individual guest, because of the volume of business (and potential repeat business) they represent. Groups are therefore generally offered a **discounted rate**, by negotiation with the group organiser.

Obviously, the group organiser may be aiming for rooms in a peak period at the lowest possible rate – while the hotel will be trying to increase occupancy in slack periods at the highest possible rate. This is what **negotiation** is for – to find an agreed solution that is acceptable to both parties.

If the group requirement is for a **slack period** when the hotel would otherwise struggle to fill the rooms, the hotel will be prepared to offer lower terms to get the business. How low could it go? It will need to make a profit on the rooms, so the lowest possible price will be what it costs the hotel to let the room: basically, the cost of any extra labour and consumables (eg laundry costs, stationery used, soap

BPP
LEARNING MEDIA

used, electricity costs) which would not be incurred if the room was empty. (This is called the '**marginal cost**' of letting the room). However, the hotel also has to bear in mind (a) the need to make a profit, and (b) the 'opportunity cost' of letting a room at a lower rate, when it might be able to let it at a higher rate.

If the group requirement is for a **peak period** when the hotel knows it can fill the rooms with customers who will pay the full rack rate, the hotel will be in a stronger bargaining positioning to demand a higher group rate. However, it will also bear in mind the attractiveness of the group's business, and may accept a lesser amount for one peak-period booking in order to 'win' repeat or volume bookings for slacker periods. The level of discount offered may be attached to the number of rooms booked over a year or in 'off-peak' periods. It may also take into account the total

value of the group's business, including expenditure on meals and other extras: the hotel may try to 'lock in' extra revenue by negotiating an inclusive **package rate** to include discounted *table d'hôte* or set price meals.

ACTIVITY 5   2 minutes

Group rates are often offered on a 'twin share' (or 1/2) basis, meaning that two group members occupy a twin room: if group members don't want to share, they may have to pay 'single supplements' or higher rates for the privilege, to compensate the hotel. Can you see why a hotel would make this their policy for group bookings?

Group booking procedures

Group bookings require special attention and protocols for several reasons.

- **Cancellation or 'no show'** by a group represents a serious loss for the hotel. Reservation clerks must therefore take even stricter steps: to check the reliability and credit-worthiness of the group organiser or agency; to establish firm contracts with the organisers, enabling the hotel to gain compensation from losses suffered as a result of breach of contract; to impose strict cancellation periods and penalties; to 'chase' unconfirmed bookings; and to keep records of unreliable organisers (who may be blacklisted, or subject to payment guarantees).

> **Cancellation deadlines** are generally set in stages. For example:
>
> – Cancellation more than 90 days prior to arrival may incur no charge or penalty
> – Cancellation less than 60 days before arrival may incur a charge of 25% of the bill
> – Cancellation less than 30 days before arrival may incur a charge of 50% of the bill
> – Cancellation less than 14 days before arrival may incur a charge of 75% of the bill
> – Cancellation less than 7 days before arrival may require full payment.

- The long lead time for booking makes it difficult for group organisers to **forecast accurately in advance** exactly how many rooms they will need: they may reserve too many, resulting in last-minute cancellations or non-arrivals. (The hotel should include this likelihood in its planned over-booking.) The hotel should request more accurate updates from the organiser or agency as the arrival date approaches, with final confirmed '**rooming list**' supplied seven days before arrival.

> The **rooming list** should include:
>
> – Names of group members
>
> – Types of rooms requested
>
> – The organiser's allocation of room shares, single occupancy requests, adjacent room requests etc: if the hotel has reserved a specific block of rooms, the organiser may pre-allocate them
>
> – Special food requirements/allergies (if meals are included in the package)
>
> – Nationalities and passport numbers of guests (if available) to facilitate pre-registration.

- The group may be accompanied by a **courier or tour leader**, and perhaps also a coach driver. These representatives may be accommodated free or at reduced rates, especially if they are co-opted to help with group check-ins, payments, check-outs and so on. Any such arrangements will have to be clearly specified in advance.

- Other departments of the hotel need to be **notified** well in advance of group reservations, to ensure that preparations can be made. Housekeeping may need extra staff or different rosters to ensure that all rooms are available at the same time; porters must be available to distribute luggage; the restaurant will need to know about group meals; and so on.

Group reservation forms tend therefore to be a bit different from individual ones, and may appear similar to the example below, Figure 2.10.

6.2 Conference accommodation bookings

Hotels with meetings and entertainment rooms offer a convenient **venue** for conferences and conventions, seminars and workshops of various kinds, especially if they extend over several days or involve participants from different regions or countries, who require overnight accommodation.

Conference organisers may be focused primarily on the meetings and conference facilities of the hotel, they may, or may not, make accommodation bookings on behalf of delegates. Hotels offering conference facilities will probably have **specialist staff** to handle the requirements and liaise with conference organisers as the event is planned and prepared.

In terms of **accommodation**, conferences are similar to large group bookings, so the procedures for handling them will be similar. However, unlike group tours, conference delegates may arrive (and depart) independently, at different times. They will, therefore, be checked in individually, and may also be billed individually (depending on whether accommodation is included in the conference package price). They may make a reservation to stay on as independent guests after the conference, either at the time of booking for the conference or by extending their stay during the conference. Such extensions may require the juggling of room allocations, and separate billing – perhaps at a higher rate than the discounted rate negotiated for the conference (to reflect the fact that the room could be let at a higher rate to other incoming guests). All these issues will need to be considered.

In addition, a conference may involve the hotel in providing a wider range of facilities and services, and front office staff may need to give thought to:

- The **booking of bedrooms** for delegates *plus* **accommodation for the conference** itself: a main conference or seminar room; plus 'break-away' meeting or discussion rooms; plus a welcome or registration area; plus possibly banqueting or other rooms for social events attached to the conference.

- The reservation and/or hiring of **presentation equipment** (eg microphones, data projectors, speaker's lectern), **furniture** (chairs and tables), **signage** (announcing the time and location of conference sessions for delegates) and **back-up services** (eg e-mail, fax, telephone, photo-copying and so on). These requirements will have to be discussed well in advance with the conference organisers, and detailed checklists drawn up and communicated to guest services and other relevant departments.

Hill Town Hotel

GROUP RESERVATION FORM

Arrival date:......................... Arrival time: .... Ship/plane: ....

Departure date: .... Departure time: .... Nights stay: ....

Group Name: .... Tour operator:...

Address: ....

....

E-mail:.................................... Fax: .... Phone: ( )..............................

Contact:...

ROOMS	Number	Net rate	Comps	Adjoining	Extra (Z) beds
SB					
TB					
DB					
Other					

Special instructions/requirements

....

....

MEALS	Arrival Date:	Day 2 Date:	Day 3 Date:	Day 4 Date:...............
Breakfast				
Lunch				
Dinner				
Function				

Account/billing instructions: ....

To be confirmed: ☐   Confirmed ☐ by... Date: ....

Booking taken by: .... Date: ....

Figure 2.10: Group reservation form

- **Food and beverage requirements**: in addition to any formal catered events (which will need to be arranged by liaison with the banqueting manager), the conference organisers may request refreshment facilities (eg bottled water, tea/coffee making facilities) and/or scheduled morning or afternoon tea, to be arranged with the food and beverage department.

- **VIP and partner arrangements**: conference organisers may delegate or share with the hotel the tasks of meeting

Source: http://static.roomex.com

and welcoming important guest speakers, and/or planning a programme of activities for the partners and children of delegates. These responsibilities (and appropriate charges) need to be carefully negotiated beforehand.

The **events management or conference co-ordinator** of the hotel will have to be suitably equipped to provide information packs containing:

- Details of the hotel location and transport accessibility

- Descriptions (and perhaps photos) of conference and banqueting facilities

- Maps of conference and meetings rooms (showing entrances and exits, power points and so on)

- An inventory of furniture, presentation aids and equipment available for booking/hire (or obtainable by the hotel with advance notice)

- Sample menus and packages for conference catering

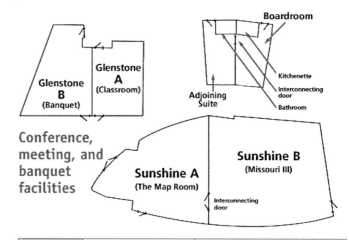

ROOM NAME	DIMENSIONS		CAPACITIES			
	Square Feet	Approx. Length/Width	Classroom	Theater	Reception	Banquet
SUNSHINE A	700	31' X 24'	20	N/A	50	40
SUNSHINE B	1100	32' X 35'	60	100	100	60
SUNSHINE A & B	1800		N/A	N/A	150	N/A
GLENSTONE A	600	29' X 20'	30	40	50	30
GLENSTONE B	700	30' X 24'	40	60	60	60
BOARDROOM	300	20" X 10"	10	N/A	N/A	N/A

Source: http://www.lamplightersouth.com

- Support services (business services, signage, flower arrangements, assistance with VIP and partner programmes)

- Descriptions of accommodation, dining/entertainment and other services and facilities of the hotel which might be relevant to delegates.

7 Reservations from other sources

7.1 Central reservation systems

In addition to reservations handled directly by the hotel (as discussed so far), reservations may come in from a number of other sources. One of these is other hotels in the same group, chain, or marketing network, via some form of **central reservation system (CRS)** or **group reservation system**.

- There may be a scheme whereby any hotel in the group can make reservations for future or onward accommodation at any hotel within the same group: an **affiliate reservation system**. One example is the HolidexPlus Reservation Network, operated by the Inter-Continental Hotels chain (including Inter-Continental Hotels and Resorts, Crowne Plaza Hotels and Resorts, Holiday Inn and other major hospitality brands). Many hotel groups now accept centralised reservations via **central reservation websites**: for example, www.marriott.com or www.hilton.com.

- A similar facility may be available for independently-operated hotels which subscribe to a **non-affiliate reservation network** (or reservations consortium) such as Leading Hotels of the World (www.lhw.com).

- A chain of hotels may also have a separate **central reservation office** (CRO) or **central booking office** (CBO), which handles reservations for all hotels in the group. Customers can contact the CRO/CBO using a Freephone or local call number. In the past, CRO staff checked availability and rates in the hotel nearest the required destination, took a reservation and then notified the hotel, which entered the booking in its own reservation system. With modern computerised systems, linked via the Internet, CRO staff can simply tap into the reservation system of the individual hotels, or a shared central reservation database, for up-to-date information on rates and availability, and to input the reservation direct to the hotel.

The main **advantage** of central reservation systems are that they support the hotel's sales by making it easy and convenient for customers (including travel agents) to make reservations within a group of hotels, whether online or by telephoning a CRO: 'one stop shopping' for hotel rooms. It also makes it easier for a group of hotels to monitor its overall booking trends.

The main **disadvantage** of such systems used to be the expense of operating CROs, the challenges of swift information exchange between the CRO and hotels, and the multiple handling of bookings (once at the CRO and once at the hotel). With internet-linked reservation systems, however, none of this is a problem. A customer can make a booking direct via a central reservation website, or the reservation clerk at any hotel in the group can tap into the reservation system of any other hotel in the group to make a reservation. This way, the bookings are only handled once, with the benefit of up-to-date availability and rate information.

7.2 Agency reservations

Another way in which reservations may be received by the hotel is via various types of booking agencies, for example travel agencies, tour operators, airlines and specialist hotel booking agencies (and their online equivalents), which book reservations with the hotel on behalf of the guest. This is a useful service for the hotel, since individual travellers would not necessarily know about the hotel, or carry out a search for available rooms, themselves. The agency directs business to the hotel, and generally charges some form of **commission** for the introduction.

- **Travel agencies** (such as Thomas Cook and Trailfinders) are a useful source of bookings and recommendations, although they charge the hotel a percentage of the accommodation charge as commission for the service. Agencies often obtain pre-payment from the guest (perhaps as part of a package of travel arrangements), and issue an accommodation voucher which the guest presents at the hotel. The hotel subsequently returns the voucher to the travel agent for payment of the stated amount (less the agency's 10% commission on the booking).

- **Airlines** may offer 'package' reservations (eg of car hire and accommodation) to their customers, and may also need to arrange accommodation at hotels near to airports, for passengers whose flights are cancelled or delayed. They also regularly book accommodation for off-duty flight crews. This means that they are commercially very powerful, and can usually insist on 'free sale' reservations: that is, the hotel allocates a block of rooms for them to use or sell – but they incur no penalty if they are not, in fact, used or sold.

- Airlines have also been at the forefront of the development of **Global Distribution Systems (GDS)** or 'intersell agencies': worldwide central reservations systems, linking various providers, so that customers have access to up-to-date availability and rate information, and can make reservations, for flights, car hire, accommodation and so on. Examples include Sabre, Apollo, Galileo, Worldspan and Amadeus.

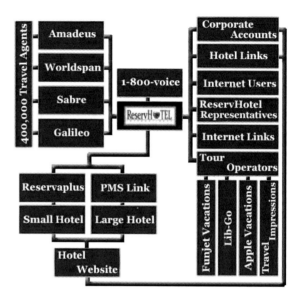

Source: www.carefreeinns.info

- **Hotel booking agencies** specialise in 'finding' hotels for enquirers who don't know an area, or who are having difficulty finding space at busy periods, or who are looking for 'last minute' bookings; they often have offices at major airports, train stations and tourist information bureaux. The customer commonly pays the agency a booking fee (a percentage of the first night's accommodation charge, equivalent to the agency's commission), and receives a receipt or voucher for presentation to the hotel, at which point the fee is credited to the guest's account. The agency has, in effect, received its commission from the hotel, via the customer. Other hotel booking agencies may specialise in finding accommodation for travel agents or conference organisers, and charge commission in the usual way.

- **Tour operators** sell holiday 'packages' to travellers, including hotel accommodation. They do *not* receive commission, because they are not introducing clients to the hotel: they are merely booking accommodation themselves (and make their money on the difference between what a package costs them to provide, and what they charge the traveller).

7.3 Internet reservations

Any customer with access to the Internet can now make reservations direct with a hotel or central reservations system, without any intermediaries. In fact, the Internet puts all the knowledge and technology previously only available to travel agencies and hotel front offices in the hands of the consumer!

In order to secure Internet reservations, the hotel will need to have its own **web site** capable of receiving reservations (ie linked into its advance reservation system) and/or subscribe to **hotel booking sites**. The hotel will also want to purchase space for advertising and reservation links on the web sites of local **tourist information organisations**, destination marketing sites (eg run by the local or regional tourist board) and destination databases, so that travellers browsing or searching for accommodation in a particular area will encounter the hotel.

E X A M P L E

You might like to check out some central reservation systems online, if you have access to the Internet.

- For an example of a global distribution system (GDS): see www.amadeus.net

- For examples of a hotel booking site, see: www.hotels.com, www.hotelreservations.com or www.hotelnet.co.uk

- For an example of destination marketing, see the website for Australia's Northern Territory: www.nttravel.com.au

- For examples of hotel groups' central reservation systems, see: www.marriott.com or www.hilton.com

SUMMARY

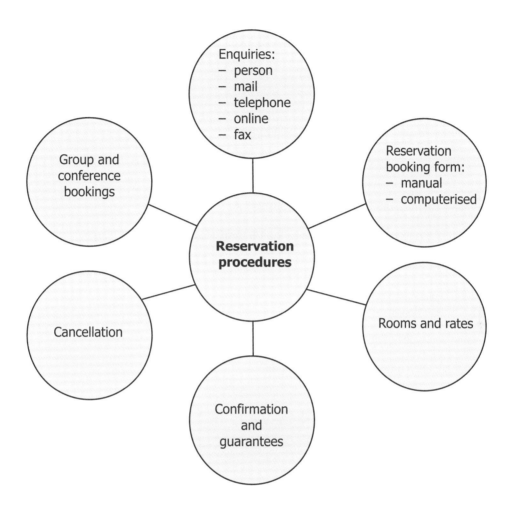

SELF-TEST QUESTIONS

1 List four ways in which booking enquires may be received.

2 What three main records are used in a basic manual reservation system?

3 A hotel is entitled to request a guest to leave the hotel if (s)he damages hotel property. True or false?

4 Define 'planned overbooking'.

5 What do 'TB' and '+S' mean on a bookings diary?

6 If rooms are not pre-allocated to guests and planned overbooking is used, the hotel will do better to use a .... chart to record its room availability.

7 What is (a) 'rack rate' and (b) 'best available rate'?

8 Which of the following corresponds to the US term 'Modified American Plan'?

    A   Room only
    B   *En pension*
    C   Full board
    D   Half board

9 Name two types of non-guaranteed reservation.

10 What should a group 'rooming list' include?

SELF-TEST ANSWERS

1 In person (walk in); by phone; in writing (post/fax/e-mail) or online.

2 Reservation form, bookings diary, and bookings control chart.

3 True.

4 Planned overbooking is the practice of intentionally taking more bookings than there are rooms available, by a pre-determined percentage, intended to cancel out forecast no-shows and cancellations.

5 Twin room with bath; double room with shower.

6 Density

7 Rack rate is the standard 'full' rate for the room, without inclusions. Best available rate is the lowest rate that can be offered for a given room type on a given day, as quoted to enquirers.

8 D: half board.

9 6 pm release; T or P (Take or Place)

10 Names; types of rooms; room share/allocation requests; special food requirements; nationalities and passport number (where relevant)

ANSWERS TO ACTIVITIES

1 It should be obvious where the items of information go. There isn't a 'right answer' to this activity: it is just designed to demonstrate how easy a reservation form can be to use.

2 A bedroom book would be a cumbersome system for very long stays (having to duplicate the entry for each day) – and would really only work if you had few enough rooms to fit on the page. So it is really only suitable for small hotels or bed and breakfast establishments with a high proportion of touring custom. However, it does give useful information about which rooms are booked and which are free; ensuring that a guest isn't changing rooms from night to night; checking that two-person parties haven't been placed in single rooms and so on.

3 Two rooms are available on the 10th (add a score in the '10' column, against the 3 and 2 rows)

Three rooms (counting down the column) are available on the 4th – but not the 5th. Rooms are available on the 16th and 17th (add three scores in the '16' column, rows 5, 4 and 3; add three scores in the '17' column, rows 2, 1 and -1).

There are three rooms available on the 8th: just follow the row in which the first empty space occurs, to the 'no of rooms' marker.

A single room is available for the 16th, 17th and 18th (add one score to the 16 column, row 2; one score to the 17 column, row -2; one score to the 18 column, row -1).

You might notice that the same day each week suffers from low bookings: you might suggest that a discounted rate be offered for booking on (or including) this night, to try and stimulate occupancy.

4 Some of the points you might have included are:

Advantages of computerised reservations	Disadvantages of computerised reservations
▪ Availability information is updated in real time as reservations are made	▪ Cost of initial systems development, hardware and software
▪ All records and communications are interlinked, for automatic updating of room status displays, arrival lists and so on	▪ Cost of training staff to use the system
▪ The system can 'juggle' bookings, without messy corrections to charts	▪ Vulnerability of the system to data corruption and theft (eg hacking, computer viruses)
▪ Data only has to be entered once for all purposes: less costly and time consuming, less likelihood of transcription errors	▪ Risk of system failure, losing all records: need for manual back-up of systems
▪ Data is stored cheaply and securely	▪ Loss of staff knowledge, understanding and experience of underlying processes and manual systems
▪ Data can be quickly and conveniently accessed	
▪ Decision support (eg for maximising occupancy)	
▪ Automatic compilation of management reports (eg on levels and sources of bookings)	
▪ Can be used to enable direct customer, group and agency bookings via a central reservation system	

5   The hotel wants to ensure that it gets as many 'sleepers' as possible for the number of rooms booked: if a single traveller occupies a twin room, the hotel only earns one lot of breakfast/meals revenue, rather than the possible two.

CHAPTER 3

CHECK-IN PROCEDURES

Chapter objectives

In this chapter you will learn

- Procedures for receiving and checking-in guests
- How to use manual and electronic room status systems
- How to deal with chance arrivals, group check-ins, foreign guest registrations and non-arrivals
- How to issue keys and 'walk' a guest
- How to deal with VIP guests and guests with special requirements
- How to offer services such as wake-up calls and papers

Topic list

Receiving and checking-in guests
Monitoring room status
Chance arrivals, non-arrivals and booking changes
Group check-in
VIP guests and special requirements

1 Receiving and checking-in guests

Several months may well have elapsed between the activities described in the previous chapter (reservation) and those covered here (receiving and checking-in guests). The purpose of many of the manual and computerised systems described in Chapter 2 were to bring the reservation – and imminent arrival – *back* to the attention of front office staff at the right time to check that everything is made ready. The prospective guest may have been deep in the reservation records and booking charts for months. But now, we are at the front page of the bookings diary; we have this week's reservation slips at the front of the pile; we have called up today's arrival list on the computer. It's time for the hotel to make good on its promises! The guest is about to walk into reception – perhaps their first face-to-face encounter with the hotel.

1.1 Pre-arrival

In order to be able to prepare for guests' arrival, the front office needs a list of all the guests expected on a given day, with their estimated arrival times, room type (or allocated room, if any), special requirements, and so on.

An **arrivals list** is an alphabetical list of all guests expected to arrive on a specific date, together with their length of stay and any special requirements or requests, enabling the hotel to prepare for their arrival.

The arrivals list is usually generated, using the data in the bookings diary, the day before the arrival date, so that it is as current as possible (allowing for the possibility of last-minute walk-in or 'chance' lettings). Separate **group arrivals lists** and **VIP/Special Attention Guest lists** may be generated a week in advance, however, because such guests generally require more preparation. These various lists will be copied, as required, to the housekeeping department (so that rooms can be prepared for new arrivals), the food and beverage manager (eg for incoming banqueting parties), and guest relations (eg if some arrivals are flagged as VIPs).

A manually-produced arrivals list is illustrated at Figure 3.1. ETA stands for **'estimated time of arrival'**. You might like to compare this with the bookings diary (Figure 2.1): note that the entries have been put in alphabetical order, so that as guests arrive, their details are easy to locate.

DATE OF ARRIVAL:	28 May 2009						
Name	No of adults	No of children	Room type	Room allocated	Length of stay	ETA	Notes
Blew	1		SS	11	1N	18.00	
Greene	2		DB	12	2N	17.00	Wheelchair access
Pincke	2		TB	13	2N	19.30	

Figure 3.1: Arrivals list

In a computerised system, daily arrivals lists can be generated automatically from the reservations data, by simply selecting all reservations made on a particular date, and sorting them alphabetically, see Figure 3.2.

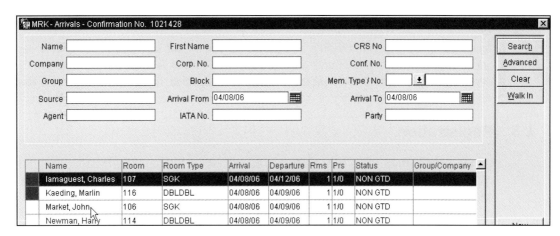

Name	Room	Room Type	Arrival	Departure	Rms	Prs	Status	Group/Company
Iamaguest, Charles	107	SGK	04/08/06	04/12/06	1	1/0	NON GTD	
Kaeding, Marlin	116	DBLDBL	04/08/06	04/09/06	1	1/0	NON GTD	
Market, John	106	SGK	04/08/06	04/09/06	1	1/0	NON GTD	
Newman, Harry	114	DBLDBL	04/08/06	04/09/06	1	1/0	NON GTD	

Source: http://www.micros-fidelio.co.uk

Figure 3.2: Arrivals list (using Fidelio's OPERA reservations system)

1.2 Welcoming or receiving guests

First impressions are incredibly important. The look of the reception area, the appearance and manner of front of house staff: everything will either match, exceed or disappoint guests' expectations – which in turn may influence how they feel about their whole stay at the hotel, how they describe their experience to others – and whether or not they come back! We will discuss these aspects in more detail in Chapter 9, but it is worth saying all this before we get further into procedural matters. It doesn't matter how good your check-in systems and procedures are, or how impressive the public spaces of the hotel: if reception staff don't welcome every guest promptly, courteously and in a friendly manner (as appropriate to the formal or informal style of the hotel), all the effort put into efficiency will be wasted.

E X A M P L E

'A Word from the FOM'

As a Front Office Manager, I cannot overstate to my trainees and staff how important the greeting of guests is. If you don't welcome an incoming guest with a smile, it can colour his whole view of the hotel: he will start *looking* for problems and shortcomings – eventually building-up into a complaint....

Guests will arrive with a variety of needs and expectations – and in a variety of moods. They may be tired and frustrated from their journeys. They may be in a foreign country where they don't know the language or customs. They are quite unlikely to be familiar with the check-in procedures you might take for granted. The job of a good receptionist is to make guests feel welcome; to make them feel that they have arrived somewhere where their needs will be met; and to facilitate them in getting their bearings and settling in. A guest doesn't need to know that you are having problems, that your system is down, or that you have already welcomed 240 people that afternoon: (s)he wants to be treated as if (s)he is the first and only focus of your attention during the moments of your encounter – and genuinely welcome.

FOR DISCUSSION

A new guest has arrived to check-in at a busy time. You are the only person at the front desk, and a queue of guests has formed, wanting various things. What will your priorities be? How will you handle the situation? How would *you* want the situation to be handled, if you were the guest in this situation?

1.3 Registration

On the guest's arrival at the front desk, the receptionist will look up the arrivals list and/or other booking records and check the guest's booking details – first of all, to make sure that there is in fact a booking, and a room available (and that the guest has turned up at the right hotel on the right day!) Guest records will have to be set up from scratch for '**chance' or walk-in guests**, for whom no advance reservation records exist.

After greeting a guest in a welcoming and courteous manner, confirming or entering the guest's booking and dealing with any urgent questions the guest may have (such as whether cars can be left standing outside, or whether there is help available with luggage), the receptionist should ask the guest to 'register'.

DEFINITION

> **Registration** is the process where a guest enters certain identifying details in a book, or on a form or card, fulfilling certain legal and administrative requirements.

Under the **Immigration (Hotel Records) Order 1972**, all hotels, boarding houses and other accommodation providers must keep a record of the full name and nationality of their guests over 16 years of age: each guest must be separately registered.

'Aliens' (generally, **foreign guests** who are not UK, Commonwealth, Republic of Ireland or European Union passport holders) must also record:

- The number and place of issue of their passport
- Their next destination after they leave the hotel: a town or region, and ideally also an address.

This is a legal provision designed to allow immigration and security authorities to keep track of visiting foreign nationals, in case of need. It may be awkward obtaining this information, and guests may not know where they will be going next: the question may have to be 'flagged' and asked again on check-out, when the guest may at least know generally where (s)he is intending to head.

Records of all this information, for domestic and foreign guests, must be kept for at least 12 months and be available for inspection by any police officer or Home Office representative.

Why do guests need to register?

Registration is helpful for both guest and hotel, in various ways.

- It satisfies the legal requirements for hotels to keep records of their guests.

- It provides a record of arrivals (as opposed to reservations), which may help to account for residents in the event of a fire or other disaster.

- It provides management information: eg about the proportion of arrivals to reservations; occupancy statistics; the national origin of guests and so on.

- It confirms guests' acceptance of the hotel's terms and conditions (if they are asked to sign the register).

- It occupies the guest while the receptionist checks booking records, allocates rooms, prepares keys etc.

Registration books, forms and cards

A register may take the form of a bound registration book. As an alternative, the register may only cover the standard details for UK travellers, with a supplementary 'Overseas Visitors Form' (or **'aliens form'**) provided to gather information from overseas visitors.

Hill Town Hotel								GUEST REGISTER		
								Overseas visitors only		
Date	Surname	Forenames	Address	Nat.	Rm	Signature	Car reg.	Passport no	Place of issue	Next destination
28/05	Greene	Mr A B	3 Blue St, Crewe, UK	UK	12	ABGreene	ABT 3MU			
28/05	Xio Hu	Alison	52 Mount St, Kowloon, HK	HK	17	AlisonXioHu	–	2083539C	HK	Crown Hotel, Hull

Figure 3.3: The registration book

Advantages of registration book	**Disadvantages of registration book**
▪ Cuts down on paperwork	▪ Cannot be simultaneously used by multiple guests checking in: may cause delays
▪ Keeps records together (for ease of reference and storage)	▪ Lacks confidentiality: guest entries are open to each other
▪ Ensures that entries are in chronological order (for ease of reference)	
▪ Protects entries from loss or alteration	

For larger hotels, with the likelihood of multiple simultaneous registrations, individual forms or cards are usually preferred. In a computerised system, a registration form or card can be printed out, with some details pre-inserted from the reservations record: saving time for the guest on check-in.

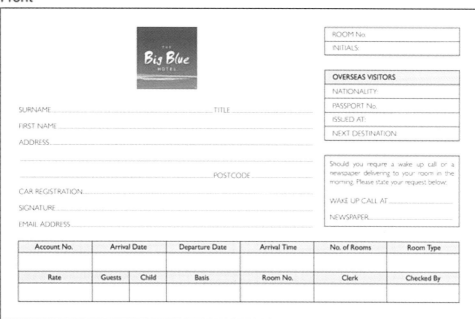

Figure 3.4(a): A simple registration card

Front

English Lakes Hotels
English Lakes Hotels Ltd., Low Wood, Windermere, Cumbria LA23 1LP
☎ (015 394) 33773 ☎ (015 394) 34275 🌐 www.elh.co.uk ✉ info@elhmail.co.uk

Registration Card

ROOM No.

RECEPTION INITIALS

NAME:

ADDRESS:

POSTCODE:

EMAIL:

HOME ADDRESS:

POSTCODE:

ARRIVAL DATE:

DEPARTURE DATE:

VEHICLE REGISTRATION NUMBER:

PLEASE INDICATE HOW YOU INTEND TO SETTLE YOUR ACCOUNT

CASH ☐   CHEQUE ☐   COMPANY A/C ☐   M'CARD ☐

VISA ☐   SWITCH ☐   AMEX ☐   DINERS ☐

CARD No.

EXP

ADULTS: CHILDREN: RATE:

TYPE:

DEPOSIT: RESERVATION No:

FOREIGN GUESTS ONLY

NATIONALITY:

PASSPORT No: PLACE ISSUED:

COUNTRY OF RESIDENCE:

WHICH NEWSPAPER DO YOU REQUIRE? ....

DO YOU REQUIRE AN EARLY MORNING CALL? .... AM

WHAT TIME DO YOU REQUIRE
A RESTAURANT RESERVATION? .... PM

SIGNATURE

English Lakes Hotels will store your name and address details for marketing purposes. If you do not wish to receive our special offers from time to time, please tick ☐

SPECIAL INSTRUCTIONS _____

_____

_____

_____

_____

_____

_____

Guests are requested to vacate their rooms by 11.00am on the day of departure.

Information on current and maximum charges for all types of room, subject to their availability, is displayed on our tariff in the Reception Area. Additional charges made for some advertised facilities are available on request.

FIRE
Your safety is our priority. Please read the instructions on the reverse of your bedroom door.

If the alarm sounds, please leave the building immediately, via the nearest available escape route and make your way to the *ASSEMBLY POINT*.

Under no circumstances should a lift be used.

Guests with any disability including impaired hearing or sight should notify Reception on arrival for special attention in the event of an emergency.

NAME:

ROOM NO:

RATE: NO. OF GUESTS:

ARRIVAL DATE:

DEPARTURE DATE:

All prices are inclusive of VAT and there is no additional service charge.

SIGNATURE

This card is used for entry into the Low Wood or Sandpiper Leisure Clubs; collection of room key; making charges to room accounts; for the duration of your stay.

LOW WOOD LANCASTER HOUSE **THE WATERHEAD** THE FAMOUS WILD BOAR **STORRS HALL**

www.elh.co.uk   *A fine family of hotels*

Source: http://www.aspenprint.com

Figure 3.4(b): A more complex registration form

Forms and cards may be more expensive to prepare and easier to mislay or misfile than using a book-form register. However, they are much more flexible. They can be filled out simultaneously by multiple arrivals – and issued in batches to groups (possibly in advance, eg for conferences). They can be pre-printed in different languages, if the hotel attracts a large number of guests of a particular nationality. And guest confidentiality is protected – unlike a book, where all entries are on display.

ACTIVITY 1   **15 minutes**

For a range of examples of registration forms and cards, so that you can see various formats – and the different kinds of information exchanged with guests at check-in, have a look at the samples posted on the web sites of stationery suppliers, when you next have access to the Internet.

Link: http://www.aspenprint.com/Registration_Cards_Suppliers.html

---

It is worth noting that, while registration documents generally have space for a guest's **address**, the law does not require a guest to give this information. Nor does it require a guest to give a **signature**, although hotels often request one to indicate the guest's acceptance of the terms and conditions of the booking. One member of a party may sign on behalf of the others (eg a tour guide or conference organiser can sign for a group), although each member must be separately registered.

Once the registration has been completed, the receptionist will check that all necessary information has been given (and conforms to the booking details, where available), and will add it to the guest's file.

1.4   Room allocation

If a specific room has not yet been allocated, the receptionist may need to **check on room status** (using various charts, discussed later) and **allocate a room**. Room status documents show which rooms are occupied, which are reserved, which are currently being worked on by housekeeping or maintenance, and which are available for immediate occupation. Available rooms can then be allocated, according to room availability – and guest preference.

When allocating rooms:

- Priority (ie allocation of the best rooms of a given grade or rate) should be given to VIPs and major clients, regulars (loyal returning guests), earlier bookings and longer stays.

- Priority should be given to the requests of guests with special needs (eg for accessibility for the disabled).

- Specially requested rooms should be flagged as requested or reserved in advanced reservation and room status charts, so that they aren't let to someone else by mistake.

- A certain number of the 'better' (preferred) rooms might be 'held back', where possible, to allow for special requests on check-in.

- Computers may be used to allocate non-requested rooms randomly or in rotation, so that all rooms are used equally over time (and available for maintenance on rotation). Computerised systems may also be used to select the best available room for a given set of parameters (rate, room type, guest preferences and yield management).

ACTIVITY 2   **5 minutes**

List some of the attributes which you think guests might particularly value in a hotel room, and which may dictate their preference for one room over another, within the same grade or type of room (ie where the rooms have broadly the same facilities).

Early check-ins

If a guest is checking-in earlier than expected, there may be no rooms ready for occupation – or the pre-allocated/requested room may not yet be vacated by an outgoing guest, or cleaned for re-letting. In such a case, the reception should:

- **Understand** that this situation is frustrating for guests, and make every effort to make them feel welcomed and reassured that they will be given access to a room as soon as possible.

- **Offer an alternative** room or room type to the guest, if one is ready to occupy immediately.

- **Register** the guests, informing them, with an apology, that their room is not yet available. Offer them the opportunity to put their luggage into storage, informing them that it will be taken to their room as soon as it is available. Direct guests to places where they can wait comfortably and/or access refreshments and entertainments: give them a time to return to reception to collect their room key, or arrange for them to be informed.

- **Contact housekeeping** to put a 'rush'/priority on preparation of the allocated room, if it has been vacated.

1.5 Booking-out or 'walking' the guest

As we saw in Chapter 2, the hotel may have deliberately overbooked some room types, in order to minimise its losses from no-shows, cancellations and shortened stays. So what happens if a guest turns up to check-in, and there are no rooms available? This is a tricky situation, because the guest has a genuine complaint against the hotel, and will probably be very displeased.

DEFINITION

> **'Walking the guest'** is one term for the process of having to book a reserved guest into another hotel because the hotel is full. It is also called **'booking-out'**.

The reservation clerk should have pre-planned for this situation. First, it will need to be **confirmed** as accurately as possible, as soon as possible, how many rooms/guests have been double-booked. The arrivals list should be **double checked**: might there have been a cancellation or room change that hasn't been recorded, so that there is, after all, a room available for the guest? Might rooms be 'freed up' in some other way (eg by offering incentives to group travellers to share a room, or using rooms reserved for staff)?

The second step will be to **prioritise bookings**, so that the least possible damage will be done to the hotel by re-locating guests. The principle of 'yield management' (maximising occupancy and revenue) – as well as guest convenience and hotel marketing – suggests that you should relocate guests on the basis of:

- **Shortest reservation** (eg one-night stays) first, since these guests will not be as badly affected as guests who had reserved longer stays – and the hotel will not lose the longer-stay revenue to another hotel!

- **First-time** (ie non-repeat, non-regular) guests first, since these guests may not have a fixed preference, and the hotel will not be risking displeasing a loyal guest in whom it already has an investment.

- **Overseas guests** before domestic guests, where these are less likely to represent potential repeat business (ie not guests from the overseas office of a major business client!).

Every effort should be made to **minimise** (a) the inconvenience and loss to the guest and (b) the damage to the hotel's reputation, as a result of relocation.

- The handling of the booking-out may be **referred** to the senior receptionist or duty manager, so that disgruntled guests feel that the matter is being taken seriously (and so that a tricky situation can be handled by the most qualified person).

BPP
LEARNING MEDIA

- Guests should be relocated in **a similar grade** of hotel, in a similar grade and type of room, and at a similar rate, ideally, within another hotel in the same group. If *better* terms can be found for the grade of accommodation, or a *better* grade of accommodation for the same terms, this may help to 'soften the blow' for the relocated guest.

- The hotel should offer to **pay the expenses** associated with the relocation: the cost of telephone calls, transport to the other hotel, excess room charges (if the accommodation found is at a higher rate) and so on. It may also offer assistance with transport, eg if there is a shuttle bus service.

- The hotel may also offer **compensation** to guests for being booked-out: eg vouchers for a subsequent stay, payment for the first night's stay in the other hotel and so on. *Dix & Baird (Front Office Operations)* argue that even after meeting all the costs of booking-out, 'it is still in the interests of the hotel to overbook by a sensible margin, to achieve the objective of a "full house"'.

Meanwhile, the arrivals list and other records will have to be amended to show that the guest has been booked-out. (The switchboard's guest index, for example, will have to show where the guest has been booked out to, so that callers and messages can be directed to the correct hotel.)

E X A M P L E

'A Word from the FOM'

Booking-out is never a desirable or pleasant situation. You need to make every effort to find booked-out guests accommodation that is close by (as location may have been one of their main considerations in choosing the hotel); and accommodation that is *at least* as good in terms of standard, rate and inclusions. Try and get them a 'better deal' if possible.

We always try to call in advance – as soon as the need to relocate the guest has been confirmed – to give the guest some warning. I advise my staff to tell the truth, acknowledge the situation and apologise sincerely. (By the way, *within* the hotel, we refer to booking-out as 'bumping' the guest – but this expression should *never* 'leak out' with guests themselves!)

We also try to follow-up afterwards, phoning the guest to check that their replacement accommodation is satisfactory. We may even drop off a small gift at their new hotel (say, a bottle of wine or chocolates), with our apologies and best wishes.

1.6 Checking the method of payment

It is usual practice at this point to:

- Confirm with the guest what the **room rate** will be, and what it includes.

- Ascertain or confirm and record the **method of payment** by which the guest intends to settle the bill, and to confirm that the proposed method is accepted by the hotel.

- Confirm the **foreign currencies** accepted by the hotel, and exchange rates applied (where relevant).

- Confirm and record any **billing arrangements** made, if a company or travel agent is settling the account (eg collecting agency vouchers and opening a bill for 'extra' charges).

- Confirm any **deposit or pre-payment** already made, and ensure that a credit is posted to (shown on) the guest's account, which is opened at this point.

- Take steps (if guests are unknown to the hotel and the account has not been pre-paid) to ensure that the guest will be **able to pay** the account on demand.

The hotel is entitled, under common law, to request that a guest pays a reasonable amount in advance (there is no obligation to offer credit) – and although this needs to be handled tactfully, to avoid offence, most guests will be amenable to complying with hotel policy.

In most hotels, it is standard procedure to request some form of deposit, pre-payment or guarantee from '**chance guests**' who walk in without a reservation. The receptionist may refer such registrations to the duty manager who may, if any suspicion is aroused, use the guest's registration particulars to conduct a credit check. A deposit would typically include one night's room charge plus an added amount to cover extras (refundable if not spent).

Even where a guest has made a reservation, it is standard procedure to request a **copy or imprint** of the guest's **credit card** (if available) for the hotel's records and as a guarantee of payment. The credit card may even be 'swiped' on arrival so that the hotel receives **pre-authorisation** from the credit card company for the authorised amount: it is effectively 'reserved' by the credit card company for the transaction. If the bill goes over this amount, a new authorisation may be required – while if it is less, the original transaction can be invalidated and the lesser sum put through instead.

Photo: http://creditact.com

If the hotel has any further doubts about a guest's ability to pay, the receptionist may ask for pre-payment (eg to allow a cheque to clear); or state that it is the hotel's policy to impose a **credit limit**, and to request an 'interim' or 'part' payment once the guest's account reaches that limit (preventing him from running up a very large bill). Obviously, this will have to be handled with great tact, and may be delegated to the duty manager if one is available.

FOR DISCUSSION

'Walking' or relocating guests and imposing credit controls are two tasks that can be unpleasant and stressful for front desk staff. Why are these tasks so 'difficult'? And what can the hotel do to *support* staff in performing them well and without unnecessary stress?

1.7 Issuing keys

Once registration details are complete and a room allocated, the receptionist can issue a key and/or key card to the guest, explaining its use if necessary. (We will discuss keys and key cards in the context of hotel safety and security, in Chapter 7.)

1.8 Information and services

In addition to all the above:

- **Additional services** may be offered to guests, such as wake-up calls or newspaper delivery (discussed later).

- The receptionist should check whether there are any **messages or mail** for the guest, which may have been sent to await their arrival.

- **Special requests** by guests may need to be logged and passed on to relevant departments (eg

Photo: http://www.fnetravel.com

LEARNING MEDIA

if special meals or medical requirements need to be notified). **Late check-out requests** may need to be approved, eg by checking that the room is not due for immediate re-occupancy. An additional charge may or may not be made for this facility, and will need to be notified to the guest at the time of request.

■ The **facilities and lay-out** of the hotel, and other information to make settling in easier for the guest, may be explained, for example, the location of the bar and restaurant, the services offered by the concierge, access to the pool or spa and so on. Alternatively, guests' attention can be drawn to the comprehensive hotel information provided in 'Welcome folders' and Guest Directories in the rooms.

■ Guests can then be **directed** to their rooms (which floor they are on, where the lifts are and so on), or reception may organise for the guest to be **escorted** by a member of the uniformed staff (who may also help with guest **luggage**). In a luxury hotel, a receptionist or guest relations person may escort guests to their room, and explain the facilities and services: porters will then deliver the luggage shortly afterwards.

E X A M P L E

Consider the following exchange at reception, between a guest (G) and Guest Service Agent (GSA).

GSA: Good afternoon, sir. How can I help you?

G: I have a reservation: name of Wright – P M Wright.

GSA: Welcome, Mr Wright…. Yes, I have a standard double reserved for one night. Is that correct?

G: That's right.

GSA: Thank you, Mr Wright. Can I ask you to complete this registration card with your name, address and signature? And just tick the box if you'd like a complimentary newspaper in the morning.

G: Sure… Here we are.

GSA: Thank you. May I ask how you wish to settle your account?

G: I'll be paying by credit card: Mastercard, if that's OK.

GSA: That's fine, Mr Wright. I'd like to take an imprint of the card, please, for our records, and to cover any extra charges… Thank you… And here is your card back, Mr Wright. This is your electronic room key: you'll see that I've allocated you Room 112, on the first floor: the lifts are just over there. Your room rate is £90 for the night, including VAT, which also includes your breakfast. Breakfast can be taken from 7.00 am in the café. Is there anything else I can help you with for the moment? Would you like help with your luggage?

G: No, I'm fine. I may want to deposit some articles for safe keeping a bit later.

GSA: You are welcome to do that, although there is also a safe in your room, you'll find the information in your welcome directory.

G: OK. Thanks.

GSA: Enjoy your stay, Mr Wright.

1.9 Follow-up administration

Once guests have departed for their rooms, reception has some follow-up work to do:

■ Updating **guest records**. In a computerised reservation system, the receptionist can simply call up the guest's reservation file, and enter the fact that the guest has in fact arrived. There should then be fields available on screen to record new data, such as the guest's preferred method of payment, credit card or voucher number and room allocation.

- Reception must **inform other departments**, where relevant, that the guest has now arrived and may require their services.

- A guest **billing account** is opened, on which daily accommodation and additional charges will be posted, and from which the guest's bill will be prepared. (This is discussed in detail in Chapter 5.)

- The various **room status and availability records** will be amended, to show that the guest's room is now 'occupied' and unavailable for let. A computerised system should do this automatically once a room number has been allocated, but a manual system will have to be updated by hand.

1.10 Automated or self-service check-in

You may have come across automated or self-check-in terminals at airports – and some large hotels are now using similar systems to allow guests to check-in outside office hours, or at their leisure, without approaching the reception desk.

- The guest usually inserts a credit card, or types in a credit card number, or inserts a bar-coded booking confirmation slip for scanning.

- The computer system will recognise the credit card or booking number of an advance reservation, and display reservation details on screen for the guest to confirm.

- On confirmation, the screen will display a personalised welcome message, allocate a suitable room type (which guests may also be able to confirm or request a change) and issue a computer-coded key card. The system may also offer a menu of services (such

Photo: http://www.uwelorenzen.de

as wake-up calls and newspapers) from which the guest can select. All these details are input to the other relevant records and reports of the Hotel Management System, to show that the guest has arrived, that the room has been allocated, that the services have been requested and so on.

- If the in-coming guest is a 'chance arrival' and does not have a reservation, the system will display a menu of room types/locations available and their rates: the guest can select a suitable room (via the menu or a touch-screen display of the hotel floor plan, say). The machine will then request the insertion or swiping of a credit card, log the check-in, and proceed from there.

Advantages of self-service check-in	Disadvantages of self-service check-in
▪ Allows guest arrival outside office hours – while saving the hotel the cost of staffing reception on a 24/7 basis	▪ No greeting or welcoming of guests on arrival
▪ Avoids problems of overnight reception: staff safety, boredom, tiredness; security of premises	▪ May alienate older guests, or others who prefer human to automated service
▪ Situation, eg at airports or tourist offices to facilitate early, convenient check-in	▪ May not offer full range of extra services, flexibility and information provided by human service
▪ Offers quicker check-in facility if reception is busy	▪ May still require separate guest registration, to fulfil legal record-keeping requirements.

1.11   Offering additional services on check-in

As we noted above, it is customary to offer certain additional services to guests on check-in, to add convenience and value to their stay. Two of the most common are wake-up calls and newspapers.

Of course, there may be other services to be offered or 'sold' to in-coming guests, depending on the establishment, its facilities and procedures. Many of these services will be explained in a detailed directory of services, provided for guest information in the rooms; many will be accessible via a phone call to housekeeping, room service, the concierge or other departments, via the in-room directory. We will discuss the 'selling' role of reception in Chapter 9.

However, practices vary widely. It is common in some small motels, for example, for reception to provide guests with fresh milk on check-in (due to the high proportion of 'chance arrivals', as well as limited staffing). You will have to familiarise yourself with the added-value services and information to be offered to incoming guests in any establishment in which you work.

Wake-up calls

Nowadays, when everyone has an alarm clock facility in their mobile phone or i-Pod, there is less demand for reception to telephone guests with a pre-arranged wake-up call or appointment reminder. However, this used to be an important service – and older guests, in particular, may still value it (and a cheerful 'Good morning, this is your requested wake-up call').

In a manual system, the receptionist might simply keep a diary or timetable for wake-up calls, writing in the room number and guest name against the requested call time. The receptionist or switchboard operator could then simply work down the list, ticking off each call as it is made and answered. Of course, there are computerised versions of the same system, illustrated at Figure 3.5.

Newspapers

Similar manual and computerised systems could be used to log the newspaper requests of different guests by room. A hotel would typically offer a small selection of local and national newspapers, which could be ordered from a local distributor for delivery (often together with share copies for the lobby, waiting areas, breakfast room and so on).

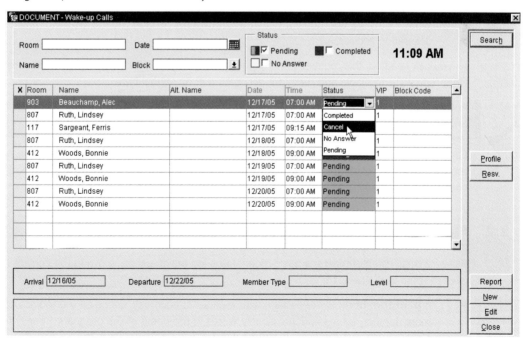

Source: <u>www.MICROS-fidelio.co.uk</u>

Figure 3.5: A computerised wake-up call log (in Fidelio)

1.12   Computerised check-in

As we have noted in our discussion of procedures, above, computerised check-in offers significant advantages – for both hotel and guest – of efficiency, speed and accuracy.

- The receptionist can simply access the reservation record of the arriving guest, and print out a registration card containing relevant details, the guest then simply has to confirm and sign.

- The system can be interrogated for real-time, up-to-date information on room status, prior to allocating rooms (as discussed further below). The entire room list can be searched by room type and specific attributes, to 'find' a suitable room – without the operator having to manually sift through the records.

- The system can be linked with an electronic key system, which will automatically prepare an electronic key and key card for the guest (and transmit the un-locking code to the electronic device on the room door) on allocation of a room number.

- The system will also automatically open an account or 'folio' for the guest, crediting any pre-payment or deposit logged, recording the guest's credit card details and so on.

2   Monitoring room status

2.1   Checking room status

We saw above that when a guest arrives to check-in, the receptionist needs to confirm:

- What rooms are **available**, if no specific room has as yet been allocated to the guest.

- Whether the room allocated to the guest (where relevant) is in fact **ready for occupancy**, that is, not being repaired or cleaned, or not subject to extension of reservation by the previous occupant.

- What rooms are **occupied,** by whom, for how long (or how much longer) and at what rate

- What rooms will shortly **become available** (if prospective guests are prepared to be flexible about arrival dates or times).

- What rooms are unoccupied, but **unavailable for letting**, due to cleaning, maintenance or re-decoration activity.

As you can imagine, this requires immediate access to a running, constantly up-to-date record of exactly what rooms are available and ready for occupation at any given time.

DEFINITION

> A **room status display** is a record or display which keeps track of the availability status of all rooms at any given time.

Each time a guest checks-in or checks-out, each time housekeeping or maintenance are active in a room, each time a confirmed reservation (with room allocation) is made, this record needs to be changed!

2.2   Manual room status records

For very small establishments, a basic room status log may be kept, showing the current letting position of each room in the hotel for each day.

- A **bedroom book** is like a diary, with a page for each day, listing all the rooms. Against each room number, the receptionist simply writes in the name of the occupant (if any) for a given night, and the rate being paid. Where there is no occupant listed, the receptionist may add symbols showing: (a) if the room was let the previous night, and is possibly not yet vacated; (b) if the room has been vacated, but is not yet ready to re-let; and (c) if the room is vacant and ready to re-let.

- A **bed sheet** (no pun intended) is an alternative method for hotels of up to 100 rooms. A sheet is prepared for each day, listing all rooms against columns marked Departures, Stays and Arrivals. An entry of the name, number of persons, rate and departure date would be made in *one* of these columns for each occupied room, on each day. Entries would then be copied forward to the next day's sheet, as appropriate, so one day's Arrivals entry would be the following day's Stay entry, and eventually another day's Departure entry – saving having to look up the bookings records afresh every time. Each room would either have an entry for Arrival (guest coming in that day), Stay (guest occupying the room that day) or Departure (guest due to leave that day) – or no entry at all, in which case the room is either available for let, or out of service for some reason (in which case a note could be made against the room on the sheet).

These are simple systems to operate – but time-consuming and prone to error. Guest details have to be written in for every night of their booking. Constant updates are needed to take account of check-outs, cleaning and so on. Such methods really only suit very small establishments without access to computer facilities.

Room racks or reception boards

DEFINITION

A **room rack (or reception board)** is somewhat similar to the racks used for displaying advanced bookings (discussed in Chapter 2), in that it is a flexible racked filing system for removable record slips or cards. However, while the advance reservations card rack system shows bookings, the room rack shows today's actual situation: who is in what room, for how long and at what rate.

The system generally involves a wall-mounted rack with a labelled slot for each room, in which can be slotted a colour-coded file card or slip showing the current occupancy situation. Guest cards (of one colour) would be filled in with basic data such as name, number of persons, date of arrival and departure and room. Different coloured cards could be used to indicate rooms being cleaned, out of service and so on. Or the system might operate a 'traffic light' system of red (for 'reserved/occupied'), amber (for 'on change') and green (for 'available for letting').

Such a system provides an at-a-glance view of room availability – but still requires considerable effort to keep up-to-date each day, and with each change of room status.

2.3 Computerised room status records

Computerised room status displays keep track of room status through check-in and check-out processes.

- As rooms are allocated on reservation or registration, the system records their 'reserved' or 'occupied' status, and removes them from lists of available rooms.

- As guests check-out, the system notifies housekeeping (with a task list of rooms to be cleaned and readied for new occupants) and marks the room as being cleaned. Once housekeeping has logged each room as ready, the system changes the room status to 'available' (or 'reserved', as the case may be).

- As guest departure dates approach, the system may display a 'departure due' status (to signal that the room will soon be available).

- Because **Hotel Management Systems** are interlinked, it is generally possible to switch between advance booking charts and room status charts (sometimes, confusingly, called 'room racks'), so you can not only see whether a room is available today, but whether it will be available for the next few days.

There are many different types of display for room status. Figures 3.6 and 3.7 are just two examples.

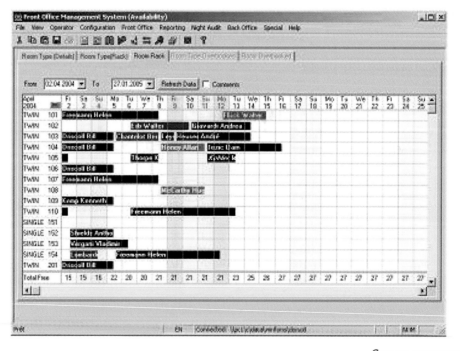

Source: http://intranet.bpc.ac.uk/widecoll/hotel/HotPerRm.html

Figure 3.6: A room control or room status chart (in Hotel Perfect)

As the inset box should indicate, the little room door icons are, in fact, colour coded with different colours for different status indications.

Source: www.pcscholl.ch

Figure 3.7: 'Room Rack' (status chart) in Front Office Management System (WinFom)

Note that this looks much more like a conventional chart (discussed in Chapter 2) and may reflect both actual room status (for part of the time period shown) and advance bookings (for a forward period). The 'refresh data' button can be used to get the latest update from the system

3 Chance arrivals, non-arrivals and booking changes

Our coverage above focused mainly on standard check-in procedures for guests with reservations. However, these may not be the only – or even the main – scenario at the front desk!

3.1 Chance arrivals

DEFINITION

Chance arrivals are guests who arrive without a prior booking, usually requiring accommodation for the same night. Some hotels – such as motorway hotels or motels – will receive most of their guests as chance arrivals.

We have already flagged some of the issues surrounding chance guests, in our discussion of check-in procedures.

- The receptionist may need to juggle existing room allocations, or offer options, in order to accommodate a chance guest, since certain types of room may be fully booked or pre-allocated.

- The chance guest is likely to be completely unknown to the hotel, which presents various security and credit risks. The receptionist's 'radar' will be particularly primed for suspicious circumstances (such as a chance guest appearing without luggage), which might suggest inability to pay or the intention to leave without paying. Measures will have to be taken – without in any way implying to guests that the hotel suspects them of dishonesty!

- The receptionist may take stricter steps to verify the guest's registration details (eg by requesting proof of identity).

- The receptionist may also request pre-payment, cash deposit or the imprint of a credit card; decline to accept payment by cheque (without a bank's confirmation or guarantee) and so on.

- It is also standard procedure to ask chance guests without credit cards to pay cash for all extra expenses within the hotel, rather than charging them to the room. (In a computerised system, charges can be automatically blocked; in a manual system, reception may have to inform other departments.) Alternatively, a credit limit for extras may be set, so that guests cannot run up a large bill; when the bill reaches that amount, the guest is (tactfully) asked to settle up for the bill so far.

These kinds of security measures are only sensible. At the same time, some hotels will get as much as 90% of their business from chance arrivals, and must value these customers accordingly!

E X A M P L E

Here's another example of a conversation between our Guest Services Agent and a 'chance' guest.

GSA: Good evening, madam. May I help you?

G: Yes, I wonder if you have a room available for tonight?

GSA: May I have your name, please?

GSA: Amanda Vickery.

G: And do you have a reservation, Ms Vickery?

G: No, I'm afraid not.

GSA: Was the room just for tonight?

G: Yes, just the one night. I'm touring the area by car, not really making any plans.

GSA: What an adventure. And is the room just for yourself, Ms Vickery?

G: Yes.

GSA: Well... I'm afraid I don't have any single rooms available, but I can offer you a nice twin room overlooking the garden: as a single occupancy, the rate for that room would be £85 per night, including VAT and continental breakfast. Or if you'd prefer a double...

G: No, a twin would be fine. I'll take that.

GSA: Thank you, Ms Vickery. Here is your registration form. If I could just ask you to put down your full name, address and passport details, and sign at the bottom of the form... You'll note that check-out time is 11 am, and that we do ask guests without a prior reservation to pre-pay in advance for a night's accommodation, plus a small sum to cover incidental expenses.

G: Oh, really? Well, I can give you cash, if that's OK?

GSA: That will be fine, Mrs Vickery.... Thank you. That will be £100, then, if you don't mind. I'll just print you out a receipt. Would you like help with your luggage?...

3.2 Non-arrivals

DEFINITION

Non-arrivals or **no shows** are people who have made a booking and then fail to honour it, by not turning up, without notifying the hotel of their intention to cancel the booking.

Cancelled bookings (and stays which are shortened at the last minute, due to a change of plans) at least give the hotel *some* notice, and a chance to re-let the room. In the case of no-shows, however, unless the hotel has a waiting list or planned overbooking in place, it may not be possible to re-let the room and the hotel will have lost revenue.

The hotel should seek to **reduce the number** of no shows by:

- 'Chasing' unconfirmed bookings (by letter, e-mail or phone call), especially for group bookings.

- Re-confirming bookings by telephone on the day before due arrival (although this may only be possible for a small hotel).

- Imposing financial penalties for non-arrival, eg taking bookings guaranteed by credit card; asking for a non-returnable deposit on booking; or imposing cancellation fees.

In addition, it should seek to **minimise the impact** of no shows, by ensuring – as far as possible – that it will be able to re-let rooms by:

- Planned overbooking (as discussed in Chapter 2).

- Advertising 'release times' (eg 6 pm release), and notifying guests of these as part of the terms and conditions of booking, that is, stating that rooms will only be held until a specified time, unless otherwise agreed, after which the hotel will be free to re-let the room.

- Waiting lists in periods of peak demand, so that once released, rooms can be offered to stand-by customers who in the meantime haven't made other arrangements.

- Notifying last-minute vacancies to appropriate agencies and organisations who may get a lot of last-minute accommodation enquiries, including hotel booking agencies and local tourist information bureaux.

The hotel may choose to take subsequent action against no-shows to gain compensation. It may not be worth the hassle of legal action for relatively small amounts, but the hotel may write a formal letter requesting compensation – if only to discourage repetition.

A C T I V I T Y   3   **5   m i n u t e s**

Occasionally, guests may arrive to check-in and the receptionist will not be able to 'find' their reservation, it may be listed under a different name (eg a company name, travel agent name, or the name of the person who made the booking); or may have been cancelled in error; or may be under the wrong date.

What should the receptionist do in this situation?

3.3   Changes to the booking

There will be occasions when, for a variety of reasons, a guest will want to **change rooms** – either immediately on inspection (because he or she doesn't like the room allocated) or at sometime during the stay (because the room proves to be too noisy, say, or a better room becomes available). There are a few key principles here.

- **Guests' wishes** should always be accommodated as far as possible, in order to ensure that they have a satisfying experience of the hotel (which they will wish to repeat and recommend to others).

- However, room changes can be **disruptive**, especially if other rooms have already been allocated.

    - Front office staff may need courteously and regretfully to inform the guest that no other room is available, if this is the case, and offer alternative solutions to solve the guest's problem where possible.

    - All relevant records and charts will need to be amended to reflect the room change, so that other departments are properly informed, and so that there is no confusion about room status or guest billing. This is comparatively easy in a computerised system, which automatically amends and synchronises all records. In a manual system, a **room change slip** should be prepared, stating the details of the move: Figure 3.8. Copies should go to all departments notified of the original room allocation (such as switchboard, billing and housekeeping) to alert them of the change, with a further copy attached to the guest's file.

A similar system may be used in the case of change to the **number of persons** staying in a room (to inform porters and switchboard of extra guests, and housekeeping of extra requirements), and in the case of **rate changes**. A guest may be offered a discounted rate on the room for an extra night, or in compensation for some problem or inconvenience during their stay), or a higher rate may be charged for a room upgrade or the occupancy of an extra person in the room. Again, the guest record and room status record will have to be amended and, most importantly, the guest accounting/billing department will have to be notified.

```
┌─────────────────────────────────────────────────────────────┐
│  CHANGE NOTIFICATION              HOUSEKEEPING               │
│ ┌───────────────────────────────────────────────────────┐   │
│ │ CHANGE NOTIFICATION            SWITCHBOARD            │   │
│ │┌────────────────────────────────────────────────────┐│   │
│ ││ CHANGE NOTIFICATION          CONCIERGE            ││   │
│ ││┌─────────────────────────────────────────────────┐││   │
```

CHANGE NOTIFICATION   RECEPTION

Name: ....

Change of room

From Room #: ....   To Room #: ....

Number of persons in residence

From: ....   To: ....

Special requirements: ....

Change of rate/terms

From: ....   To: ....

Remarks:

Date: ....   Time: ....

Signature: ....

Figure 3.8: Change notification slips

4   Group check-in

4.1   Pre-registration

From our discussion of registration, earlier, you might have gathered that a large group registering simultaneously could crowd the reception desk and cause frustrating queues and delays, both for the arriving group and for other guests who might need attention at the same time. It, therefore, makes sense to try and pre-register the group as far as possible.

As we saw in Chapter 2, the reservations department should receive a **finalised rooming list** of group names and room preferences from the group leader or organiser some days in advance of arrival. Front office staff can then pre-prepare a set of individual registration cards, to which room numbers are added (when allocated) and room keys attached. The card and key, together with the group's programme (eg conference or meal arrangements) and a map and brochure of the hotel, say, can be put into individual envelopes or '**Welcome Packs**' for each group member.

When the group arrives, they should, where possible, be directed to a **separate desk**, **area or room**, where they can be handed their envelopes and asked to sign their registration cards, for collection and return to reception. Meanwhile, the group can proceed direct to their rooms without further business at the reception desk.

Alternatively, it may be possible to supply the tour leader with pre-prepared registration cards, and have the group fill them in prior to arrival, eg during transfer from the airport. As guests arrive, the cards are handed to the receptionist in exchange for room keys or welcome packs.

BPP
LEARNING MEDIA

Computerised systems make this process – like so many others – easier and more efficient.

- In the '**Group Check-In**' area of the programme, enter the identification code for the group. The programme should display a list of the group's members: with room numbers, if pre-allocated.

- It should also specify, or allow you to specify at this point, the **package and billing terms** agreed for the group. What charges will be allocated to the master bill for the group (usually under the name of the group leader or organiser) and what will be separately charged to individual guest bills? If individual guests are responsible for meals or other extra charges, what methods of payment will they be using?

- As each member of the group is registered, **room numbers** can be allocated or confirmed, and appropriate room keys and/or Welcome Packs can be handed out.

4.2 Group check-in arrangements

For a large group, group check-in presents certain challenges!

- **Pre-allocation** of rooms to the group will probably be required, in order to place group members as close to each other as possible – not only for their convenience, and to simplify portering of luggage, but for the convenience of other guests (as groups can be noisy, moving about the hotel).

- If a group checks in comparatively **early,** which may be the case if they arrive on morning flights, or have afternoon programmes prepared, not all rooms may be ready for occupation and some group members may have to wait to access their rooms. Arrangements will have to be made to store luggage and to offer waiting facilities, where necessary.

- The **porter's desk** will be responsible for ensuring that coach transport (where relevant) is suitably parked; mail and messages (if any) distributed to the guests; and the group's luggage distributed to the rooms. The total number of bags may be tallied, to ensure that the same number of bags are loaded on departure.

- Arrangements should be made for guest **charges/billing** during the stay. The hotel should have a clear arrangement with the tour operator as to what charges it will be responsible for, and what 'extras' the group members will pay for themselves.

5 VIP guests and special requirements

A C T I V I T Y   4   **5   m i n u t e s**

Most hotels pay 'special attention' to 'high priority' guests who are important in some way. Why, in general, would they want to do this? What is the benefit to the hotel?

5.1   Who are 'important guests'?

'Important' guests for a hotel may include:

- **Very Important Persons (VIPs)**: eg celebrities; guests booked into the very expensive rooms or suites of the hotel; guests with special security risks (eg politicians or diplomats); and perhaps visiting senior managers from the hotel's head office.

- **Commercially Important Persons (CIPs)**: eg the executives and guests of major company account-holders (who may be in a position to influence the continuance of the account); business travellers (who may be in a position to recommend the hotel to their companies, offering a significant amount of business in future); travel agents and tour company staff (who may be in a position to recommend the hotel to travellers, or not); and perhaps journalists or media representatives (who may give positive or negative media coverage to the hotel).

VIPs may have special requirements for **security** and **privacy**, and may even be travelling *incognito*, that is, not wanting their identity to be known. Front office staff will need to be flexible and alert to these needs, and support the guest's security and privacy in various ways.

- The guest may have **rooms assigned** in advance of arrival, in some cases, with special room allocation criteria (eg the best rooms, or a number of adjoining rooms for the guest's *entourage*, or closing off a block of rooms or a whole floor to maintain security).

- The guest may be **escorted** straight to the room on arrival, and invited to register in the room, to avoid exposure and delays at reception.

- Front office staff will need to be vigilant in avoiding the **disclosure of information** about the guest to unauthorised enquirers (especially members of the press), and may also support the guest's privacy by discouraging members of the public (eg protestors, fans or autograph hunters) from pestering the guest in public areas.

In general, both VIPs and CIPs will be given a special level of care and attention. They may have their room preferences prioritised and rooms allocated prior to arrival (even where this is not the norm for the hotel). They may be greeted and escorted on arrival by guest relations staff, to whom they may also be given access if they have needs or requests at any time during their stay, the guest relations representative acting as a 'facilitator' for them within the hotel, so that they only have to deal with one person. VIPs and CIPs may also be given complimentary or exclusive use of hotel facilities, eg complimentary transport (whether by limousine service or hotel shuttle bus); access to special lounges or business facilities (eg the Executive Lounge) within the hotel; and so on. They may also be given complimentary in-room extras, from extra towels to flowers, champagne, fruit or chocolates on arrival.

FOR DISCUSSION

'VIP guests are more trouble than they're worth.'

Discuss the pros and cons of having 'celebrity' and high-profile guests in the hotel.

5.2 Special attention guests (SPATTS)

Special attention guests are guests who may require extra care or assistance for some reason. They may include disabled or partially-disabled guests, the elderly or infirm, or guests suffering from some illness which has been notified to the hotel. They may also, depending on the level of service aspired to by the hotel, include long-stay and regular/loyal guests, and guests who have (on a previous or the current visit) suffered some inconvenience or service failure, for which the hotel wishes to 'make up'.

As with VIPs and CIPs, the needs of such guests will be catered to in various ways. Rooms may need to be pre-allocated to take account of special needs: wheelchair access, proximity to lifts or ground floor rooms to avoid stairs, proximity to bathrooms (if not *en suite*) and so on. Assistance may be required with check-in and registration procedures for sight-impaired guests, and special arrangements may be required for delivering telephone messages to hearing-impaired guests. Front office staff will need to be flexible, understanding and discreet in these matters: medical information is highly personal and confidential.

Long-stay and regular guests, and guests to whom the hotel wishes to offer recompense for problems, may also be offered priority room allocation or upgrade (subject to availability); greeting and escort by the guest relations or front office manager on arrival; and complimentary extras.

5.3 Notification requirements

A **VIP/SPATTs list** will often be compiled and circulated in advance to all relevant front office and operating departments, to let them know who is coming, to what rooms, when and for how long, and what special provisions have been made: who is to greet and escort the guest; whether a fruit basket or champagne is to be provided in the room on arrival; whether any special security measures will be applied; etc.

SUMMARY

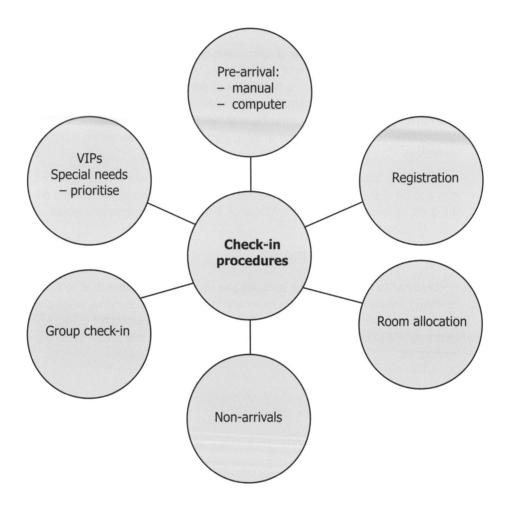

SELF-TEST QUESTIONS

1 What do (a) ETA and (b) CIP stand for?

2 All guests over 16 years of age must give their nationality on registration. True or False?

3 If a hotel needs to 'book-out' guests, what category of guest will be booked-out first?

4 What does credit card 'pre-authorisation' mean?

5 What records need to be updated once a guest has checked-in?

6 What are the disadvantages of self-service check-in?

7 Name three methods of displaying room status.

8 How can a hotel reduce the number of no-shows?

9 What will a hotel do if a group checks-in early?

10 What three categories of guest will be earmarked for special attention?

SELF-TEST ANSWERS

1 Estimated Time of Arrival; Commercially Important Person

2 True

3 One night stays (or first time and non-VIP guests)

4 The hotel swipes the guest's credit card for a certain amount, which is 'reserved' by the credit card company, guaranteeing this amount is available for payment.

5 Guest record; other department records (via notifications); guest account/bill; room status and availability records

6 Self-service check-in doesn't offer a greeting or welcome; may alienate older guest; may not offer flexibility or range of services; and may still require registration.

7 Bedroom book; bed sheet; room rack (or reception board)

8 Chasing unconfirmed bookings; reconfirming bookings; imposing financial penalties for non-arrival.

9 The hotel may have to store the group's luggage and offer waiting facilities.

10 Very Important Persons (VIPs); Commercially Important Persons (CIPs); and Special Attention Guests (SPATTs).

ANSWERS TO ACTIVITIES

1 Your own Internet research. You could also collect copies of Registration cards from various hotels you visit in the course of your studies (or your own travel).

2 Some attributes which guests particularly value in rooms, and which may dictate their preference for one room over another within the same grade or type of room, include:

- Familiarity (eg rooms that a guest has stayed in previously)

- Location (eg close to facilities – or *away* from noisy areas such as lifts or public areas)

- Views (eg of the ocean, gardens, city skylines etc – particularly valued by tourist and special occasion guests)

- Accessibility requirements (eg ground floor rooms for disabled or elderly guests)

- Room size (especially for multiple occupancy and long-stay guests), and perhaps also the amount of wardrobe space, or the ability to take extra occupants on pull-out or sofa beds

- Bathroom (eg bath rather than shower) facilities.

3 In the case of a 'missing' reservation, the receptionist should first ask the guest for details of the booking, and any documentation the guest has for it (ideally, without alerting the guest that there is a problem), before checking the records. If no record is found, but the guest has confirmation documents, normal check-in procedures should be carried out as far as possible. If the guest has no confirmation, and is unknown to the hotel (ie not a repeat guest), (s)he should be treated as a chance arrival.

4 Having VIP guests stay (particularly if they become regulars) may enhance the reputation and prestige of the hotel, or their business may be particularly lucrative in financial terms, over time (eg in the case of a large corporate account). And in any case, important guests may have higher expectations about how they will be treated – so 'special attention' is required to keep them satisfied (which is the hotel's aim with *any* guest).

CHAPTER 4

CHECK-OUT PROCEDURES

Chapter objectives

In this chapter you will learn

- Procedures for posting charges, recording deposits and prepayments
- Procedures for preparing and presenting guest bills
- Procedures for accepting guest payment, using different methods of payment
- Procedures for processing visitors paid outs (VPOs), disbursements and petty cash
- Procedures for foreign currency exchange
- Procedures for express check-out, late check-out and group check-out
- Measures to protect the security of cash and other forms of payment

Topic list

Checking-out guests
Preparing and presenting guest bills
Payment procedures
Other cash transactions
Security issues

1 Checking-out guests

In our last chapter, we checked guests into the hotel – and now it is time to send them on their way! It may be tempting to think that most of the 'public relations' work of the front office has been done by this time; that it's too late now to make guests feel welcomed, valued and served – and all you're really doing is getting them out the door. But this isn't the case.

For one thing, a guest is a guest right until the moment (s)he walks out the door – and beyond. The hotel's hope will be that each guest may plan to return, and will be so pleased with the service (s)he has received that (s)he will tell family, friends and colleagues about the hotel. **Good service** is cost-effective marketing, generating future business without incurring any advertising costs! The hotel may well keep in touch with guests after their departure, for this very reason, reminding them of their stay, reinforcing the message that they will be welcome to return, and perhaps offering incentives to do so (such as a special offer on their next stay).

For another thing, **check-out** is an opportunity to **offer further services** to guests to enhance their stay and their onward travel experience. Front office staff may offer assistance with the handling of luggage. They may also offer assistance with onward travel arrangements, ordering a taxi or shuttle bus service to the nearest airport or train station, say; or confirming reservations at the next destination hotel – or perhaps recommending and making a reservation at a sister hotel at the guest's next destination.

Check-out is also a great opportunity to do some **selling and information gathering**. For example, a satisfied departing guest may be open to joining the hotel loyalty scheme (if any), or accepting the recommendation of a sister hotel. Departing guests will also be in an excellent position to fill out Customer Feedback forms, with the good points and bad points of their stay fresh in their minds. This will be valuable information for hotel management to identify how the hotel's facilities and service can be improved.

On the other hand – and equally importantly – check-out is a point at which the hotel is **vulnerable** to getting it *wrong*. Guests may be feeling sad or stressed on departure: their holiday is over; there are uncertainties about onward travel arrangements; or there may be worries about the bill. Checking-out of the hotel should be made as relaxed, positive and trouble-free as possible.

A C T I V I T Y   1   1 0   m i n u t e s

Why is check-out time a period of particular 'vulnerability' for a hotel? Identify some of the activities and circumstances that may cause stress to guests and hotel staff.

So front office staff certainly can't take their minds 'off the ball' when it comes to check-out time...

1.1 Check-out procedures

As with check-in, the hotel will have a standard set of basic procedures for the departure and check-out of guests.

- **Check-out times**. Most hotels inform their guests on reservation and check-in, and again via in-room information, about the standard check-out time. The registration form, for example, may state: 'Guests are requested to vacate their rooms by 10 am on the morning of departure'. This standard check-out time (usually 10 or 11 am) is designed to ensure that rooms are vacated in time to be cleaned and prepared for incoming guests (who may arrive mid-afternoon).

- **Confirming departures**. Although reservation and registration documents clearly state a departure date, some guests may wish to extend their stay at the last minute, and it may not occur to them to give the hotel advance notice of their change of plans. Many hotels, therefore, seek to confirm with the guest that they are due to depart as planned, usually the night before.

BPP
LEARNING MEDIA

- This is also an opportunity to check whether the guest requires **early or late check-out**. If the guest needs to leave before reception is staffed, the bill may need to be presented and settled the night before, and instructions given for returning the keys on departure. If the guest wishes to stay in the room later than standard check-out time, this will have to be approved. Housekeeping will have to be notified to delay cleaning, and the room status will have to be monitored (to ensure that it is not allocated to a new guest who has notified an early arrival). There may be a charge for late check-out.

- **Departure services and information**. When confirming departure, front office staff may also offer additional services such as an early wake-up call, assistance with luggage, airport transfers or help with onward travel arrangements. Guests may also be provided with a **Departure Pack** including their bill (for checking prior to payment); a reminder of check-out times, procedures and services; a customer feedback form (asking the guest to evaluate the facilities and service offered to them during their stay); promotional brochures for the hotel and/or hotel chain (as a reminder for future travel needs); and perhaps a letter or card thanking them for their stay.

- **Departure notifications**. On confirmation, other departments of the hotel will have to be informed that the guest is departing. Switchboard will need to know not to put calls through to the room. Housekeeping will need to know which rooms to prepare for re-letting. The bar, restaurant and other internal services will need to know not to extend further credit to guests who have already settled their bills, and so on. These notifications may be made via a **Departures List** (often combined on the same sheet as the Arrivals List): a list of all anticipated departures on a given day, in room number order. However, as we noted above, guests can change their minds at the last minute: some may leave unexpectedly, while others may extend their stays. Some hotels, therefore, circulate periodic **updates of actual departures**, so that the Departures List can be amended. In a computerised system, these notifications, and the updating of all relevant records (housekeeping task lists, room status displays, departure lists), are done automatically as each guest is checked out on the system.

- **Bill preparation, presentation and settlement**. The **guest bill** (**room account** or 'folio') will be prepared for presentation to the guest, either at check-out or (in case of early check-out, or to allow the guest to check the bill) the night before departure. On check-out, the guest settles the account, using one of a range of payment methods accepted by the hotel. These are major check-out tasks, and we will discuss them in detail, later in the chapter.

- **Key return**. It is the responsibility of front office to ensure that the guest returns room keys on check-out, to avoid the hassle and security risk of keys being lost or taken away by departing guests. Keys will often be stored on room-numbered racks, or in room-numbered pigeon holes (along with guest mail), allowing an at-a-glance check that keys have been returned. Electronic key cards may need to have their room access data 'erased' (blocking subsequent use) before storage. We will discuss this in more detail in Chapter 7.

- **Updating records**. Once the guest has left, there is some immediate record updating to do. On a computerised system, this is done automatically as the guest is checked-out, but in a manual system, front office staff will have to update:

  - The **room status records** or room rack, to show that the room is first being prepared ('vacant but not ready') and then available for re-letting. If a rack system is used, the guest's card can simply be removed from the rack and disposed of.

  - The **guest list** or index (used by switchboard to locate the room numbers and extensions of guests by name)

- The **guest file**. Copies of the guest's bill and payment details will be added to the guest's file (already containing the reservation form, confirmation, any correspondence and the registration card), which will be stored in the 'past guests' filing system for 12 months.

- **Guest history records**. Hotels wishing to offer a personalised service to returning guests keep records of their details and preferences, updated for each stay. This allows front office staff to 'recognise' returning guests (even if the staff have changed), anticipate their particular needs and wants, send birthday cards and so on. This would probably not be worthwhile for any but luxury hotels, or loyal regular guests, except for computerisation, which makes it achievable for any establishment. We will discuss the use of such records further in Chapter 6.

ACTIVITY 2   20 minutes

You have been given the task of instructing and coaching a new front desk staff member in check-out procedures.

Write out the key points of the check-out procedures discussed above, in such a way that they will provide a quick **checklist** or **guidelines** for a new staff member.

1.2 Computerised check-out systems

As with reservation and check-in systems, the computerisation of check-out procedures has a number of advantages for speed, efficiency and accuracy. All the relevant data is **stored** electronically and easily **accessed** from various data points (eg by date, name or room number).

Records can be easily **updated**, and, since they are all interlinked, related records and status reports will be simultaneously updated. When a guest checks-out, room status displays will immediately show that the room is 'vacant, not yet ready'; housekeeping tasks lists will show that the room is available for cleaning; the departures list will be updated; the guest index will indicate that the guest has left; and the guest's record will be 'filed' under 'past guests' without the physical transfer of any files.

Guest accounts can be maintained in the computer system, with some transactions automatically entered by the system itself: pre-set room charges will be posted each day from the reservation records, for example, and restaurant/bar bills may be directly input to the account from Electronic Point of Sale systems in the relevant departments. The **posting of charges** can be done swiftly and automatically allocated to the relevant room accounts, with updated running totals.

Final **guest bills** are therefore calculated and generated automatically by the system: far less time-consuming and error-prone than manual and mechanical systems, and more professionally presented in a final-version, correction-free, smartly printed form.

Check-out and settlement are **speeded up** (a major advantage at one of the busiest periods at front desk) by facilities such as: automatic foreign currency conversions; automatic verification of company account status; and express/self check-out (discussed below).

1.3 Express and self check-out

As express check-in, the hotel may offer facilities for guests who may need to check-out early, before reception is open – or who simply wish to avoid a busy period at the cashier's desk.

In a manual system, this may be done by gaining authorisation from the guest to debit the entire amount of the bill to the guest's credit card. An **express check-out form** may be supplied to guests on check-in, or on request, or made available with in-room information, for completion in advance of departure. The guest supplies all relevant credit card details on the form (or the cashier may take a credit card imprint) and signs a declaration that (s)he authorises the hotel to debit the full amount of the bill to the designated credit card, and to send the bill and receipt to a given address: this substitutes for a signature on the credit card voucher.

The guest may be supplied with a copy of the bill as it currently stands, the night before departure, as a guide to the approximate total of the account. When the guest leaves, (s)he simply puts the express check-out form – and room key – in a designated '**drop box**'. The credit card payment can then be processed by the cashier, in the usual way, and a copy of the finalised bill and credit card voucher/receipt posted or e-mailed to the guest.

In a computerised system, as for self check-in, the guest may be able to simply use a **kiosk or computer terminal** at reception (or even in-room), which:

- Asks the guest to key in the name and room number, and/or to swipe the electronic key or credit card previously logged on the system.

- Displays and/or prints out the account to date.

- Invites the guest to confirm/accept the bill (or flag items for query).

- Invites the guest to insert or swipe their credit card, in order to process a credit card payment.

- Issues a receipt (or logs the need to send a copy bill and receipt to the guest at his or her registered address).

FOR DISCUSSION

'Self check-out is convenient for some guests – but it is a missed opportunity for the hotel.'

Looking back to the beginning of the chapter, if you need to, discuss the potential 'lost opportunity' for the hotel in not handling guest check-out personally.

1.4 Group check-out

Just as with group check-in, the main issue will be to **minimise chaos**! A separate group waiting area or room may help to get the group out of its rooms (so that housekeeping can begin preparing them for re-letting), in one place (so the group leader can keep them together) – and away from the front desk (so they do not overwhelm the cashier and other departing guests).

The front desk should have a departures list for the group, so that it can follow a checklist for ensuring that:

- All keys have been returned.

- The tour leader has countersigned a voucher itemising all the accommodation and meal charges the tour company will be responsible for.

- Individual guests' extras bills (if any) have been paid.

- All luggage cleared from the rooms and any storage areas.

The hotel may co-opt the group leader to gather keys and remind guests about extras bills, in order to minimise to-ing and fro-ing. If the group is due to leave later than the standard check-out time, the hotel may offer a **waiting or 'hospitality' room**, enabling group members to rest, store hand luggage and use bathroom facilities during the period between check-in from individual rooms and departure. This is a valued service for tour guests – but it also enables the hotel to clear individual rooms for servicing at the usual time, and to avoid having groups milling around reception.

2   Preparing and presenting guest bills

At first glance, you might think that preparing a guest bill is a simple matter: multiply the number of nights by the quoted rate per night, or just take the agreed package price – and there you go. Not quite.

For one thing, guests may have **paid a deposit** (or even the whole accommodation amount) in advance, to confirm their reservation, this will have to be deducted from the total bill, to provide the balance still owing.

For another thing, guests may have incurred a number of **additional charges** during their stay: extra nights' accommodation; meals and drinks from the hotel restaurant, bar or room service; drinks and snacks from the in-room mini-bar; newspapers (if charged for); laundry services; telephone calls made from the room phone; additional services (eg treatments in the hotel spa); and so on. In most hotels, these items will not be paid for as they are purchased: they will be 'charged to the room'. In the restaurant or bar, for example, guests may give their room number and sign a voucher or 'chitty' for the services they have received. In the case of the mini-bar, they will be asked to fill out a form with the items they have consumed. These details will be passed to reception and added to the guest's main room account.

Keeping track of all these items involves a lot of record-keeping! *Abbott & Lewry* (*Front Office*) suggest that the process is both complex and sensitive, with particular challenges arising from the fact that:

- The hotel is effectively giving guests **credit** for the duration of their stay: allowing them to consume goods and services now, and pay later. This is not unusual in business dealings, of course, but hotels are in the unusual position of giving potentially substantial credit to people about whom they may know very little. There's a risk of inability or failure to pay, which must be planned for.

- Guests may be incurring additional charges in different departments of the hotel, right up to departure. There needs to be **fast, accurate notification** of this information to the billing or accounting section, in order for all charges to be included on the guest's bill at check-out.

As we saw in Chapter 1, the keeping of guest account records and preparation of bills is usually the responsibility of a billing or accounting section (in large hotels), while the handling of settlement (payment) is the responsibility of the hotel cashier. In a smaller hotel, this may all be handled by available front desk staff, so receptionists need sufficient numerical (and cash handling) skills to cope with whatever accounting procedures the hotel uses.

2.1   Guest accounting and billing systems

As we will see in Chapter 5, many hotels now use **computerised guest accounting and billing systems** – which keep a running total of what each guest owes (taking into account deposits, pre-payments and additional charges) as each item is entered or 'posted'. Front office staff can print out the running total at any time, if a guest wishes to know the current status of his or her account (sometimes also called a 'folio').

With a manual system, each guest account needs to be balanced and totalled daily in a **tabular ledger**: the hotel's running log of each day's business, including for each room:

- The running total owed (outstanding charges), brought forward from the day before

- The day's accommodation and meal charges, as appropriate to the rate or package terms agreed

- Itemised additional charges incurred under various headings: bar, restaurant, phone and so on

- A running total of outstanding charges at the end of the day

- Any payments made against the amount owing (eg prepayments or deposits) and any outstanding amounts to be carried forward to the next day. The payments made *plus* amounts carried forward should therefore *equal* (balance) the amount owing for each day. On settlement of the final account, at check-out, there will be no amounts carried forward: payments should balance the amount owing.

Whichever method is used, the main objective of the person dealing with the preparation of guest accounts is to be as **accurate** as possible: the bills or folios presented to guests *must* accurately reflect the services used, pre-payments made and the charges notified to the guest. Errors – whether over- or under-charging – will inevitably reflect badly on the hotel.

A C T I V I T Y   3   **5   m i n u t e s**

What might the consequences be for a hotel, if a guest feels that he has been (or has actually been) overcharged or undercharged for the services he has received?

We will look at **guest accounting** and **billing systems** in more detail in Chapter 5: here, we will just touch on the procedures most relevant to guest check-out.

2.2 Recording deposits and pre-payments

As we noted above, one of the key tasks in guest accounting is to record deposits and pre-payments, so that these are deducted from the final bill – and the guest isn't charged for them twice!

- Receipt of a **deposit or pre-payment** should immediately be recorded in the reservations status records. If pre-payment is required to guarantee a reservation, any deposit made will be shown clearly in the booking confirmation documents and invoice, requiring the prospective guest to pay the outstanding balance by a stated date. The guest will normally be sent a receipt for any deposit or pre-payment received.

- A deposit or prepayment will be entered in the **advance deposit ledger**. The amount will also be entered in guest account or billing records when the guest checks-in and the bill is opened – so that the guest has an opening credit balance reflecting the deposit.

- The reservation records, confirmations and guest account should be **cross-checked**, to ensure that the received/acknowledged deposit amount tallies with the amount shown on the guest account.

- There will be a separate ('**ledger account**') entry for arrangements whereby the hotel will claim the amount of a guest's bill from another party at a later date (eg a tour company or a corporation with a credit account at the hotel), by issuing an invoice or statement. The guest may have pre-paid a tour company or conference organiser for accommodation and/or meals, and present a voucher or coupon confirming this fact to the hotel. Having checked that this is a legitimate, agreed arrangement (and received authorisation), the charges covered can be recorded as a ledger entry.

2.3 Agency (commissionable) bookings

Reservations made by travel agents and hotel booking agents (including online booking agencies) are normally made on the basis that the agent will earn a commission (percentage) payment on the room rate, as its 'reward' for making the sale on the hotel's behalf.

Commissionable bookings should be noted in the remarks column of the bookings diary, or in the computer reservation form (as discussed below), so that when the guest checks-in, their account can be marked as commissionable. Two separate accounts (or a **split folio**) may need to be opened for the guest, so that the commission can be calculated on the accommodation part of the bill only.

If guests are having their main accommodation charges settled by a company or tour organiser, they may also require a split folio: that is, there will be a master account or folio for the room charges (which will be sent to the company) *plus* a folio for the extras or incidentals, which will be settled by the guest.

2.4   Posting charges

During the guests' stay, extras such as drinks, afternoon tea, newspapers, telephone calls and other items can be added to their accounts.

Information about charges will have to be passed from the departments concerned to the front office, for inclusion on the guest's bill. This is called '**posting charges**'.

- Charges may be recorded **automatically**: eg by a telephone call logging system, or via an Electronic Point of Sale system (linking the bar or restaurant cash register to the front office billing system).

- They may be **pre-agreed** with the guest, and signed for at reception on registration (eg a daily charge for newspapers or extra towels).

- They may take the form of **reimbursements** (repayments) of payments made by the hotel on behalf of guests, or '**visitor paid outs**' **(VPOs)**. For example, the hotel may have had to pay COD (cash on delivery) for a parcel delivered to a guest by courier, or may have sent someone out to fill a guest's medical prescription.

- They may be confirmed by the guest and notified to reception via **vouchers or 'chitties'**, with the name of the guest, room number, date/time, details of the service provided or items purchased, and their cost. Guests will often be required to sign the chitty to confirm their agreement with the charge, prior to sending to the billing section: this is useful in the event of a later dispute (so signed chitties are usually retained in the guest file until departure).

E X A M P L E

A guest is getting ready for dinner, and dials out from his room telephone to make a reservation at a local restaurant: the computerised telephone system logs the call, and automatically charges the call charge to the guest's room account.

Meanwhile, the guest has had a beer and a packet of peanuts from his in-room mini-bar: he writes a '1' against these items on the printed price list, adds up the subtotal, and signs his name and room number on the form. Housekeeping will pick up this form the next day, when the mini-bar is being checked and re-stocked, and the form will be sent to reception for adding to the guest's account.

Unfortunately, the restaurant was fully booked, so the guest decides to entertain his guests in the hotel. They meet at the bar for pre-dinner drinks. When their table is ready, the bar tender presents the guest with a bill for the drinks: the guest signs his name and room number, and takes the top copy – while the bar tender sends the bottom copy through to reception.

Similarly, at the end of dinner, the guest is presented with a bill. The restaurant has an Electronic Point of Sale system, so when the guest gives his name and room number, and signs his bill, the 'cash register' automatically logs the amount and transmits it to the main Hotel Management System, which logs it on his guest account.

The guest had previously arranged with the concierge for flowers to be delivered to his room, as his wife is joining him the next day. The concierge has arranged for the delivery with a local florist, and paid for the flowers. A 'visitors paid outs' amount has been logged on the guest's bill.

The following morning, the guest also receives the newspaper he asked for on check-in, and the price of the newspaper is charged (as he was told it would be) to his room account.

In a manual system, hand-completed chitties may be pre-printed with information headings, to cut down on the amount of filling-in required. They should identify the department in which the charge is made (eg being colour-coded or differently designed for restaurant, room service, housekeeping, concierge and so on). This enables the hotel to analyse the spending of guests on different services, as well as making it easier to follow up guest queries about posted charges. Chitties may also be serially numbered, making queries easier to follow-up.

The system only works if staff in other departments are **accurate** in filling out vouchers, and **efficient** in sending them swiftly to front office. This is a particular challenge with charges incurred on the morning of a guest's departure, eg overnight mini-bar expenses and breakfast charges. (This is why breakfast is often included in the room rate and charged in advance.)

The posting of charges is thus an important area in which there needs to be excellent communication between front office and other departments:

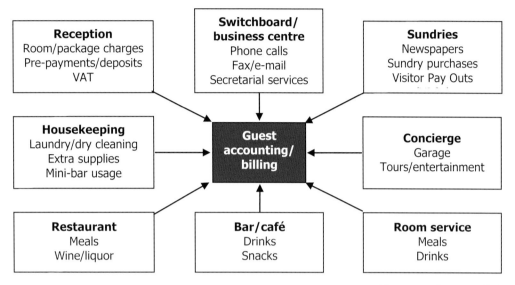

Figure 4.1 Sources of charges

Chitties can also be printed out from cash registers or computerised **point-of-sale systems** for guests to sign, and in **computerised systems**, the charge is also automatically transferred to the guest account from the point of sale terminal. Hand-held electronic devices may even be used, with charges displayed and guests signing on-screen. Even if a computerised system is used, however, it is still useful to have a paper print-out with guest signature, in case of subsequent queries.

The example computer screen at Figure 4.2 below shows a facility (in Hotel Perfect) for multi-room posting of charges. This allows charges to be posted in batches, making it a relatively quick daily task for a quiet period. It is linked to individual guest accounts (by name and room number), so the system can 'pick' the charges for each guest/room and insert them in the guest account for billing: Figure 4.3.

2.5 Presenting the bill

Accounts are usually prepared early each morning, after final postings have been made, for all guests on the departure list (although this may also be done the night before for longer stays, allowing guests to check through the bill at their leisure). Each guest's bill will be:

- **Written out**: itemising pre-payments and posted charges (often against pre-printed headings), and totalling the outstanding amount *or*

- **Printed out** from a **billing machine** or **computerised billing system**: automatically itemising pre-payments, credits and posted charges, with relevant details

- **Checked** for accuracy against reservation and confirmation records and guest account records.

The final bill (or bills, in the case of split folios: split bills for accommodation charges and extras) can then be presented to guests for checking, agreement and payment. An example of a printed bill is shown in Figure 4.4.

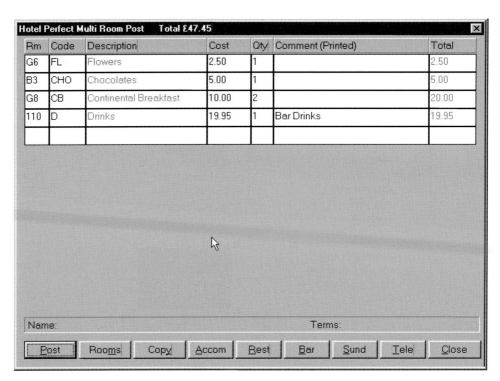

Figure 4.2: Multi-room posting of charges (in Hotel Perfect)

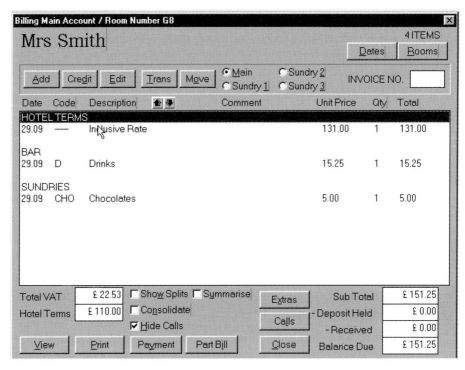

Figure 4.3: Guest account/billing system (in Hotel Perfect)

Hill Town Hotel

Guest Bill

Guest:	Mr Paul Martin Wright	**Arrival date:**	11/06/09
Room:	112	**Departure date:**	15/06/09
Folio no:	2609527	**Rate:**	£99 (room only)

Item	Date	Description	Amount £
1	11/06	Telephone	6.93
2	11/06	Bar	24.42
3	11/06	Telephone	14.26
4	11/06	Restaurant	63.20
5	11/06	Room	99.00
	11/06	BALANCE	207.81
6	12/06	Breakfast	12.99
7	12/06	Newspaper	2.00
8	12/06	Reimbursement: postage	6.00
9	12/06	Telephone	12.33
10	12/06	Mini-bar	15.75
11	12/06	Room	99.00
	12/06		355.78
12	13/06	Payment (Mastercard ending **09)	(350.00)
13	13/06	Breakfast	12.99
14	13/06	Newspaper	2.00
15	13/06	Internet access (30 minutes)	15.00

Date: 13/06/09	Time: 15.20	Balance due: **£ 35.77**

Figure 4.4: Standard guest bill or folio

BPP LEARNING MEDIA

2.6 Group billing arrangements

Payment and credit terms for the group (including protocols for handling any payment disputes) will have been agreed in a detailed contract with the tour operator or group organiser at the time of reservation. The operator's credit status will have to be checked before the booking is accepted, since a group account may add up to many thousands of pounds.

The group organiser should have sent a **voucher**, itemising the expenses for which it will be responsible, with the final guest/rooming list. A copy of this voucher can then be counter-signed by the tour leader on the group's departure, to confirm that the promised services have been delivered.

The group's account is completed and authorised by the cashier, and sent to the tour operator, together with the vouchers, for payment.

2.7 Handling account queries

As usual, we'll focus on the customer service angle first: how you handle a guest query or complaint about a bill is much more important than who is right or wrong! Billing questions and disputes must be handled efficiently and with good humour and understanding – regardless of who is responsible for any error or misunderstanding. If errors are found, apologise clearly and simply (grovelling is not required) and put the matter right.

ACTIVITY 4   5 minutes

What kinds of questions and disputes might arise on presentation of a guest's bill?

We will deal with the handling of guest complaints in more detail in Chapter 9, but briefly, good practice for a dispute on check-out might be as follows.

- Take the guest aside, so that the matter can be handled discreetly – and so that other guests can continue their check outs (if other staff are available) without disruption

- Assure the guest that the matter will be immediately looked into, and ask him to wait for a moment while this is done. Reservation documents, chitties and other documents can then be checked for errors, and authorisation for legitimate reductions or adjustments sought.

- If time is short (reception is busy and/or the guest has to leave immediately), the cashier may have – or seek – authorisation simply to alter or delete the disputed charges, to settle the issue without further conflict which might reflect badly on the hotel.

- Authorisation from a manager may be required to offer a refund or reduction, or to write-off disputed charges. It may also be advisable to get confirmation from the guest that this has been corrected and accepted, in case of follow-up disputes. This can be done by getting both guest and manager to sign an Adjustment or Allowance slip, attached to the hotel's copy of the final bill.

- Both the hotel's and the guest's copy of the bill should be altered to show any adjustment. In a computerised system, the billing details can simply be amended to show the adjustment and the bill re-printed. In a manual system, a hand-written correction may be made and countersigned.

- Any adjustments must be recorded in the guest accounts (eg the tabular ledger or computer system) as 'adjustments', 'allowances' or 'refunds' – so that at the end of the day, the recorded payments received will still tally with the recorded amounts due.

Again, remember that this is just procedure and record-keeping: a positive attitude will make all the difference in whether this satisfies the departing guest or not...

3 Payment procedures

Once the guest has agreed the account, (s)he will offer payment in a variety of ways. The hotel may **accept** various forms of payment – and may **prefer** some more than others. What dictates this preference?

- **Liquidity**: the swiftness with which the payment becomes available for the hotel to spend (to purchase goods) or bank (to earn interest). Cash is a highly liquid form of payment: it can be immediately deployed. If a guest pays on credit, on the other hand, it may take 30, 60 or 90 days (depending on the hotel's credit terms) for the money to reach the hotel's bank account.

- **Security**: the safety with which the payment can be handled, stored and transported. Cash poses a risk, because of the ease of theft, requiring strong security measures. Forms of payment requiring signatures or PIN numbers (such as traveller's cheques, credit and debit cards) are more secure, as there is less likelihood of theft.

- **Worth**: the total amount of money received by the hotel once the transaction is completed. Different payment methods (notably credit cards) attract a variety of handling charges, commission and delays in payment, which will all cost the hotel money. On the other hand, if hotels accept payment in foreign currency, for example, they can *make* money on the transaction, by offering guests a rate of exchange which gives them a margin of profit.

There are eight major **methods of payment** commonly accepted by hotels:

- Cash
- Foreign currency
- Cheque
- Traveller's cheques
- Credit cards
- Debit cards
- Credit accounts
- Vouchers

Let's look at each of these in turn.

3.1 Cash

Cash is the only 'legal tender': this means that a hotel *could,* theoretically, insist on full payment of bills in cash – and only accepts other methods of payment as a courtesy. Cash is still the most commonly used payment instrument for low-value transactions – and the receptionist will inevitably handle some small cash payments, eg for drinks

and snacks, phone cards, newspapers and so on. However, as accommodation prices have increased and other methods of payment (safer and more convenient for travellers than carrying cash) have developed, cash tends to be used less for payment of main accounts – and other methods of payment are accepted in order to attract and retain guests.

Where sales are made for cash, it is normal practice to have a cash till, which records the sale, calculates any change required, produces a receipt for the purchase and stores the cash received. Alternatively, the cashier may simply operate a secure cash box or tray, locked away when not in use, and never left unattended or on view to the general public. Either way, there will be a cash **'float'** (a standing amount of cash in different small denominations), allowing the receptionist to give change when required.

The use of cash requires good accounting records and security (because of the risk of theft). Guests must be given a receipt, or their bill should be marked 'paid by cash', to give them a record of payment.

Advantages of accepting cash	Disadvantages of accepting cash
▪ High liquidity: money can be reused (or banked to earn interest) without delay	▪ Low security: high risk of theft, counterfeit notes
▪ Fairly high worth: no processing costs associated with cheques and card-based payments	▪ Worth: bank charges for depositing cash, plus cost of transport, staff time, security
▪ Convenient for small-value transactions	▪ Time taken in 'cashing up', banking etc
▪ Anonymous (where privacy desired)	▪ Prone to errors in counting, change giving
▪ No special equipment required	▪ Inconvenient for large purchases

3.2 Foreign currency

A hotel may choose to accept payment in a foreign currency, if it has significant international trade, or regular outgoings in foreign currencies, eg if it can re-use euros or US dollars for its own purchases. Some larger hotels also offer foreign currency exchange facilities for guests (as discussed later). The hotel can make a profit by accepting the currency at an advantageous exchange rate. In addition, the hotel will charge a commission, to allow for any charges the bank may apply when the currency is deposited. This is a legitimate charge for a service provided to guests.

Receptionists and/or cashiers need to be knowledgeable about which currencies are readily accepted by UK banks, and by the hotel. They should also be familiar with – or able to look up – the design of currencies (in order to avoid the accepting of fake or counterfeit money) and their exchange value. Current rates of exchange can be found on the Internet – or the hotel may request its bank to supply a list of daily exchange rates. Management can then determine the rate, or percentage difference from the central rate, offered by the hotel. (We will discuss this further below.)

Only banknotes should be accepted as payment from guests, most banks will not accept foreign coinage. Change must be given in pounds sterling or euros, unless the hotel is registered as an authorised foreign exchange dealer. If the hotel is *not* so registered, it is illegal to supply foreign currency. Receipts should be given for all currency transactions, in case of dispute.

Advantages of accepting foreign currency	Disadvantages of accepting foreign currency
▪ Worth: can charge a commission and earn a profit on difference in buying/selling rates	▪ As for cash, plus
▪ Customer service: convenience for foreign guests	▪ Risk of errors in exchange calculation
	▪ Cost of staff training/information for exchange calculation
▪ No special equipment required	▪ Risk that bank may not accept some currencies

3.3 Cheques

For a long time, cheques were one of the most common forms of payment, as most travellers had access to bank accounts, and the use of cash declined. A cheque is a paper-based form of payment, effectively, a promise to pay the amount stated. A typical cheque is illustrated at Figure 4.5.

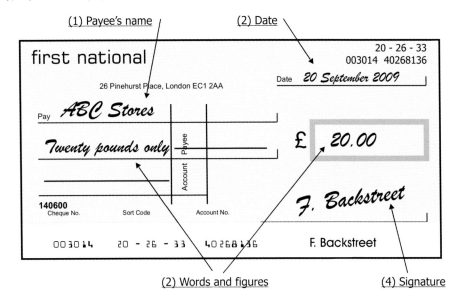

(1) Payee's name   (2) Date

(2) Words and figures   (4) Signature

Figure 4.5: A cheque

Payment by cheque suffers from some disadvantages of liquidity (the cheque will take at least three working days to 'clear' following banking, before the funds are received) and security (the cheque may not be honoured due to forgery, incorrect completion or lack of funds in the drawer's bank account). Front office staff need to keep to very strict rules when accepting cheques. If you accept a cheque and the guest has the benefit of services before the cheque has been cleared, you could have a situation where the guest does not in fact have sufficient funds to cover the cheque, which is returned to you unpaid – perhaps after the guest has departed.

Front office staff should, therefore, follow procedures to establish that the cheque is correctly completed, valid, and backed by available funds.

- **Check** that the payee's name (the hotel) is correct; that the date is today's date; that the words and figures for the amount of the cheque are the same; and that the cheque has been signed, in the presence of the receptionist (in case of forgery). If any of these details are incorrect, the guest should be asked to amend them and to initial the amendment.

- The hotel should have a policy to accept cheques only if accompanied by a **valid cheque guarantee card**, the citing of which (by the receptionist writing the card number on the back of the cheque) guarantees that the cheque will be honoured up to a certain amount. Since this is normally only £50 or £100, and hotel bills are often larger than this, the hotel may only accept cheques in payment of larger amounts from known guests. The receptionist must check that the guarantee card has the same name and account number as the cheque, is not defaced or altered in any way, and is not past its expiry date – otherwise the guarantee will not apply. Only one cheque per transaction is guaranteed by the card; the use of two £100 cheques doesn't guarantee a payment of £200.

- The hotel may ask guests paying by cheque, where possible, to settle the main account **three to four days before** their scheduled departure, to allow the cheque to clear.

- If none of the above securities are available, the hotel is entitled to request the guest (politely) to **settle the account by some other means**. This should have been discussed on reservation, so that it doesn't come as an unpleasant surprise to any guest!

Advantages of accepting cheques	Disadvantages of accepting cheques
▪ Better security than cash: less worth stealing, as funds can only be obtained by the designated payee	▪ Security: can 'bounce' (returned for lack of funds), or errors or forgeries can result in the bank refusing to honour a cheque
▪ Less handling than cash for large amounts	▪ Liquidity: takes time to clear
▪ Cheaper than cash to operate with	▪ Worth: handling charge imposed by banks

3.4 Traveller's cheques

Traveller's cheques, with their system of signature and counter-signature, were designed to provide travellers with a secure and replaceable document that a wide range of organisations would be willing to accept in exchange for cash, goods and services.

A hotel with significant international trade will often be given traveller's cheques in payment and/or to exchange for cash in the local currency. This will involve the receptionist in foreign exchange rate calculations, as with foreign currency payments.

The cheques are issued in fixed denominations by major banks, travel agents and building societies in predetermined multiples of various currencies. American Express, for example, currently issues traveller's cheques in nine different currencies: US dollars, Canadian dollars, pounds sterling, Swiss Francs, Australian Dollars, Japanese Yen, South African Rand, Saudi Riyal and euros.

The traveller's specimen signature will be put on each cheque at the time of the purchase: a counter-signature is required when the cheque is used. When accepting a payment by traveller's cheque, the cashier must watch the guest sign and date the cheque, and verify that the signature matches the one already on the cheque. It is also common to request some proof of identity (such as a passport or driver's licence), for verification purposes. Banks also issue **lists of invalid (lost or stolen) traveller's cheques**, and the cashier should check the serial number of any presented traveller's cheque against this list.

The hotel will typically use the normal bank clearing system to receive funds from the issuer of the travellers' cheques, or the issuer's paying agent for a particular currency.

Advantages of accepting TCs	Disadvantages of accepting TCs
▪ High security: reduced risk of theft due to non-transferability	▪ Liquidity: take time to 'clear' before funds are available
▪ Customer service: convenient and safe for travellers, with better exchange rate and no expiry date	▪ Worth: banks charge a small commission for exchanging them

3.5 Credit cards

Credit cards of all type are a very popular method of payment for any goods and services: most hotels will accept at least one or two major credit cards (such as Mastercard or Visa, American Express or Diners Club). Credit cards are convenient for travellers: they allow payment to be made without the need for insecure cash or bulky cheque books – and provide an opportunity to pay on credit, as well as to receive loyalty benefits such as Air Miles.

Credit card companies levy **commission charges** (usually between 2% to 5% of the transaction amount), making them comparatively expensive (low worth) for the hotel, and this will be one reason why management may decide not to accept particular cards. However, business travellers, in particular, like to pay by credit card (because it is a company card, or because they can get their expenses reimbursed before they actually have to pay the debt). A hotel with a high proportion of business trade may have to accept a range of cards – although it may also pass on the commission charge to the guest, in return for the service.

When accepting a credit card payment, most hotels nowadays use electronic machines linked by telecommunication links directly to a bank. Card details are collected from the magnetic strip on the back of the card when the card is 'swiped' through the machine.

- The cashier inserts or swipes the card, and enters the sales amount and the hotel's identification code.

- Details are transmitted to the bank's computer system for approval (eg on the basis that the card has not expired, is not stolen, and has sufficient available credit). The machine signals that the transaction has been approved, and provides an authorisation code.

- The guest is generally requested to enter their Personal Identification Number (PIN) into the keypad, to confirm identity, and to accept the transaction.

- The machine produces a two-part voucher or receipt, which may (if PIN numbers are not used) require signature by the guest.

- The cashier verifies that the signature on the receipt matches that on the back of the card.

- The top copy of the receipt is given to the guest and the other copy is retained for the hotel's records.

Some small hotels may still use the manual system by which the cashier fills out the top copy of a multi-sheet sales voucher, and places it over the credit card in an 'imprinting' machine, which by sliding a weight across the card and voucher, makes an imprint of the raised credit card details on the voucher: the completed voucher is then handled in the same way as the computerised print-out version.

Credit card charges are paid into the bank with cash and cheques and credited to the hotel's account in the normal way (minus any commission charges).

Advantages of accepting credit cards	Disadvantages of accepting credit cards
- High security: less cash held on the premises, less risk of theft, payment is guaranteed	- Liquidity: take time to 'clear' before funds are available
- Customer service: convenient and safe for travellers	- Worth: banks charge commission for use, plus the hotel incurs costs of equipment, training etc
- Can be used to accept payment by phone, mail and online (eg for deposits and pre-payments)	- Need to purchase or rent equipment, and develop contract with the credit card company
- Encourages higher spending on impulse buys	- Security: danger of credit card fraud

E X A M P L E

'A word from the FOM'

Despite the convenience and widespread use of credit cards, we are finding that hotels are becoming a 'cash economy' again. The hotel may pass on a credit card surcharge to guests (to cover the commission it has to pay to the credit card company), and many guests prefer to avoid this by paying cash. Cash suits the hotel because it is extremely 'liquid', requires no special handling and incurs no fees. Despite the risk of theft, it is also looking increasingly safe, given the widespread threat of credit card fraud and identity theft.

Just recently, we had a person telephone and ask to pre-pay a room reservation 'for their son', by credit card over the phone. Staff are instructed to decline such bookings politely: without sight of the credit card, and checking of the signature, we have no way of knowing whether the person using the card was its legitimate owner.

3.6 Debit card

Many banks now provide their customers with a debit card, such as Switch or Delta. These cards look similar to credit cards, but their function is very different: payment is immediately transferred by Electronic Funds Transfer at Point of Sale (EFTPOS), directly from the guest's bank account to the hotel's bank account.

The procedure for accepting a debit card payment is the same as that for a credit card. The advantages and disadvantages of accepting them are much the same, too.

However, debit cards also make it possible to offer a **cash-back** service, whereby an extra amount is added to the total amount owing, for the customer to receive in cash. For example, a guest may pay a hotel bill for £242.99 by debit card, and ask for £50 cash back. The cashier would enter the total amount as £292.99, and give the guest £50 in cash. Many guests may find this a useful way to obtain cash, rather than make a separate trip to a bank or ATM machine. (It does not cost the hotel anything extra to offer the service, because organisations accepting debit card payment pay a fixed commission to their bank or merchant services provider – *not* a percentage.)

3.7 Travel agents' vouchers

Some guests may have paid a **travel agent** for their accommodation and/or meals in advance (perhaps as part of a single invoice for multiple travel and accommodation arrangements). In such a case, the travel agent will usually issue some kind of voucher, showing the services booked and the amount paid.

- One copy will go to the hotel, to confirm the booking, and be held in the guest's reservation file.

- Another copy is given to the traveller to present to the hotel on check-in, confirming the guest's identity – and alerting the receptionist to any misunderstandings or changes.

- The receptionist should ensure that both (s)he and the guest are clear on what is covered by the voucher. An imprint or swipe of the guest's credit card may still be taken to cover any extra charges incurred during the stay, additional meals, optional services and sundries.

- The amount covered by the voucher is recorded in the 'ledger' column of the guest accounts (so that the 'payments' eventually balance with the amounts owed), and the amount transferred to its ledger account: these are amounts owing to the hotel, for which payment will be invoiced later.

- At check-out, the guest's bill should show the amount pre-paid (quoting the voucher), plus any extra charges incurred. Even if there is a zero balance owing (ie there have been no extra charges), the guest should be asked to sign the bill, to show that they have taken up the services paid for, in case of subsequent query.

- Vouchers are collected and sent, usually monthly, to the issuing travel agents for subsequent payment (deducting the agent's commission on the booking).

Group tours are often paid for by group vouchers. The tour guide or organiser agrees the total number of persons/nights of accommodation, meals and other services covered by the voucher, prior to departure, on the group's behalf. Individual 'extras' bills will still be presented and settled in the usual way.

3.8   Credit accounts

Tour companies, and businesses paying for their employees' travel, will often find themselves making regular, high-frequency bookings. They may find it inconvenient and costly to pay for each stay separately, and may ask the hotel to set up a credit account.

The hotel will have to carry out checks on the company's reliability and ability to pay (ie its '**credit-worthiness**'): we discuss this in Chapter 5. Once credit is approved, an account can be opened, and guests can ask for their stays to be billed to the account. The company may supply the hotel with a list of guests/stays to be covered by the account, or may issue travellers with some kind of voucher or corporate purchasing card confirming their authorisation to charge their expenses to the account.

At check-out, the hotel will record the billed amount in the '**ledger' column** of its guest accounts, and transfer the amount to its **ledger account**. At regular intervals, usually monthly, the hotel can then send the company an **invoice or statement of account** showing all the transactions charged to the account during that period (with details of guest names and dates of stay and/or copies of itemised bills). The account holder can then pay for the 'batch' of charges with a single cheque, bank transfer or credit card payment.

This requires a little extra bookkeeping on the part of the hotel, but it is an added value service which can be offered to large, regular (and therefore valuable) clients, and which may induce more frequent stays and higher expenditure. It also reduces the payment-handling tasks of front office. However, there is an added risk of failure to pay, and a cost associated with low liquidity. The account may take 30, 60 or 90 days to be paid, depending on the agreed terms, during which time the hotel isn't earning interest on a banked payment.

3.9   Summary: comparison of methods

Let's look again briefly at each of the **payment methods**, for liquidity, security and worth.

Method	Liquidity	Security	Worth
Cash	Immediate	Little payment risk to hotel (unless counterfeit), but high risk of theft	100%
Foreign currency	1 day	Little payment risk to hotel (unless counterfeit: added risk of unfamiliar design), but high risk of theft	102 – 104 %
Cheque	3 days	Payment risk (if forged or not honoured) but low risk of theft (worthless to thief)	98%
Traveller's cheque	4 days	Little payment risk to hotel (unless forged), low risk of theft (worthless to thief)	98%
Credit card	7 days	Guarantees payment, but risk of fraud and theft (despite blocking measures etc)	96%
Credit account	30 days	Payment risk to hotel from default, but no security risk	100% (but lost interest)
Vouchers	60 days	Payment risk to hotel from default, but no security risk	89% (commissionable)

3.10 What happens if a guest can't pay the bill or fails to do so?

Credit status checks, payments in advance, guaranteed bookings and interim or staged payments are all designed to minimise the hotel's losses from guests' lacking funds to pay their bills at check-out. However, if a guest has 'slipped through the cracks' and finds – or confesses – that (s)he has insufficient funds to cover the bill, or lacks acceptable means of payment (perhaps because traveller's cheques have been lost or stolen), the hotel has some options.

- It may retain **possession of the guest's luggage and valuables** (by a legal principle called the 'right of innkeeper's *lien*') as security, until the account is settled. After six weeks, if the matter has not been settled, the hotel can legally auction the goods, retain the amount of the bill (plus expenses) and return the balance to the guest.

- It may give the guest the opportunity to contact a bank, employer, friend or relative who may be willing to **make or guarantee the payment** on their behalf.

It is worth noting that a hotel *cannot* physically restrain a guest from leaving the premises, if (s)he tries to leave without paying; this may constitute an assault.

Walk-outs, skippers and runners

Unfortunately, not all failures to pay the bill are due to incapacity or innocent mistake. Some guests may simply leave without paying: these are known, variously, as 'walk outs', 'skippers' or 'runners'.

- Some guests may genuinely **forget to pay**, or believe they have paid (forgetting the 'extras' bill), or think that someone else in their party has paid or is going to pay. Because of this possibility, the matter should be handled tactfully. Inadvertent walk-outs will probably be embarrassed and willing to rectify their mistake immediately.

- Some guests may **opportunistically take advantage** of poor hotel security procedures: access the car park without passing reception; honesty systems for notifying reception of mini-bar consumption; failure to confirm that a cheque will clear before the guest leaves; etc.

- Still others will **deliberately and repeatedly 'skip' without paying**, and will probably show up on hotel blacklists. The hotel can only maintain its vigilance in such cases. Reception staff may develop a 'sense' about people who are reluctant to provide registration and credit card details, or who have no luggage. Housekeeping may report guests who appear to have removed their luggage from a room the night before check-out.

In the UK, the law (under the **Theft Acts** and various amendments) provide that:

- 'A person who by any deception dishonestly obtains services from another shall be guilty of an offence' and

- 'Any person who, knowing that payment on the spot for any goods supplied or services done is required or expected from him, dishonestly makes off without paying as required and with intent to avoid payment shall be guilty of an offence.'

Unfortunately, if the hotel chooses to take a 'skipper' to court over this matter, its claim may not be as easy to prove as you may think. In the UK legal system, you have to prove, beyond reasonable doubt, both that the person did what you allege (ie stayed at the hotel and left without paying) but that (s)he *intended* not to pay, or never to pay. The defendant could claim in court that (s)he intended to pay at some later date...

Abbot & Lewry argue that walk-outs don't really cost the hotel very much (other than the opportunity cost of letting the room and the cost of food and drink consumed), so it may not be worth the cost and hassle of legal proceedings. But it will certainly worth trying to avoid the scenario, and we will discuss how this can be done in Chapter 5, as part of the hotel's 'credit control'.

EXAMPLE

'A word from the FOM'

Credit control is a very important part of the front office role. Don't underestimate (a) the risk of identity theft and credit card fraud (b) the risk of people trying to leave the hotel without paying. Our hotel sees people attempt both – frequently.

Front office staff need to develop a 'radar' for these things – and a determination to stick to security procedures and protocols. Insist on sight of the credit card, and check signatures carefully. Be alert to suspicious behaviour. Ask for pre-payments and guarantees where necessary. It isn't pleasant, but it is necessary – and you can still be courteous and helpful to guests. Most *bona fide* guests understand the problem, and the need for hotel policy. If in doubt, call the duty manager to deal with the situation.

Another frequent problem is guests 'forgetting' to notify us of late charges. The terms and conditions printed on our reservation form includes a statement that the guest agrees to be 'responsible for all charges' – so we are authorised to charge any 'late charges' to the guest's credit card. For guests who have paid by other means, we send a letter requesting payment for late charges.

4 Other cash transactions

A number of other cash transactions may be required to meet guests' needs. These may occur at any time during a guest's stay, but we will cover them here, since we have been talking about payments and foreign currency.

4.1 Petty cash

It is always advisable to have a small amount of cash handy in the cashier's department or reception, in order to make low-value cash purchases that crop up from time to time. The front office may require cash for the payment of casual wages (eg window cleaners), or for the 'emergency' purchase of stationery, postage stamps or small items required in the office (or reimbursement of staff who have made these purchases out of their own pockets). It would be costly to require a cheque to be drawn up each time these types of expenses are incurred, so instead a small amount of cash is kept for these purposes, known as a **petty cash float.**

The most common method for dealing with petty cash is called an **imprest system**. A certain amount of cash, say £100, is paid into the petty cash box as a starting float. In order to withdraw money from the box, staff have to fill in a **petty cash voucher** (with a purchase receipt for the same amount attached, where available). The voucher is authorised by a responsible manager, and handed to the petty cashier, who pays out the money and places the cancelled voucher in the petty cash box. This means that at any given time, the value of the remaining cash in the box *plus* the value of cancelled vouchers equals the amount of the original float (£100).

PETTY CASH VOUCHER		
Number: 0497		
Details		Amount
Envelopes		2-50
Paper		2-06
	Net	4-56
	VAT	0-79
	Gross	5-35
Claimed by: J. Raine		
Authorised by: M. Harris		

PETTY CASH VOUCHER		
Number: 0496		
Details		Amount
Train fare		16 - 20
	Net	16 - 20
	VAT	—
	Gross	16 - 20
Claimed by: J. Goswell		
Authorised by: M. Harris		

Figure 4.6: Petty cash voucher

At the end of each day, the cashier will go through the vouchers, and write details of all the payments made out of petty cash into a **petty cash book**. At the end of the day or week, the cash in the petty cash box is topped up to the imprest amount (eg by completing a cheque requisition form for the balance amount, and using the cheque to withdraw cash from the hotel's bank account). The top-up amount, when paid in, is also recorded in the petty cash book, so that all the figures balance: Figure 5.4.

Note that for security purposes:

- Vouchers are sequentially numbered, which ensures that they can be accounted for.

- Vouchers are signed by the person claiming the petty cash *and* authorised by a responsible manager, so that transactions can be traced if necessary.

- Cash floats are securely locked away at all times, with restricted access to the keys.

- There should be rules preventing misuse of the system (eg for routine purchases, the cashing of staff cheques or IOUs).

Receipts				Payments				
Date	Details	Amount £		Date	Voucher	Details	Amount £	
1 Sept	Balance b/d	50	00					
				2 Sept	9–1	Coffee	1	89
				4 Sept	9–2	Stationery	11	75
				10 Sept	9–3	Taxi	5	00
				15 Sept	9–4	Cleaner	15	00
				25 Sept	9–5	Repairs	5	88
						Total vouchers	39	52
						Balance c/d	10	48
		50	00				50	00
	Balance b/d	10	48					
30 Sept		39	52					

Figure 4.7: Petty cash book

4.2 Visitors paid outs (VPOs) or disbursements

Visitor Paid Outs (VPOs) or disbursements are cash payments made by front office on behalf of guests. Examples may include amounts paid to accept cash on delivery (COD) parcels for a guest; or a staff member being sent out to purchase 'emergency' supplies (toiletries or medications) for a guest; outside service providers being used to supply services requested by a guest (eg a florist or baby-sitting service); or theatre tickets or tours obtained for the guest by the concierge.

Such expenses are generally handled through the main cashier's float. As with a petty cash system, a **VPO or Guest Disbursement voucher** (similar to a petty cash voucher) will be filled out, stating the name and room number of the guest, details and amount of the expenditure, and the signature of the guest (or person receiving the money). Where possible, a purchase receipt should also be attached.

The amount of the disbursement can then be posted to the guest's account, and the voucher placed in the cashier's float, to be exchanged for cash (or logged as 'paid in' to management with other cash takings) at the end of the day or shift.

VPOs are normally **pre-arranged** with guests, so that the hotel doesn't find itself paying out amounts that the guest has not authorised – and may refuse to be responsible for. (This may also mean that the facility is not extended to chance guests.)

4.3 Foreign currency exchange

Large hotels which have a high proportion of foreign trade may, as we noted earlier, offer foreign exchange facilities – both as a value-adding service to overseas guests, and as a potential source of revenue for the hotel (through beneficial exchange rates and the charging of commission).

- The hotel may rent space to a **foreign exchange bureau** (*bureau de change)*, which can both buy foreign currency (ie exchange it for pounds sterling) and sell foreign currency (eg exchange pounds sterling for other currencies required by guests for their next destination).

- Unless it is specially registered to offer a full currency exchange service, the hotel itself may only **buy foreign currency** (and exchange it for pounds sterling), if a guest wants other currencies, (s)he will be referred to a nearby *bureau de change* or bank. Most hotels only change notes and foreign currency traveller's cheques, since coins are too costly to handle and may not be accepted by banks.

The exchange rate is not fixed by law, so the hotel can offer whatever price it wishes in order to make a profit on the transaction. The hotel will find out what the central exchange rate is on a given day (from the Internet, or by notification from its bank), and set a slightly more advantageous rate (as determined by management). The hotel's rates can then be listed at the reception or cashier's desk, for the information of overseas guests.

Guests may wish to exchange a particular amount of a foreign currency (eg US$100), or may wish to purchase a particular amount in pounds sterling, and staff will need to be able to make the appropriate calculation.

- When **converting from a foreign currency into £ sterling**, you divide (÷) the amount by the rate of exchange (ROE): so, for example, US$300 ÷ 1.85 = £162.16.

- When **converting £ sterling into foreign currency**, you multiply (x) the amount by the ROE: so, for example, £100 x 1.42 = $142.

In addition, the hotel may charge a **commission** (eg 2% of the total transaction value) for the service.

In a **computerised** system, there are special programmes for calculating, recording and receipting such transactions: staff simply add updated exchange rates (although these, too, may be automatically 'synchronised' from the internet or head office systems) and transaction amounts.

Most hotels issue a **receipt** for currency exchange transactions, stating the guest's room number, the exchange rate used, the amount of currency 'bought', the amount of sterling provided in exchange, plus any commission charged. The record retained enables the cashier to balance the amounts of foreign currency to be paid in to the bank, minimising the risk of fraud.

Foreign currency should be banked as soon as possible (the procedures for which will be discussed in Chapter 5), to avoid the risk of the hotel's losing money because of fluctuations in the exchange rate.

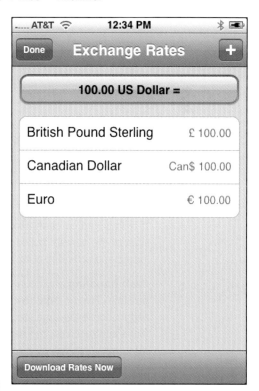

An American guest at your hotel asks you to exchange $50 in US currency, and give him pounds sterling. If your hotel's exchange rate for the dollar is currently £1 = $1.85 dollars, how much would you give him.

If the exchange rate was to decrease to £1 = $1.40 dollars, what would the impact be on the traveller's spending budget?

5   Security issues

As you may have gathered from our discussion of different methods of payment, earlier, there are significant security issues to handling cash and credit cards. There may be risks of:

- **Theft of cash** left unsecured or unattended (by staff, guests or other people with access to the premises)

- **Armed robbery** of the premises, if it is known that significant amounts of cash are kept there

- **Fraud** of various kinds: the use of counterfeit banknotes, forged cheques or stolen credit cards; staff processing 'cash back' transactions on debit cards but keeping the money for themselves; staff altering guest account ledgers and keeping the difference between logged payments and actual payments for themselves; and so on.

The level of security will depend on the circumstances and policies of each hotel. We will discuss security and safety issues in detail in Chapter 7, but at check-out and payment time, the following points will be most relevant.

5.1   Safe handling of cash and other forms of payment

Some commonsense measures for handling cash and other forms of payment safely at check-out include the following.

- If substantial amounts of money are involved, it may be necessary to transfer cash and cheques from front office to a **back-office safe**, immediately following peak check-out times and at intervals during the day.

- All **'standing' cash** used in front office operations – such as cashier's floats and petty cash – should be kept in a safe, ideally in separate cash boxes, when not in use.

- If cash is kept in **cash boxes or drawers** at front office, these should be kept locked and out of sight of the general public when not in use. If cash is kept in a cash register, this must also be locked and attended at all times.

- **Cash handling** and counting should always be done out of sight of the general public, if possible. Two or more responsible members of staff should count cash takings, when required, and reconcile the amounts with what is expected from accounting records (eg cash payments made and received, the cash 'float' amount and so on). Cash should be kept in a secure, locked safe until collection by a security company or members of staff for transportation to the bank.

- The number of people having **access to safes and lock-boxes** (and their keys or access codes) should be kept to the minimum required for efficient customer service. Authorised individuals must not hand keys or reveal access codes to other people – however busy they may be at check-out time! Under no circumstances should keys or notes of pass codes be left 'lying around' (even in desk drawers or filing cabinets). If safe or lock-box keys are lost,

the matter must be reported to a relevant manager, who must make arrangements for locks to be changed as soon as possible.

- Where possible, staff should attempt to **limit the amount of cash** on the premises (and there may be notices posted to this effect, to deter would-be thieves), by encouraging cheque or credit-card payments; transferring excess cash into safes; banking cash as soon and as often as possible; and avoiding making large payments (eg staff wages) in cash.

- If the hotel operates a **cash register**, records should be kept to show which member of staff used the till at a particular time and date and ideally (in computerised systems) who undertook a particular transaction. Cashing up should be done as soon as possible after the close of cashier services each day, the cash drawer removed, and the empty till drawer left open (to prevent unnecessary damage by would-be thieves). The same protocols apply to the security of cash drawers and boxes (eg holding cash floats and petty cash).

- **Guest credit card details** should be kept secure at all times: unauthorised parties – including hotel staff – may use stolen credit card numbers (together with known names, expiry dates and authorisation numbers) to make Internet or telephone purchases (for which signatures are not required). This will mean restricting access to guest files (whether manual or computerised) which include such details. Documents referring to credit card payments (eg confirmations of deposits or billing receipts) should identify the credit card by the last four digits only, avoiding giving further details. Signed hotel copies of credit card vouchers/receipts should be kept securely. If old-fashioned 'imprinter' machines are used for credit card transactions, the cashier should offer to destroy any carbon paper used in voucher preparation (which carries card numbers and signatures).

- All procedures for **checking the validity of payments** should be followed. Front office staff must learn to identify suspected counterfeit bills and fake foreign currency. They must get used to going through a series of checks of cheque, traveller's cheque and card transactions: verifying names, checking expiry dates and signatures, looking for signs of tampering and so on. Credit card fraud is particularly widespread, and cashiers need to look for signs that the person using the card is not the real owner: payments made on the basis of an invalid card will not be honoured by the issuing organisation.

This may all seem a bit scary – or mistrustful. But theft and fraud do occur, particularly in situations where people are relative strangers, and there are constant comings and goings. Get used to being 'alert but not alarmed'. We will discuss this further in Chapter 7.

SUMMARY

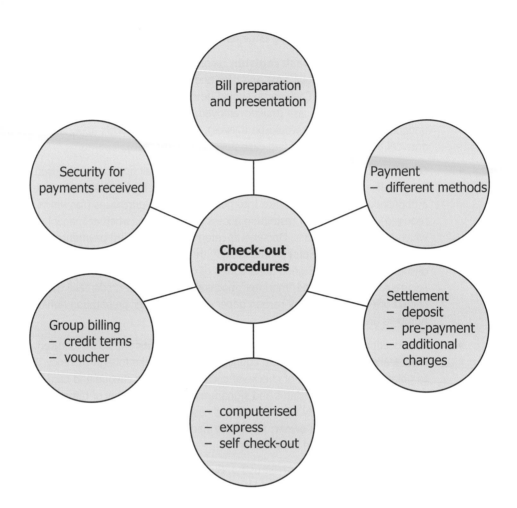

SELF-TEST QUESTIONS

1 What is the usual check-out time in a hotel?

2 How does a computerised check-out system speed up the check-out process?

3 What are the two main requirements to fill out an express check-out form?

4 What is a tabular ledger?

5 What is a split folio, and why might it be needed?

6 What is a 'chitty'?

7 Identify the three criteria by which different methods of payment are evaluated.

8 List eight methods of payment commonly accepted by hotels.

9 Cash and cheques are the only legal tender. True or False?

10 What is (a) a VPO and (b) ROE?

SELF-TEST ANSWERS

1 10.00 or 11.00 am

2 Faster preparation of the bill and receipts; automatic foreign currency calculations; automatic verification of account status; express/self check-out facilities.

3 Credit card details; and authorisation for the hotel to charge the amount of the bill to the credit card.

4 The hotel's running log of each day's business (charges and payments) in regard to guest accounts.

5 Two separate guest accounts: one for the main accommodation charge (for payment by the tour operator or company, and calculation of commission where appropriate) and one for the extra or incidental charges to be paid for by the individual guest.

6 A voucher signed by the guest to authorise the charging of a bill for expenses in various departments of the hotel (such as the restaurant or bar) to his account.

7 Liquidity, security and worth (value).

8 Cash, foreign currency, cheque, traveller's cheque, credit card, debit card, credit account and voucher.

9 False. Only cash is legal tender.

10 Visitors Paid Outs; Rate of Exchange.

A N S W E R S   T O   A C T I V I T I E S

1 It is usually a very busy time, with a potentially large number of guests checking out within a fairly short period: queues and delays can be frustrating for out-going guests, particularly if they have onward travel deadlines (eg flights or trains to catch). The presentation of bills and the receipt of payments also has the potential for errors, queries and conflicts, if there is a discrepancy between the hotel's and the guest's views of the amounts owing. There are also security issues in the handling of payments – and, perhaps, the risk that some guests will be unable to pay their bill, or attempt to leave without doing so.

2 No answer is provided for this activity, because it depends on your own creativity in laying out the points already provided in the text in a creative and helpful way of your choice.

3 If the bill is fair and accurate and in line with what the guest was expecting, he will pay without stress and leave feeling satisfied that he has received good service and value for money. If he has been overcharged, he is entitled to become irritated – and may start to feel he has not received good service. Even if the problem is sorted out in a constructive way, the guest may leave feeling less than satisfied with the hotel. You might think that a guest would like to be undercharged, but in fact this is no better, for the guest will gather that the hotel is inefficient, and – having 'escaped' with a lesser charge, may be shy of returning to the hotel (losing it potential repeat business). Moreover, if the guest does not point out the error, or the cashier fails to spot it before the guest leaves, the hotel will lose income to which it is entitled.

4 On receiving the bill, guests may find that the accommodation rate or terms are not what they had agreed to, or thought they had agreed to. They may not have received, or remembered that they received, some of the items charged. Or they may be unwilling to pay the amount owed, because they have, or feel that they have, received poor service – or because they have been unable to enjoy what they have paid for (eg if extreme discomfort or noise has prevented them from sleeping).

5 If the exchange rate for the dollar is currently £1 = $1.85 dollars, you would give the guest £27.02 in exchange for his $50.

If the exchange rate was to decrease to £1 = $1.40 dollars, the same $50 would be equivalent to £35.71.

CHAPTER 5

GUEST ACCOUNTING

Chapter objectives

In this chapter you will learn

- The basic purpose and nature of front office accounting systems
- How to use manual, machine and computer billing systems
- How to conduct banking procedures, including documentation and reconciliation
- How to administer cash floats
- The purpose of night audit procedures and reports
- The use of ledger accounts
- The importance of credit checking and credit control

Topic list

Front office accounting
Billing systems
Banking
Cash floats
Night audit
Credit control

1 Front office accounting

First of all, as we start this chapter, please don't panic at the sight of the words 'accounting' and 'statistics'! You may not have a head for numbers – and perhaps you hoped to have left the study of maths behind you forever. But it's an important fact of life. No hospitality business could survive without keeping an accurate record of what each guest has purchased, what has been paid (or part-paid) for, and what is still owed. (Imagine the complaints of overcharging, the loss from undercharging...) And no hospitality business could survive, especially in today's harsh economic climate, without calculating how many rooms it needs to let, and at what price, in order to make a profit.

As a member of front office staff, you will need to be able to prepare guest bills efficiently and accurately, in order to avoid chaos and complaints at a busy cashier's desk. And you will need to be able to support the business, and managerial decision-making, by being able to compile some basic statistical and financial reports.

Again: don't worry. The concepts and sums in this chapter (and the next, on yield management, statistics and reports) aren't too complicated, and we hope you'll see the use and relevance in everything we cover.

FOR DISCUSSION

'It's more important for a Front Office staff member to be a "people person" than a "numbers person". '

How far do you agree that this is the case?

1.1 The purpose of front office accounting and billing systems

The main purposes of front office accounting and billing systems are:

- To keep an **up-to-date record** of what any given guest owes at any given time – to enable both the hotel and the guest to keep track of what is owed. This generally means posting pre-payments, credits and charges to guest accounts at regular intervals throughout the day (as we saw in Chapter 4) so that an up-to-date balance is maintained.

- To allow **control checks** to be carried out, so that there is a record of every transaction; the posting of charges can be verified against chitties and payments against receipts; cash takings can be confirmed against recorded cash transactions; and so on. These checks should be made as a matter of internal control, to protect the whole system from fraud, theft and error. The records also provide a method of verifying transactions and calculations in the event of guest queries.

- To allow an **accurate bill** to be presented to guests, reflecting what they have paid, what they have spent, and the outstanding balance owing – in such a way that they can feel confident (and confirm) that they have been charged fairly. As we suggested in Chapter 4, over- and under-charging are *not* good for the reputation or finances of the hotel!

- To provide the hotel accounts office with accurate **financial data** for the compilation of the hotel's accounts, financial reports and statistics (eg on revenue and expenditure).

1.2 The front office accounting cycle

We looked briefly at the preparation and presentation of guest bills in Chapter 4, as part of the check-out process. From our discussion there, you should be able to see that front office accounting follows a chronological **cycle** which mirrors progress through the **guest cycle**.

Accounting cycle stage	Guest cycle stage	Main activities
Opening of guest account	Pre-arrival and check-in	<ul><li>Determining and confirming the rates/tariffs to be applied</li><li>Checking guest's intended method of payment</li><li>Checking credit worthiness and establishing credit limits</li><li>Checking corporate and agency settlement agreements</li><li>Opening a master folio and extras folio for the guest</li><li>Crediting the amount of any deposit or pre-payment</li></ul>
Maintaining the guest account	During occupation	<ul><li>Posting of credits and charges to the guest account as they are incurred</li><li>Verifying the postings (night audit)</li><li>Monitoring the guest's credit balance against credit limits, and obtaining interim payments if required</li></ul>
Settling and closing the guest account	On check-in or following departure	<ul><li>Posting of final charges</li><li>Preparation of final guest bill(s)</li><li>Presentation of final bill(s) to guest for checking, agreement and payment (or signature on bills to be paid by companies)</li><li>Checking payment and posting final credit to balance the guest account (or posting amounts to be paid by companies to the ledger account)</li><li>Forwarding master folios to companies for payment</li><li>Taking follow-up action to obtain payment of walk-outs, late-posted charges and late payments</li></ul>

ACTIVITY 1   15 minutes

See if you can draw the accounting cycle as a 'cycle diagram', similar to the one we provided for the guest cycle in Chapter 1. Show the stages of the guest cycle, the accounting cycle and the activities in the accounting cycle.

We will now look at different systems for opening and maintaining guest accounts, and preparing guest bills, in more detail.

2 Billing systems

2.1 Manual billing systems

For a small, old-fashioned hotel, without access to computerised accounting systems, a manual accounting and billing system will consistent of keeping **ledgers**.

Ledger accounts

DEFINITION

A **ledger** (or **ledger account**) is simply a book, in which transactions are recorded as part of the accounting records of an organisation.

The main accounts of the hotel, administered by the accountant, will include:

- A **Sales Ledger** (recording amounts owed and paid by each of the hotel's credit customers or debtors).

- A **Purchases Ledger** (recording amounts owed and paid to each of the hotel's suppliers or creditors).

- A **Main or General Ledger** (recording all the various income and expenditure, assets and liabilities of the hotel).

Two main types of ledger are kept by Front Office, under the general heading of '**accounts receivable**' (that is, what guests owe the hotel).

- The **Guest Ledger** (recording all debit and credit transactions made by registered guests of the hotel, that is, charges incurred and payments made).

- The **City Ledger** (recording all amounts 'receivable' from – or owed by – *non-registered* guests who use the services of the hotel on credit terms).

We'll focus on the guest ledger first.

The tabular (guest) ledger

DEFINITION

The **guest ledger (or tabular ledger)** is like a 'sales day book', recording all the various transactions made by registered guests, against each room on each day.

In a tabular guest ledger, there is a page for each day, with a number of 'tabs' or labelled columns, identifying where transactions will be entered.

In a **horizontal tabular ledger**, the tabs/columns list the various types of charges across the page:

- **Room and guest details**: the room number, guest name, number of sleepers (relevant if the rate is per person, rather than per room) and rate (as agreed with the guest).

- A **starting balance** brought forward from the previous day (where relevant), showing the outstanding balance on the guest's account, as totalled-up at the end of the previous day.

- **Debit charges** to the guest's account (that is, amounts the guest owes) are grouped on the left-hand side. These may include columns for the room charge, breakfast, lunch and dinner (split into separate amounts for accounting purposes, even if the rate reflects inclusive room-plus-meals terms), bar charges, telephone, mini-bar, newspapers, sundries and Visitor Paid Outs (VPOs: discussed in Chapter 4) – plus a column for the *total* of all these debit charges.

- **Credit charges** to the guest's account (that is, amounts the guest has paid) are grouped on the right-hand side. This would typically include columns for:

BPP LEARNING MEDIA

- Cash or payments, under which are entered any deposits, pre-payments or part-payments made on the day. 'Cash' is a shorthand term for 'bankable' forms of payment such as cash, cheques, traveller's cheques or credit cards. If the hotel wishes, the cash/payments column can be subdivided accordingly.

- Credits or allowances, under which are entered any refunds made by the hotel, or credits made to cancel out wrongly posted charges or over-charges.

- Ledger, which covers arrangements by which the hotel has claimed or will claim back an amount from someone else after the guest's departure: eg a group organiser, company or travel/booking agent, and some credit card companies, such as American Express and Diners Club, which require the hotel to send a statement to the card company to obtain payment. The ledger column may be sub-divided into Ledger Received (for payments already obtained by this means) and Transfer to Ledger (for payments which need to be transferred to the City Ledger for future payment).

- A balance carried forward to the next day (where relevant). If the debit charges are equalled by the credit charges on a given day, there will be a zero balance to carry forward – and this should be the case for a guest who has paid his or her final bill! If the debit charges do not equal the credit charges, the balance will be inserted as the starting balance for the following day's sheet. It will also offer a useful guide to how much of a bill the guest has 'run up' so far, for the purpose of credit control (eg if the hotel has imposed a credit limit on a chance guest).

Each column will be totalled-up at the end of the day, providing analysis totals: how much has been spent on accommodation, meals, alcohol, phone calls; how much has been paid in by cash, credit card or ledger; and so on. This gives useful information on guest spending and the sales performance of different departments and services.

We hope this makes some sense, just from our description, but of course it will help to see what it looks like! A simple manual version is illustrated at Figure 5.1, overleaf. It would look quite similar if the hotel set it up as a computer spreadsheet, for example, in Microsoft Excel – except that the spreadsheet software would automatically keep running totals for you, and you could have many more columns in your record, without the constraints of space as on a paper page.

A C T I V I T Y   2   1 0   m i n u t e s

Mr & Mrs Yale-Howe are staying in Room 6, on a specially discounted room rate of £37.50 (bed and breakfast, of which the cost of breakfast is £7.50).

Their outstanding balance of account on the 6th June 2009 was £53.40.

It is now the evening of the 7th June, and you are just getting a chance to catch up on entries to the tabular ledger.

- There is a chitty signed by Mr Yale-Howe for lunch (£24.20 of which £5.20 is from the bar)

- There is another chitty signed by Mrs Yale-Howe for dinner in the restaurant (£63.90 of which £18.46 is from the bar)

- The Yale-Howes took morning newspapers for £2.40.

- The switchboard logs several outgoing phone calls from Room 6, totalling £8.14.

- There is a note from the cashier to say that Mr Yale-Howe complained during the day, because a bar chitty from Room 11 (for £23.50) was wrongly charged to his account the day before. The cashier has authorised an adjustment to be made to the Yale-Howe account to correct this mistake.

- The Yale-Howe's accommodation and breakfast has been pre-paid by a travel agency.

See if you can add an appropriate record to the tabular ledger overleaf. You will need a calculator!

Hilltown Hotel

Date: _Sunday, 7 June 2009_

Rm	Guest Name	Slprs	Rate	B/fwd	Accomm	Break-fast	Other meals	Bar	Phone	VPOs	Sundry	TOTAL	Credits	Cash	Ledger Rec'd	Trans > Ledger	C/fwd
7	Orinde	2	47.50	–	40.00	7.50	76.80	–	1.80	–	4.75	130.85	–	–	–	–	83.35
18	Whyte	2	55.50	59.90	48.00	7.50	–	–	–	–	–	115.40	–	–	47.50	–	115.40
4	Purpeulle	1	47.50	123.25	40.00	7.50	24.98	8.95	–	7.50	1.20	213.38	–	200.00	–	–	13.38
19	Blewgray	2	55.50	–	48.00	7.50	83.40	15.75	2.40	–	18.99	176.04	–	–	–	154.65	21.39
5	Baycz	1	47.50	93.20	40.00	7.50	39.85	14.20	–	–	–	194.75	–	194.75	–	–	0.00
TOTALS																	

In a **vertical tabular ledger**, the columns represent the room numbers – and the *rows* represent the different categories of charges: debit charges at the top, and credit charges at the bottom: Figure 5.2. This format may be used to prepare the guest bill at the same time as the tab, by having billing stationery in the same format, and using carbon paper (or no-carbon-required document sets), so that as entries are written onto the tab, they are duplicated on the bill.

Using the tabular ledger

Whichever format is used, a number of operations can be carried out using the tabular ledger.

- At the beginning of each day, current occupancies will be carried forward in room order, but when a new guest **checks-in**, a new tab entry will simply be added to the end of the list.

- **Room charges** for new guests can be entered on check-in, and all other room charges entered at a set time of day (eg 6 pm).

- Other **debit charges** are posted periodically as vouchers come in from other departments, with the vouchers being crossed through once they have been dealt with.

- **Credit charges** are also posted periodically, as pre-payments or allowances are made.

- All entries to the tabular ledger will be **copied to the guest bill** (either manually or using duplication sets with a vertical tabular ledger).

- Amounts in the **'transfer to ledger'** column are copied to the City Ledger.

- At the end of each day, the tabular ledger must be **'balanced'**. That is, the record is checked for accuracy by verifying that everything 'tallies'.

  - Total debit charges (amounts owing) should equal total credit charges (amounts paid or recorded as owing).

  - Amounts of cash taken should equal the cash column on the tabular ledger.

  - The amounts in the ledger column should equal amounts featured in, or transferred to, the city ledger.

  - The total 'balance carried forward' should equal the total of outstanding guest bills.

When the guest **checks-out**, the bill is totalled and the top copy presented for payment. Once the guest has paid, the payment is entered as a **final credit charge** in the tabular ledger. The account is then totalled and balanced: the total debit charge *equals* the amount billed *equals* the total credit charge, leaving a **zero balance outstanding**.

Advantages and disadvantages of tabular ledger systems

From our example, and the activity (if you attempted it), you might note that a manual tabular ledger system has a number of advantages and disadvantages for a small hotel.

Advantages of tabular ledger	Disadvantages of tabular ledger
- Cheap and simple to use	- Time consuming making entries
- Flexible, as headings can be inserted as required	- Requires manual/calculator calculations: time-consuming and subject to error
- Easy to check by balancing	- Requires additional time for checking, balancing, bill-preparation

(The bill would go *underneath,* so that the ledger entries for room 106 will be carbon copied to the bill.)

GUEST LEDGER

SLEEPERS _____ DATE

ROOM NO,	101		102		103		104	
NAME	Jarrold Mr.&MrsT.		Spain Miss B.		Slaney Mrs.C.		Ray. Mr.&Mrs	
RATE	R.O. £90 (2		R+B £60 (1		R+B £60 (1		R.O. £90 (2	
B/F	101	90	181	18	68	12		
APARTMENTS	96	00	55	00	55	00	90	00
PENSION								
BREAKFASTS	12	00	5	00	5	00		
LUNCHEONS					4	80		
TEAS			4	20				
DINNERS	42	90						
EARLY TEAS								
BEVERAGES	2	00			1	40		
WINES	12	90			2	80		
SPIRITS & LIQUEURS	14	40						
BEERS								
MINERALS	1	75						
TELEPHONES	8	30			v/c 11/6 4	40		
V.P.O'S			8	60			5	00
NEWSPAPERS			1	80				
TOTAL	286	45	255	78	141	52	95	00
CASH			200	00				
ALLOWANCES			o/c TEL 4	40				
LEDGER								
BALANCE C/F	286	45	51	38	141	52	95	00

GUEST BILL

DATE:

ROOM NO: 106

NAME: ....

RATE: ....

	DAILY TOTAL	
B/FWD:	351	20
Room:	290	00
Pension:	—	—
Breakfasts:	22	00
Luncheons:	4	80
Teas:	4	20
Dinners:	42	90
Early teas:	—	—
Beverages:	3	40
Wines:	15	70
Spirits:	14	40
Beers:		
Minerals:	1	75
Phones:	13	00
VPOs:	13	60
Newspapers:	1	80
TOTAL:		
Cash:	778	75
Allowances:	200	00
Ledger:	4	40
BALANCE c/f:	—	
	574	35

Source: adapted from *Dix & Baird, Front Office Operations*

Figure 5.1: Vertical tabular ledger with bill

The City Ledger

DEFINITION

> The **City ledger** is the ledger in which Front Office records payments owing by credit customers who are *not* themselves registered guests with the hotel.

A functions organiser may put down a deposit on a banquet. A local company may keep an open account at the hotel for entertaining and/or accommodating visiting clients. A business traveller may have her bill paid for by her company, which has a credit account with the hotel. A tourist may have pre-paid a travel agent, who will be invoiced later by the hotel for the amount. All these transactions are examples of amounts owing by credit customers who are not themselves registered guests with the hotel.

E X A M P L E

Bardi (*Hotel Front Office Management*) gives the following examples of transactions affecting the Guest Ledger and the City Ledger respectively.

Guest Ledger	(Registered guest activity)
Pre-arrival	Deposit of future reservation Return of deposit on reservation due to cancellation
Check-in	Pre-payment of account
Occupancy	Charge for room and tax Charge for food and beverages Charge for purchases in the gift shop Charge for parking, phone calls, value, in-room movies, cash advances etc
Check-out	Payment of outstanding balance Return of credit balance to the guest Transfer of charges to another account (> City Ledger) Correction of posting errors (allowances)

City Ledger	(Non-registered guest activity)
Food and beverage	Deposit on upcoming function Return of deposit due to cancellation Charge for food and beverage/payment for food and beverage
Concession rental	Rental/concession charge/payment of rental charge
Parking rental	Parking charge/payment of parking charge

2.2 Machine billing systems

Billing machines were introduced in the 1950s, at which stage they were electro-mechanical (relying on gears and cogs powered by an electric motor): more modern equivalents are electronic.

Billing machines essentially fulfil the same functions as a combined bill/tabular ledger entry system, except that they carry out the calculations for you.

- Instead of a tabular ledger record, the machine stores the various charges in a register (or *memory*), and prints out a '**summary sheet**' of the cumulative totals for each category/ department. (The transactions are listed on an '**audit role**', allowing checking if necessary.)

- Guest bills (or '**guest folios**') are printed out, usually in duplicate sets: the top copy being presented to the guest and the sheet beneath retained for the hotel's records.

The operation of billing machines varies widely – and you are unlikely to come across them, since they have been replaced by computer packages. So we won't go into their operation in detail here, but:

LEARNING MEDIA

- On check-in, the operator types the guest's details at the head of a **blank folio card**, and inserts the folio into the machine. The folio is opened by entering the room number and the opening balance (0 – or a negative number if a deposit or pre-payment has been made).

- When charges are posted, the relevant **folio and vouchers** are inserted into the machine. The billing machine stores the transaction amounts in its memory; prints each item on the guest folio and creates a new balance; prints the same item with the room number on an 'audit roll' (which can be checked against vouchers in the event of queries); and cancels the voucher by overprinting it.

- At the end of the day or shift, the machine prints out a **summary** of the total balance carried forward (from its previous summary); total debits; total credits; and total balance carried forward. These figures can then 'balanced' as for a tabular ledger.

- A summary sheet is then printed, showing the totals of each different type of charge (for analysis). The machine's memory can then be '**cleared**' for the following day's transactions.

- **On check-out**, the guest's folio is inserted into the machine, and the operator enters the amount of payment (or transfer to the ledger account). The machine prints out the final guest folio.

Advantages and disadvantages of billing machines

Like anything else, a billing machine has its good points and bad points for a hotel.

Advantages of billing machines	Disadvantages of billing machines
▪ Calculations are handled automatically: greater accuracy, less staff time	▪ Still potential for error in inputting of charges
▪ Vouchers are cancelled automatically: less risk of being charged twice in error	▪ Print-out for guest bill (folio) may be confusing, with codes, abbreviations etc
▪ Guest bills (folios) are printed rather than handwritten: may look more professional	▪ Cost and time required to train staff to use the system competently
▪ Easier checking and balancing	▪ Machines are mainly obsolete: can be hard to obtain replacement parts!

2.3 Computer billing systems

As we noted in Chapter 4, guest accounts can be maintained in the computer system.

- **Charges** can be posted in batches (as a multi-room post), with individual room accounts automatically updated for the charges that apply to them.

- Some transactions can be **automatically entered** by the system itself: pre-set room charges will be posted each day from the reservation records, for example; restaurant/bar bills may be directly input to the account from Electronic Point of Sale systems; and telephone call charges may be automatically logged by the computer-linked phone system. Meanwhile, charges to be paid on credit (eg for corporate account customers) are automatically posted to the **City Ledger**.

- Each guest account will be automatically **updated** with running totals and outstanding balances, so that the cashier can always provide a current balance (or copy of the account-to-date) for the guest.

- **Adjustments and corrections** (eg the reversal of wrongly posted charges, or transfer of the account if a guest changes rooms) can be done easily.

- The system will carry out all **calculations**: eg for the addition of VAT to relevant charges; the calculation of commission on commissionable bookings; and the calculation of foreign currency exchange and related commission charges.

- The system can **alert the cashier** if guests exceed their pre-set credit limit, and have to be asked for an interim settlement.

- The system automatically carries out the various **'audit' functions** required to check and balance the various accounting records (as discussed later in the chapter).

- Final **guest bills** are calculated and generated by the system: far less time-consuming and error-prone than manual systems, and more professionally presented in printed form, with all debit and credit charges clearly itemised.

- **Invoices and statements** can be generated for corporate account customers from the guest data already in the system.

- **Reports** can automatically be generated to show payments which are outstanding (eg charges posted after a guest has left; amounts owing by 'skip outs'; and late payments by credit customers) for the purposes of 'chasing'.

- **Management reports** can also be automatically generated to show total revenues by division or point of sale; average revenues per room etc.

The main advantages of this – as for all other computerised applications – are speed, efficiency and accuracy, and the freeing up of valuable staff time to focus on guest service!

E X A M P L E

The following is an example of one of the 'open folio' screens available in the MICROS-Fidelio system.

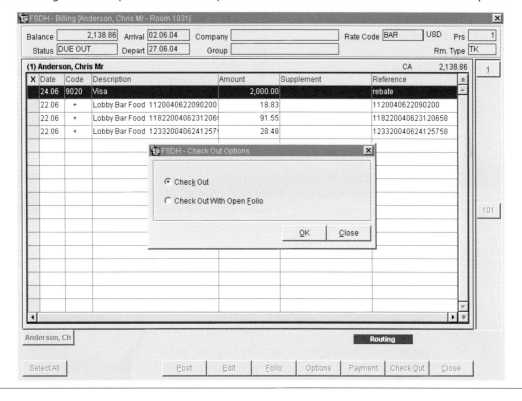

F O R   D I S C U S S I O N

'Now that computer packages are available, why would a hotel require its front office staff to know about manual guest accounting and billing systems?'

How might you answer this question?

3 Banking

3.1 Banking procedures

At the end of each day (or more often if necessary to remove cash from the premises for security reasons), the 'takings' (money received) from the various operations of the hotel should be 'banked', that is, paid into the hotel's bank account.

The various front office sections, and other departments of the hotel which receive payments for products and services, will usually 'pay-in' their takings to the cashier's office at the end of a shift. All payments, in any form, are gathered together, and handed in to the cashier together with a summary, which is generally written out on an internal **paying-in slip**. This breaks down the totals of foreign currency and foreign currency traveller's cheques, plus sterling cash (broken down by denominations), sterling traveller's cheques, personal cheques, credit card vouchers, petty cash and/or VPO vouchers and so on – allowing the cashier to make a quick count and check. The petty cash and VPO vouchers can then be processed, and the cash, cheques and credit card vouchers from all the departments consolidated for paying-in to the bank.

A **paying-in book** is used to record the amount to be banked in each transaction. You may be familiar with the system from the 'deposit' book you use to pay cash and cheques into your own personal bank account. The main difference is that the hotel's paying in book may have duplicate or triplicate sheets, so that the top copy of each paying-in slip is given to the bank together with the cash and cheques being paid-in, the duplicate remains in the book for the hotel's financial

Photo: https://www.softprochecks.com

control purposes – and, if the hotel is part of a chain or group, a third copy can be sent to head office (as a report on the day's revenue).

One obviously important element of the paying-in of cash and cheques is to ensure that the paying-in book is **correctly and accurately filled out**. Cheques are listed individually, with the name of the drawer (payer), bank and amount. Separate pages are used for foreign currency (calculated at the bank's current exchange rate) and credit card payments.

However, it is also important that the 'money' is properly **presented to the bank**. Banks have sophisticated machinery for counting piles of notes and bags of coins, but some preparation is required.

- Piles of **bank notes** must all be facing the same way up, and should be packaged in bundles of £100 or £500 wherever possible.

- **Coins** should be bagged, in separate bags for each type of coin. The bags provided by banks detail how much of any coin should be included: bags for 50 pence pieces may be for £10 worth (20 coins), say.

The most obvious method of paying money into a bank is to take the money to the bank during its opening hours and pay it in over the counter. However, most hotels will still be receiving payments (eg in the restaurant) long after the banks have closed, and on weekends. Their options are therefore:

- To collect the total takings for the day and keep them in the cashier's safe overnight to be paid into the bank the following morning.

BPP))) LEARNING MEDIA

- To pay in some of the day's takings during the day, perhaps last thing before bank closing time. The remainder can then be kept in the safe overnight, to be paid into the bank the following morning – meaning two trips to the bank each day.

- To collect the total takings for the day and deposit them into the bank's night safe facility.

3.2 Bank reconciliation

DEFINITION

Bank reconciliation is the process of comparing the balance of cash in the hotel's accounting records to the balance held by the bank. Differences between the balance on the hotel's bank statement and the balance in the cash book must be identified and satisfactorily explained.

Each month (or more often if appropriate), the hotel's bank should send it a **bank statement**, itemising the balance on the account at the beginning of the period, receipts into and payments from the account during the period, and the balance at the end of the period.

When the hotel gets its bank statement, the hotel accountant should check to ensure that the bank's account of these transactions tallies with the hotel's own records (eg the cash book).

- There may be **errors** in **calculation**, or in recording income and payments – and these are just as likely to have been made by the hotel as by the bank.

- There may be **deductions** made by the bank (eg bank charges or interest on overdrafts or loans), which the hotel did not anticipate.

- There may be **timing differences**, creating discrepancies in the figures. The hotel's records may included paid-in cheques or credit card vouchers, for example, but these may not yet have been 'cleared' and the amounts added to the hotel's bank account.

Of course, the computer can reconcile for you too: Figure 5.3.

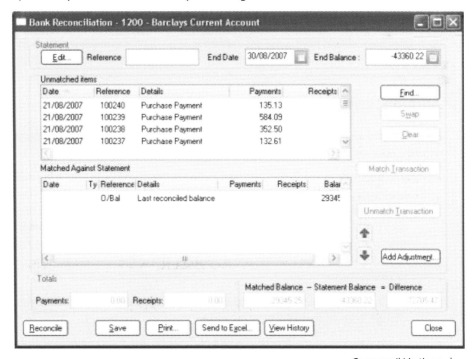

Source: wiki.bath.ac.uk

Figure 5.2: Bank reconciliation screen (in Sage software)

4 Cash floats

As we saw in Chapter 4, front office – together with the restaurant, bar and other sales areas – will need to keep a small stock of 'ready money' to enable it to give change (when guests pay their bills), to offer currency exchange facilities (where available) and to allow for Visitors Paid Outs (VPOs). These small stocks of cash are called **'cash floats'**.

A small hotel may keep a single cash float, administered by the cashier. A larger hotel may require a number of different floats, to cover a range of points of sale: the restaurant, the bar, the shop/kiosk etc.

4.1 How much should be kept in a cash float?

The amount to be kept in a cash float will depend on:

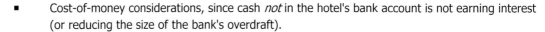

- The type, value and number of cash transactions handled.

- The hotel's policies on upper limits for cash transactions (eg VPOs or currency exchange).

- Security considerations, since as little cash should be exposed to the risk of theft as possible (and large cash floats may attract theft or robbery attempts).

- Cost-of-money considerations, since cash *not* in the hotel's bank account is not earning interest (or reducing the size of the bank's overdraft).

Basically, the aim will be to cover anticipated customer needs – and this may mean planning for worst case scenarios, such as multiple guests making small purchases and paying in high-denomination bills: the higher the number of cash transactions, the bigger the float will need to be. If the hotel takes a lot of foreign currency payments, it will also need a bigger float, because the currency paid in *won't* be available for use in giving change.

Each sales point should have a pre-established float amount and make-up (different note and coin values), and this should be the same from day-to-day, for efficiency and ease of control.

4.2 Administering the cash float

Cash floats are stored in secure cash drawers (or cash registers/tills), with compartments separating the different notes and coins. The cashier or receptionist is responsible for:

- The **security** of the float: keeping it locked away when not in use, and never leaving it unattended or within sight or reach of the general public. Cash floats are issued at the beginning of each day, and signed for by the personnel who will be responsible for them: at the end of the day, they are signed back in to the cashier's office. In other words, someone is accountable for their security at all times. If there is a handover from one shift to another, the total amount in the cash drawer must be counted and agreed on, before the float is passed to (and signed for by) the incoming cashier.

- The **accuracy of payments and change giving**: paying close attention to the calculation of change, and which notes/coins are picked up (when in a hurry).

- The **balancing** of the float at the end of the shift. The total contents of the cash drawer or till at the end of the shift *minus* the float at the beginning of the shift should equal the recorded cash sales for that shift. Any variation between the actual cash and the records (the total on a till roll, sales day book or tabular ledger) will indicate that: cash has been received or taken out without being recorded; that transactions have been inaccurately recorded; that the end-of-shift cash total has been miscounted; or that the opening or closing float has been wrongly counted.

Once the float has been balanced, cash receipts can be '**paid in**' to the cashier and prepared for banking (as discussed above), while the correct float is counted back into the cash drawer for the following shift. It can then be securely stored in the cashier's office overnight, or signed over to the incoming shift.

FOR DISCUSSION

Why do hotels have strict rules *against* staff 'borrowing' cash from the cash float and putting an 'IOU' into the cash drawer? Isn't this just a helpful facility for staff cash 'emergencies'?

5 Night audit

'Auditing' may sound like a complicated accountancy term, but it really just means 'checking'. A variety of checking or control procedures is required in a hotel, to minimise the risk of mistakes and misunderstandings – as well as the possibility of theft or fraud. While each outgoing front office shift is expected to 'balance up' its accounts, cash floats and so on before handing over to the next shift, hotels will normally also '**close**' **the day's trading** at night, and seek to '**balance up**' for the day as a whole.

5.1 What is night audit?

DEFINITION

Night audit is the process of carrying out various controls and checks on the hotel's accounting systems: posting outstanding charges, checking records against each other, balancing the hotel's daily accounts, and preparing management reports. This is generally carried out by the hotel night shift.

In a small hotel, the night auditor may be the night manager, receptionist and security officer all rolled into one. But (s)he will also use this otherwise quiet period to perform the methodical work of processing, checking and balancing, so that the hotel's records are fully up-to-date and 'ready to go' for the following day, and the busy check-out period. In a larger hotel, there may be a dedicated night auditor or night audit team for this purpose.

5.2 Night audit tasks and reports

Some of the tasks which may be carried out by the night auditor, in a manual system, are:

- **Posting outstanding guest charges** which have come in during the evening or night (such as late arrivals, dinner, room service or telephone calls), to keep guest accounts fully up-to-date for morning check-out time.

- **Verifying posted entries**: checking that vouchers have been posted to the correct accounts – and correcting them, if not. For example, if a guest has a restaurant charge on their account, a corresponding amount should be listed in the restaurant till roll, and there should be a signed restaurant chitty for the transaction.

- **Balancing the tabular ledger**: ensuring that each guest's total debit entries *minus* total credit entries *equals* the balance carried forward to the next day's entry; and ensuring that all column totals balance.

- **Balancing the accounts**: checking that total sales/takings recorded by each department add up to the total of debit charges recorded in the tabular ledger. So, for example, the total recorded on the bar's till roll or other revenue report should equal the total amount in the 'bar' column of the tabular ledger.

- **Verifying cash balances**: checking that cash balances shown in the accounts correspond to the amount of cash in the safe, and that total cash minus the day's takings equals the stated cash float amount – to ensure that no cash has 'gone missing' during the day!

- **Checking the safe**: verifying that guest valuables logged for safekeeping in the safe are (still) there!

- **Verifying room status records**, by cross-checking the **front office room status display** (or 'room rack') against:

  - The **housekeeper's report** on room status, to identify discrepancies which may need correction or further investigation: eg rooms logged as 'vacant' when they are really 'occupied' – *or vice versa*.

  - The **financial records** and **guest accounts**. A room may be listed as vacant but have an outstanding guest account open – or a room may be listed as occupied, but without a guest account. Or charges may have been recorded for one occupant, when the room rack – or housekeeper's report – says that two people are staying in the room. Such discrepancies indicate that there is an error somewhere, which must be sorted out.

- **Checking and clearing the reservations file**. The auditor will prepare a list of no-shows (a no-shows report), so that the cashier can prepare a bill (and/or process a credit card payment) for those with guaranteed bookings.

- Preparing **management reports**, such as revenue reports; daily occupancy reports; guest statistics; and so on. We will discuss a range of these in Chapter 6.

ACTIVITY 3   5 minutes

What kind of discrepancies may crop up between the front office room status records and the housekeeper's report on 'actual' room status (vacant, occupied, how many people have slept in the room)? What might be the implications of these discrepancies, and what should the hotel do about them?

5.3   Anticipating bad debts

Another of the key tasks of the night auditor is to check through the open guest accounts and try to identify the potential for 'bad debts' (people who may fail to pay what they owe) so that appropriate measures can be taken.

Bad debts may be caused by 'walk outs', but they may also be caused by forged traveller's cheques, dishonoured personal cheques, and credit account customers who fail to pay when invoiced, for a variety of reasons. There may be a misunderstanding over payments for guaranteed bookings, if a corporate customer or travel agent claims to have cancelled the booking within the approved cancellation period. The corporate customer may be in financial difficulties, which were unforeseen by the hotel when it extended credit facilities. We will look at credit control further, below.

In terms of immediate bad debt risk, the night auditor will look for credit risks and potential 'walk outs'.

- (S)he may simply compile a list of all bills over a certain amount. The following day, the cashier can then check these guests' credit limits, credit status and so on.

- (S)he may also compile a list of individual guest accounts showing unusual (often extravagant) spending patterns on extras, which may indicate an intention to 'skip out' without paying. The following day, the cashier, security officer or duty manager could then do some further investigating, and take whatever steps are considered necessary.

5.4 Computerised audit functions

As you should be used to hearing by now, computerised systems can assist – or even replace – night auditors in completing a range of tasks, freeing them up for other work.

Computerised front-office systems are designed to be **self-balancing**: the system automatically checks that charges have been correctly posted to rooms; that the revenue totals for points of sale cross-balance with the amounts paid into reception; that actual room status (as reported by housekeeping) matches front desk room status reports; and so on.

The system can also issue credit limit and potential bad debt alerts, and compile and format a range of management reports, summarising the day's activities, the following day's plans and so on.

However, there is a significant drawback to **relying** on computers for audit functions: staff may become complacent, because the computer will 'catch' their errors. In fact, a computer can only catch certain types of error, such as discrepancies between two sets of figures: it can't tell whether a member of staff has mistakenly (or deliberately) entered wrong information into the system! As *Abbott & Lewry* note: 'If room rates have been entered incorrectly, or charges posted to the wrong accounts, then the final bills will be just as wrong as if they had been done by hand'.

So computerised records need to be **printed out** at the end of each day, and subjected to night audit cross-checking. In particular, cash balances and items in safe deposit must be physically verified: the computer can only say that they 'ought to be' there – not that they actually are!

In addition, the night auditor will have the responsibility of over-night **computer housekeeping**:

- Deleting or archiving all cancellations and departed guest files, to 'clear' some of the computer's memory.

- Directing the computer (if the system does not do this automatically) to reset or update all relevant records for the new day: eg setting daily totals to zero, updating cumulative totals, setting 'today's date' for arrivals and departures and so on.

- Making a back-up copy of the entire system, and printing out essential records and reports from the system for the following day (in case of systems failure).

6 Credit control

Credit control is basically a term for the various measures taken by a hotel to ensure that customers settle their bills in full at the agreed time.

Credit control (or **credit management**) is necessary to achieve a healthy balance when allowing guests and other customers to enjoy credit, that is, to consume the hotel's services now, and pay later. The hotel will **benefit** from extra sales (because corporate clients and agencies value credit facilities, and guests prefer not to have to pay cash for charges as they are incurred). But the hotel also has to bear the **costs** of potential 'bad debts' (people defaulting on payment) and higher finance costs (because it doesn't have immediate payment with which to make payments, earn interest or reduce overdraft payments).

Credit control may involve a range of measures, such as:

- Setting limits and restrictions on granting credit, as a matter of credit policy

- Assessing the creditworthiness of individual customers (credit risk assessment)

- Agreeing credit terms with individual customers (deciding how much credit each customer should be allowed, and on what payment terms)

- Taking steps to avoid '**walk-outs**' or 'skips' (that is, customers leaving without settling their accounts)

- Being diligent in 'chasing' and collecting payments in accordance with the agreed credit terms, to minimise late settlements (eg by companies or travel agents)

- Keeping records and circulating reports of 'walk-outs', late payers and so on, to minimise the risk of repetition.

Credit management is the responsibility of the credit manager or hotel accountant, but as you can see from this brief survey, it also requires specific measures to be taken by various departments of the hotel, at appropriate phases of the guest cycle.

EXAMPLE

'A Word from the FOM'

There will often be 'late charges' – that is, items that have not been posted to the guest's account in time to be included on the final bill.

If the terms and conditions on the registration card state that the guest will be 'liable for all charges', and the guest has signed the form, we are entitled to charge the guest's credit card for any late charges. We will then send a letter or e-mail informing them that this has been done, with a copy of the credit card voucher. If the bill has been paid by some other means, it is still worth 'chasing' large late charge amounts by sending a letter requesting payment.

In case of a disputed late charge, however, we always err on the side of the guest.

6.1 Credit policies

Individual customers should only be **granted credit** in accordance with the hotel's policies on credit terms – and established procedures for assessing creditworthiness.

Credit accounts

Most hotels will need to be prepared to offer reasonable credit terms to **corporate and agency clients**, in order to win and retain their business. The aim of credit policy should, therefore, be to control the credit terms offered; to check the credit-worthiness of the customer prior to granting credit; and to monitor the ability and willingness of credit customers to pay on time, on an on-going basis.

A credit policy should set out the standard **payment terms** the business is prepared to offer (eg payment within 30 or 60 days of invoice), and these terms can be written into the terms and conditions of business and brought to the attention of new customers. They may also be asked to sign a form agreeing to comply with the terms offered, in order to open a credit account – or as part of the hotel's contract with a tour operator for a specific group booking, say.

The hotel might also have policies which act as an **incentive** to credit customers to pay on time. For example, early settlement discounts and/or penalties for late payment.

Guest credit limits

In addition, there will need to be policies in regard to the credit extended to individual guests, to charge their hotel expenses to their room account. The hotel will need to check the credit-worthiness of guests in advance, and, where necessary, set **credit limits** (sometimes called the '**house limit**'): the maximum level to be reached by the guest's account before payment or partial/interim payment is requested.

6.2 Why grant credit to some customers and not others?

Essentially, the decision of whether to offer or grant credit to a customer will come down to:

- The **volume and value of business offered** by the customer over time. Offering credit facilities is risky and costly to administer – so the potential returns need to be worth it.

- The extent to which valued customers (or Commercially Important Guests) **want or expect** to have credit facilities made available to them – and whether they might take their business elsewhere if such facilities are not offered or granted.

- The **credit-worthiness** of the customer: that is, the extent to which the hotel can be reasonably certain of getting paid, by virtue of the customer's integrity, credit record and/or available funds. Credit is generally offered to guests who have guaranteed bookings with the hotel (rather than chance guests); guests whose accounts will be settled by their employers (with whom the hotel has established credit agreements); and guests who pay by credit card.

- The willingness of the customer to offer **assurance of payment** (eg via deposits or guarantees, credit card imprints, willingness to sign contracts and so on).

- The customer's **history of payment** with the hotel over time. Credit facilities can be withdrawn from customers who routinely fail to pay on time, or dispute payments, or whose payments routinely 'fail to go through' (eg if cheques or credit card payments are not honoured due to lack of funds).

6.3 Establishing credit-worthiness

The key point about credit control, from the point of view of front office, is to ensure (as far as possible) that the hotel only extends credit to customers who are likely to repay the debt in full and on time.

As we saw in earlier chapters, this applies to an individual hotel guest checking-in for a night (especially chance guests), as well as to a company or tour operator seeking to open a credit account – because the hotel is effectively extending credit to any guest who hasn't pre-paid or guaranteed the booking. Guests may run up a large bill in accommodation, restaurant, bar and other extra charges, on the understanding that they *will* pay on check-out – and the hotel will have to ensure, as far as possible, that this will be the case.

Of course, the need for risk management is even greater for credit accounts, where guest bills are charged to the 'standing' account of a company, travel agent or tour operator: accounts of many thousands of pounds may be built up this way, for later payment upon presentation of the hotel's invoice to the account holder.

So how do you ascertain a potential account customer's credit-worthiness? These days, it is a comparatively easy matter to search an online credit database, to obtain **credit ratings** for prospective customers. If they have a low rating, or have outstanding county court judgements against them (for non-payment of debts), it would be best either to refuse credit or impose strict controls (such as credit limits or payment guarantees).

Other sources of information for assessing the credit status of a new customer include:

- Credit reference agency reports

- Information provided by the customer, on a credit application form

- Bank references or bank status report (which may be obtained on request, with the customer's permission)

- Trade references (from other businesses with whom the customer has credit accounts)

- The Insolvency Register (listing individuals and businesses notified as bankrupt)
- The Register of County Court Judgements (listing decisions about legal disputes over payment)
- The published financial statements and reports of corporate customers

6.4 Other credit control measures

We have already highlighted a number of measures, in relation to each stage of the guest cycle, which may be considered as part of credit control.

Guest cycle stage	Measures
Pre-arrival	- Inform guests that non-guaranteed and late bookings may have limited credit facilities - Ensure that the correct room rate is quoted (so that guests can plan to have funds available) - Request prepayments and deposits where required
Check-in	- Ascertain, confirm and record the method of payment - Take a deposit, prepayment or credit card imprint (especially for chance guests) - Verify settlement arrangements (eg agency vouchers, corporate credit accounts) - Inform guests clearly of acceptable payment methods, charges for which they will be responsible, and any credit limits that apply
During occupancy	- Require all departments to verify guests' credit status before allowing them to charge services to their accounts - Monitor posted charges and guest balances against authorised credit limits, and issue 'high balance reports' of guests whose accounts are near to or in excess of credit limits: computerised systems do this automatically. - Inform guests politely but firmly when credit limits have been reached and interim settlement is required. (This may be the responsibility of the credit manager, cashier or other senior staff.)
At check-out	- Ensure (as far as possible) that last-minute charges have been posted - Ensure that guests check and sign accounts to be billed to companies - Observe all protocols for verifying and checking payments - Record and receipt all payments - Balance the guest account
After departure	- Transfer corporate and agency payables to the ledger account, to be invoiced - 'Chase' late payments - Report on late or defaulted payers

ACTIVITY 4   5 minutes

How might you identify a guest who is a 'skipping' risk: what might you look for?

What can front office staff do to minimise the risk of guests' 'skipping out', at any stage of the guest cycle?

FOR DISCUSSION

What is the one issue or procedure covered in this chapter that you feel *least* confident about? What can you do to increase your knowledge, skills or confidence in this area?

S U M M A R Y

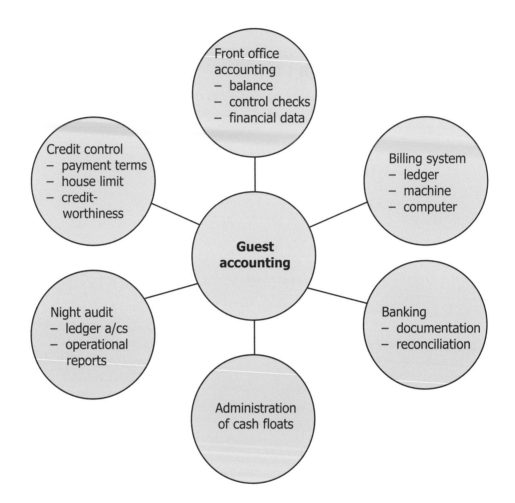

SELF-TEST QUESTIONS

1 What are the three stages of the front office accounting cycle?

2 Charges for food and beverages incurred by a local business with an entertainment account at the hotel's restaurant would be recorded in the .... ledger.

3 Amounts the guest owes are entered on the tabular ledger as credit charges. True or False?

4 What are 'allowances'?

5 Give three examples of credit charges that would be 'transferred to ledger'.

6 What is the 'register' of a mechanical billing system?

7 What two steps should the hotel take to present cash appropriately for banking?

8 Identify four considerations in deciding the size of a cash float.

9 What does 'balancing' mean for a night auditor?

10 List three sources of information for assessing a prospective customer's credit status.

SELF-TEST ANSWERS

1 Opening guest accounts; maintaining guest accounts; settling/closing guest accounts.

2 City

3 False; they are 'debit' charges. *Payments* are credit charges.

4 Amounts entered into the tabular ledger to reflect amounts credited to the guest's account as a correction or adjustment.

5 Accommodation charges to be settled by a group organiser/travel agent; accommodation charges to be settled by a credit account customer; payments made by American Express or Diners Club cards, to be paid by the card company.

6 Its memory.

7 Bundle notes, facing the same way; separate and bag coins.

8 Type/value/number of cash transactions; hotel policy on cash limits; security considerations; and cost of money considerations.

9 Making sure that debit and credit entries and totals 'cancel each other out', eg that total takings equal the total debit charges.

10 Any three of: credit references; bank references; trade references; information provided on credit applications; the Insolvency Register; the Register of County Court judgements; and published financial statements.

ANSWERS TO ACTIVITIES

1 The following is from *Baker, Bradley & Huyton* (*Principles of Hotel Front Office Operations,* p 161).

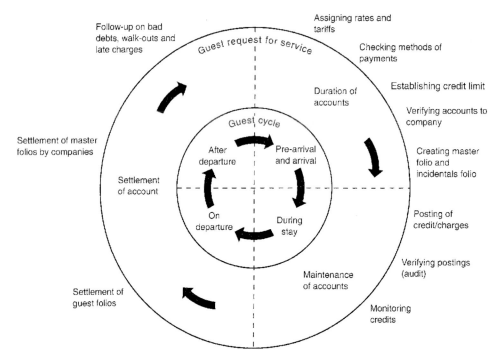

2 The debit side of the ledger would look as follows:

Rm	Guest Name	Slprs	Rate	B/fwd	Accomm	Break- fast	Other meals	Bar	Phone	VPOs	Sundry	TOTAL
6	Yale- Howe	2	37.50	53.40	30.00	7.50	19.00 45.44	5.20 18.46	8.14	–	2.40	189.54

And the credit side:

Credits	Cash	Ledger Rec'd	Trans > Ledger	C/fwd
23.50	–	37.50		128.54

3 If the front office record shows a room as occupied, but the housekeeper's report shows it as vacant, the room rack may need updating (because reception has forgotten to record a chance arrival, say) – or there may have been a 'walk out' (which needs investigating!). If the front office record shows a room as vacant but the housekeeper's report shows it as occupied, the room rack may need updating (because reception has forgotten to record a departure), or someone may be attempting to use the room without a record being kept: this may be a 'scam' whereby a chance arrival pays cash to the receptionist, who pockets the payment. There may also be discrepancies in the number of people who have slept in the room: which is a problem if the hotel charges a per-person rate.

4   Look for signs that guests may intend to make a 'swift exit'. They may have very little luggage – or their luggage may not weigh as much as it should: bags may be empty, intended to be left behind. They may load baggage into a car the night before departure. To minimise skip outs:

- Require deposits, guarantees or pre-payments from, and/or impose strict credit limits on, any guests who may be suspected of the intention of skipping.

- Monitor expenditure patterns and credit limits. Guests intending to walk out may not try to be inconspicuous: they may 'spend up big' in restaurants, shops, bar or room service facilities.

- Porters may collect guests' luggage from their rooms in advance of check-out, to have it waiting for them at reception: guests can't then access their luggage until their account has been paid.

CHAPTER 6

YIELD MANAGEMENT, STATISTICS AND REPORTS

Chapter objectives

In this chapter you will learn

- The nature and use of yield management
- How front office can contribute to maximise occupancy and revenue
- How to gather and use guest, occupancy and revenue statistics
- What notifications and operational reports are exchanged between front office and other departments of the hotel
- How to maintain and use guest history records

1 Yield management

We have emphasised throughout this Study Guide that hotels, and similar establishments are in the business of providing hospitality and guest service – but the fact is, that they are still 'businesses'! Their main responsibility is to make money for their owners: to maximise revenue and profit. This is the only way they stay in business, pay their staff, and have funds to reinvest in maintaining the hotel.

DEFINITION

> **Yield management** is the process of planning to get the best possible revenue returns from letting accommodation, by maximising the hotel's **occupancy** (the number of rooms sold) in any given period, at the **best possible rate**.

There are various pieces to the yield management 'jigsaw'. You can increase the hotel's revenue *either* by securing higher occupancy (letting more rooms) *or* by raising the rate at which you let rooms – but if you can do *both*, you get the best possible returns.

In the past, hotels sought to maximise their revenue by setting higher rates for better quality rooms; setting higher rates for weekly and seasonal periods of peak demand (when people were prepared to pay more to secure a room, in competition with others); and setting lower rates for weekly and seasonal periods of low demand (stimulating demand by offering off-peak 'bargains'). But broadly, guests who stayed in a similar grade and type of room on the same night would pay the same rate. If the set rates didn't attract customers on a particular night, rooms went empty – and the hotel lost revenue.

It was the airlines who first tackled the problem of uncertain demand and lost revenue. They saw the need to attract more **advance bookings** – so that the airline could secure at least a 'base' amount of revenue for a given flight. As the time of the flight got closer, it could then **respond flexibly to demand**: if demand was strong and there were fewer and fewer seats, it could raise seat prices; if demand was slow, it could discount seats to stimulate demand – if necessary, on a day-to-day basis.

At the same time, the airlines recognised that some **categories of customer** (or market segments) would pay more, while others would not, and that revenue could be maximised by **seeking bookings from more profitable segments**. Essentially, pricing became **flexible** – and different types of customer, or different customers, might be paying different fares for the same services: depending on how far in advance they booked; whether they placed a guaranteed booking (with no cancellations or amendments allowed); when they booked; what preferential terms they negotiated – and so on.

Hotels have gradually realised that the same kind of situation applies to them. Like an airline, they need to consider:

- Which types of bookings or business are most **profitable** for them – and should, therefore, be prioritised.

- How they can secure profitable, guaranteed bookings in **advance**, to provide a 'base' revenue.

- How they can use **different room rates** (or 'differential pricing') to secure bookings from the most profitable market segments.

- How they can use **flexible room rates** and bookings to manipulate demand: charging higher rates when demand is strong, and lower rates when demand needs to be stimulated to increase occupancy.

EXAMPLE

'A Word from the FOM'

In a hotel which operates a policy of yield management, the performance of reservations staff will be measured against a monthly budget with targets for the 'average daily rate' (ADR) at which rooms are let, or a 'yield percentage' which measures the amount of room revenue the hotel has earned, compared to the maximum possible (a 'full house' at rack rate).

Even if statistical yield management techniques aren't used, it is good for the hotel to pay attention to revenue and profits: getting the best revenue from letting rooms, where possible. We like to take advance bookings – to get some revenue 'under our belts' – and then start 'flexing' room rates, three months in advance, to respond to demand.

1.1 Decisions involved in yield management

There are number of factors to be taken into account when trying to maximise yield. Let's follow the logic through step-by-step.

The profitability of different types of business

Hotels make different amounts of money from different types of guest.

- **Corporate account holders**, especially those who are prepared to guarantee a certain volume of bookings per year, may have a negotiated rate which is anything from 40% – 90% of rack rate, depending on volume. On the other hand, the guaranteed volume business makes them particularly profitable for the hotel.

- **Travel agents and tour operators** commonly charge a 10–20% commission on accommodation bookings, depending on volume, which is effectively a discount on rack rate.

- **Independent leisure guests** are nowadays likely to be quoted discounted 'best available rates' in return for guaranteed advance bookings (which represent secure income) or online bookings (which save on administration costs), but they are more likely to pay something close to the rack rate.

At the same time, however:

- **Business customers** tend *not* to be 'price sensitive': that is, their choice of hotel isn't mainly driven by competing or changing prices. They are often prepared to pay higher rates (and to spend more on extras during their stay) because the company is paying their expenses.

- **Leisure customers** are generally **more 'price sensitive'** because they are paying their own bills; they have a longer planning horizon to make price comparisons and go 'bargain hunting'; and they have a much wider choice of destination. (Tourists can choose to go to a cheaper hotel or destination, where a business traveller may be tied to a particular location and/or a hotel with which his employer has an account.)

Advance bookings

Guaranteed advance bookings offer **stability** and **secured revenue** for the hotel, and again, different market segments show different patterns in this respect.

- Leisure travellers tend to book in advance, when they plan their holiday arrangements.

- Group tours (and conferences) tend to have particularly long 'booking horizons', because they need to reserve large blocks of rooms: they may make reservations up to two years in advance, so that they can secure accommodation for the group (particularly in busy tourist destinations) and advertise hotels in advance to prospective customers.

- Business travellers tend to make last-minute bookings, because many business trips are scheduled at short notice.

The dilemma (in a nutshell)

These two main variables create a dilemma for the hotel.

Leisure travellers book up well in advance – but they generally earn the hotel less revenue, overall, than business customers. If the hotel fills up with advance leisure bookings, it may have to turn away later – but more lucrative – corporate bookings. (Worse: the business customers you turn away will go to a competing hotel, which may therefore earn more than you do!)

On the other hand, if you turn away leisure bookings to reserve rooms for late-booking corporate customers, you are running the risk that the bookings may not materialise – and some revenue is better than the risk of none at all!

A C T I V I T Y   1   **1 0   m i n u t e s**

Explain the nature of the yield management dilemma to a friend, colleague or fellow student, in your own words.

So how does the hotel 'manage yield' to resolve this dilemma? How does it know how many low-rate leisure bookings to take early on – and how many rooms to 'reserve' for later, higher-rate corporate bookings?

In order to be able to manage its sales 'mix' effectively, the hotel ideally wants to be able to forecast the total level of demand/bookings for a given period, and the likely bookings of each type and when they will come in: this information will enable it to juggle the type and timing of bookings to get the best possible mix of occupancy and revenue.

Detailed forecasting techniques are beyond the scope of this book, but some common statistical approaches are:

- **Simple moving average**: the forecast for a coming period is an average of demand in recent past periods. So if bookings ran at 100%, 60%, 40% and 60% for the last four months, we might anticipate that next month's bookings would be 65%. This isn't very accurate, however, as it doesn't take into account the fluctuations hidden by the average.

- **Weighted average**: giving extra weight to more recent past periods in calculating the average, and less to earlier ones: adding some accuracy by reflecting more recent trends.

- **Time series (trend) analysis**: examining past booking patterns and occupancy, identifying underlying trends (upward or downward movements over time) and projecting these trends into the future. If bookings in September have increased by an average of 3% in each of the last three years, we may forecast a 3% increase this year, say. However, the hotel will also have to check for factors which may disrupt the statistics: a local special event this September might increase demand – or a competing hotel may have opened since last September, decreasing demand.

- **Regression analysis**: identifying connections between measured variables (such as advertising spend and bookings) and predicting the effect of changes in one variable (eg increasing hotel advertising) on the other (hopefully, increased bookings).

EXAMPLE

It's not just individual hotels that may be interested in forecasting occupancy: the tourist industry as a whole will be concerned to do this – and the information compiled may help individual hotels to anticipate periods of peak demand (in addition to their own historical records). The following, for example is a chart showing hotel bed occupancy percentages in Scotland in the years 2000 – 2002.

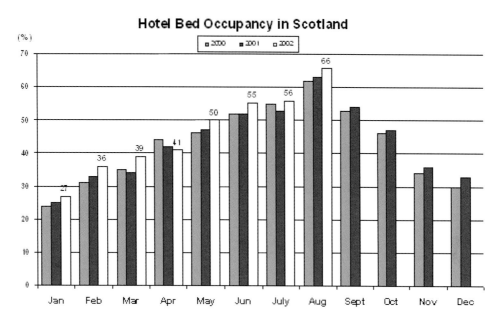

Source: http://www.scottish.parliament.uk/business/committees/historic

You can clearly see the pattern of peak and off-peak times. You can also see that hotels should be able to forecast a slight rise in occupancy in 2002 on 2000 and 2001 levels, for the remaining months of the year – if conditions generally remain the same. But what if something happened? What if September 2002 saw flooding in Scotland, say, or an outbreak of 'foot and mouth' disease? Trends can be interrupted...

ACTIVITY 2   10 minutes

Brainstorm a list of all the factors you can think of that might cause fluctuations in demands for accommodation at a given hotel. What things might create more demand – and what might create less – than the average for the time of year. You might get some ideas from your known knowledge, some from colleagues, and some from the newspapers and TV! (Think of the effect of the 2009 economic recession, for example, or the outbreak of Mexican or 'swine' flu on travel and tourism.)

Statistical methods are unlikely to be able to take into account all the various environmental factors which may cause fluctuations in demand for hotel rooms. A number of more subjective or **'qualitative' methods** may therefore be used, based on personal information gathering and judgement by yield managers. They may take into account **information** about some of the environmental factors identified (such as upcoming events or competitor plans), the **opinions** of experts in the industry, plus perhaps customer or market **research**. (What level of bookings do corporate customers anticipate in the coming year? What time of year do people envisage taking their holidays, and where?)

Rates, marketing efforts and other factors – which are within the control of the hotel – can be used to get the best possible revenue returns from fluctuating **demand**.

If actual demand is **high** (or higher than forecast) in a given period, the hotel will be able to **raise its rates** (or 'close off' lower rates), because people will pay more to secure a booking, and because the hotel can afford to turn away lower-rate bookings in the knowledge that it will be able to let the room elsewhere at a higher rate. There are various ways of **'flexing' room rates**. Reservations staff may be instructed to reduce the discount offered on agency and group bookings; to raise the 'best available rate' quoted to enquirers (or even to accept only rack rate for certain dates); or to reduce the number of leisure bookings accepted (in the expectation of getting more profitable business bookings). They may be instructed to turn away lower-rate bookings – even when there are vacancies – in the anticipation of higher-rate bookings eventually turning up.

If actual demand is **lower than forecast** in a given period, the hotel may need to **lower its rates** (or 'open' lower rates), to create an incentive for people to book for that period. Reservations staff may be instructed to increase the discounts available, accept more leisure bookings, and/or offer highly competitive 'best available rates' (especially for confirmed long-stay bookings).

FOR DISCUSSION

Traditionally, reservations staff have measured their success by maximum occupancy or a 'full house': selling as many rooms as possible – or getting 'bums in beds'! A yield management orientation, however, might require them to turn *away* prospective lower-rate customers (telling them that the hotel is fully booked, even though there are a number of vacancies), on the *anticipation* that higher-rate bookings will (eventually) come along.

Why might this way of looking at things be difficult or stressful for front office staff, and what can the hotel do to support them?

Fortunately, most hotels will issue clear **instructions** to reservations staff if they operate a yield management policy. The Reservations Manager will specify blocks of rooms to be 'reserved' for higher-rate bookings; issue instructions for 'switching' blocks of lower-rate rooms to the higher rate if demand is forecast to be high; issue instructions for 'switching' higher-rate rooms to the lower rate if demand is forecast to be low; and post charts showing the 'best available rates' to be offered for a given date.

Fortunately, too, **customers** are increasingly savvy about the realities of yield management: they know that in peak periods, such as New Year's Eve at a city hotel, they will be asked to pay full rack rate – or more – because that's what the hotel is confident it can get. ('I'm sorry: we are very busy at that time, and the best available rate I can offer you is rack rate.') They also know, however, that bargains will be available in periods of low demand – and, thanks to the Internet, they have access to plenty of information about 'best available rates' offered by different hotels in different periods: they can 'shop around' for bargains if they have the flexibility to do so.

1.2 When is yield management appropriate?

Yield management depends on reserving blocks of rooms for more profitable market segments – and only making those rooms available to less profitable market segments when necessary to stimulate demand. However, this will only work when **overall demand is high**, so that it is possible to anticipate and exploit late, high-yield bookings. In periods when demand is less than 100% (which is most of the year for most hotels), *any* booking will be regarded as better then none. Realistically, many hotels won't be able to afford to turn away lower-rate bookings on the 'chance' of higher-rate ones.

Moreover, as a formal technique, yield management depends on large amounts of statistical data, forecasts and calculations. It is, therefore, most appropriate for **large, busy hotels** (of at least 50 rooms) which generate sufficient amounts of information on occupancy and revenue to make such analysis (a) meaningful and (b) cost-effective to perform!

At the same time, the statistical nature of yield management means that it may fail to take into account important qualitative factors such as the need to retain the goodwill of **important and loyal customers**. They may pay less and book later – but that hotel can't afford to 'sacrifice' them to one-off guests willing to pay rack rate, just because that will maximise immediate revenue. The hotel will have to accept lower immediate revenue, in some circumstances, in order to do the right thing by its loyal customers (which should in any case support the business in the long-term). To reverse what we said at the start of the chapter, the hotel may be a business – but it is also in the hospitality business!

Nevertheless, as a general orientation, yield management does helpfully focus management (and sales staff) attention on **revenue, rather than just on occupancy**. We will see the crucial difference this makes in section 4 of this chapter, when we look at occupancy and revenue statistics.

1.3   Computerised yield management systems

A computerised yield management system automates all the 'juggling' out of yield management calculations and reservations, sparing staff a complex and time-consuming task. It is able to keep track of a wide range of **forecasting data**, and responds more **flexibly** to changes in booking levels: swiftly recognising where demand is getting ahead of, or falling behind, forecast, at any given time. The system can then support reservations clerks in making the optimum choices about what bookings to take and at what price.

The system accesses the database of all historical guest information, fluctuations in demand, room rates and sources of business. In addition, data can be input on local events and other factors which might attract higher demand in a certain period. On query by the operator, it can:

- Analyse the profit potential (and affect on average room rate) of each booking

- Analyse 'what if' questions about the impact of different combinations of bookings on yield

- Suggest room rates, alternative booking dates or room allocations, and other courses of action (eg refusing a booking because of the likelihood of better profitability later) to maximise yield.

E X A M P L E

The following is a Yearly Forecast screen, showing 'rooms left to sell', in Hotel Perfect.

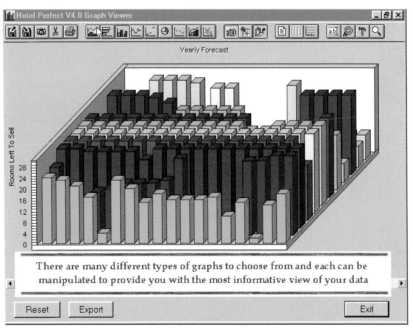

Source: http://intranet.bpc.ac.uk/widecoll/hotel/HotPerMg.html

Let's now look at a range of other uses for '**front office statistics**': that is statistics compiled from data gathered by front office staff, in the course of managing the guest cycle.

2 Guest statistics

Guest statistics are data compiled about the guests who have stayed in the hotel. Much of the data on individual guests will be gathered in any case, during reservation, registration and guest accounting. When these compiled in various ways, they present a picture of activity in the hotel, which can be used to support staffing, marketing and other types of decisions.

2.1 Average length of stay

Question: How many people are typically staying at any one time, and how long, on average, do they stay?

Purpose: This information will be used to support a range of managerial decisions: staffing levels and rosters; facilities to be offered (are you just catering for short-stays or longer-staying guests who need more varied facilities?); housekeeping requirements (how often do linen and towels need to be changed?; how frequently are rooms prepared for re-letting?); and so on.

Calculation: There are two main ways of calculating an 'average' length of stay. Let's start with some 'raw' data from the records.

Let's say a hotel has the following figures for June.

Length of stay (nights)	Number of guests	Sleeper nights sold
1	12	12
2	25	50
3	13	30
4	6	24
5	4	20
	60	136

- The **mean average** is the total value of items *divided by* the number of items.

$$\frac{\text{Total number of sleeper night sold in a given period}}{\text{Number of guests}}$$

So with 136 total sleeper nights sold in June, and 60 guests, each guest stayed an average of 2.26 nights.

- A **mode** is the most frequently occurring item in a set of statistics: in this case the most frequently occurring length of stay – from our data, two nights.

We can also see that 40 out of 50 (or 80%) of our guests stay for two nights or less: the hotel will either want to focus its facilities on this type of guest, or work harder to attract long-stay guests.

2.2 Guest origin

Question: Where do guests come from?

Purpose: This information will be used to support hotel marketing (which areas offer 'ripe' audiences for advertising and sales campaigns?) and services offered (eg which languages will most likely be spoken by guests, which may require translation or the presence of multi-lingual staff? What cultural differences will need to be taken into account?)

Calculation: The nationality of guests is logged at registration. A computerised system can automatically provide a breakdown of guests by nationality and (for UK guests), city, region or postcode, but a similar breakdown can be done by hand. The number of guests from each country/region can then be calculated as a percentage of the total number of guests. To calculate a percentage, you simply multiply your fraction by 100.

$$\text{Segment \%} = \frac{\text{Number of guests from a region/country}}{\text{Total number of guests}} \times 100$$

So if 15 of our hotel's 60 guests in June were from the USA, this would be 25%.

Statistics which represent comparative percentages or proportions of a total amount are often shown visually as bar charts (with different height bars for each country/region, according to percentage) or pie charts (with different-sized 'slices' of the pie, according to percentage).

ACTIVITY 3   20 minutes

The Hill Town Hotel's reported figures for July are:

Length of stay (nights)	Number of guests
1	26
2	43
3	22
4	8
5	14
	113

Of these 113 guests, 53 were from the UK; 26 from the USA; 13 from Japan; 12 from France; and 9 from 'other' countries.

(a)   Calculate the average length of stay for the hotel's guests in July.

(b)   Calculate guest origin percentages for each of the hotel's national segments, and display the information in any way that you think would make it 'user friendly' for staff and management.

2.3 Average guest expenditure

Question: How much do guests spend, on average during their stay?

Which categories of guest (corporate, travel agency, groups) and/or which guest nationalities spend more or less, on average, during their stay?

Purpose: This information can be used to identify the most profitable guest 'segments', so that the hotel can maximise revenue by seeking more of their business (through marketing and sales targeting) and by giving them reservation priority over less profitable segments, where relevant.

Calculation: This can be simply calculated, using the mean average.

$$\text{Mean average expenditure} = \frac{\text{Total amount of guest bills in a given period}}{\text{Number of guests}}$$

The period analysed could be a single day (average daily spend per guest), but a number of different days should be analysed, to take account of variations. Average expenditure figures will be more useful if broken down by nationality or source of booking, so that the hotel knows which categories of guest tend to spend more, and are, therefore, particularly worth attracting.

2.4 Source of booking

Question: Where do the hotel's bookings come from: corporate, travel agency, tour operator, individual/personal booking or chance guests?

Purpose: This information can be used to identify which sources offer the highest proportion of bookings and the highest revenue (when used to break down average expenditure statistics), so that the hotel can target its marketing to the most effective sources, and plan facilities and services for the needs of different types of guest (eg corporate, personal or chance).

Calculation: Source of booking data should be collected on reservation, and can be broken down into relevant categories by a computerised system or by hand. The number of guest nights (or revenue earned) from different segments can then be expressed as a percentage of the total and shown as a bar or pie chart.

$$\text{Segment \%} = \frac{\text{Number of guests (or revenue) from booking source}}{\text{Total number of guests (or revenue)}} \times 100$$

A computerised system may also allow you to call up a list of the **'Top 10' customers** in each segment, as measured by number of guest nights and/or total expenditure in a given period. This allows the hotel to prioritise reservations, if there is a choice between taking a booking from a bigger (or bigger-spending) customer.

3 Occupancy and revenue statistics

3.1 Measuring business performance

Statistics and reports are a great way of measuring how a business is doing. Once you have gathered the information, you can compare:

- **actual performance** with **planned or forecast performance**, to identify where the business did better than expected, where it 'fell short' – or where plans and forecasts need to be adjusted.

- **this year's performance** with **last/past year's performance**, to identify whether the business – and/or business conditions – are getting better or worse.

- the performance of **your hotel** against that of **competitors**, or other hotels in your group, or 'benchmark' hotels that you measure yourself against, or hospitality industry averages.

- the performance of **one shift or team against another**, to see which are deserving of extra reward, which are 'falling short' and need extra training or motivation, and so on.

So what measures might a hotel use to evaluate its performance? The most common ones are as follows.

Measure	Comment
Occupancy statistics	Most hotels derive the main part of their earnings and profit from the sale of accommodation, so a key measure of performance is how fully the hotel is occupied. This is usually expressed as a percentage: the number of rooms sold compared to the total number of rooms (room occupancy); the number of guests compared to the total possible number of guests (guest or sleeper occupancy); and the income from occupancy compared to the total possible income (income occupancy).
Room statistics	Hotel performance can be expressed via various statistics to do with the occupancy and revenue achieved from the rooms. Such measures may include: room and guest/sleeper occupancy statistics; and the average rate at which rooms are being sold; revenue per room (or room yield); and profit per room.

Measure	Comment
Yield percentage	As discussed earlier, yield measures the hotel's success in achieving maximum occupancy at the highest room rate possible. It is measured as revenue actually achieved from the sale of rooms, as a percentage of the possible maximum revenue.

3.2 Occupancy statistics

There are a number of basic measures of occupancy, using percentages. Again, let's start with some 'raw' data to use as an example.

E X A M P L E

Raw data for the following calculations

The Hill Town Hotel has the following room breakdown for July.

Rooms			Beds	Occupancy
50	Single rooms	=	50	45 occupied
80	Twin rooms	=	160	45 occupied by two people, 30 occupied by one person
70	Double rooms	=	140	25 occupied by two people, 30 occupied by one person
200	Rooms		350	175 rooms let (245 sleepers)

Room occupancy percentage

Room occupancy is the percentage of rooms occupied in a given period.

$$\text{Room occupancy} = \frac{\text{Rooms sold/occupied}}{\text{Total rooms available}} \times 100$$

In our example: $\dfrac{175}{200} \times 100 = 87.55\%$

On this showing, the hotel isn't doing too badly – although not as well as it would probably like, given the aim of 100% occupancy. The hotel has sold a good proportion of its rooms.

In general, the figure for 'total rooms available' is the number of rooms in the hotel: adjustments tend not to be made for rooms which are temporarily 'out of service' (eg for maintenance, decoration or staff use), as this gets in the way of meaningful comparisons. It is important to know if 'out of service' or non-revenue-earning rooms are impacting on the hotel's performance.

Sleeper occupancy percentage

Sleeper or **bed occupancy percentage** is the number of guests, as a percentage of capacity.

$$\text{Bed occupancy} = \frac{\text{Number of beds/sleepers}}{\text{Total possible beds/sleepers}} \times 100$$

In our example: $\dfrac{245}{350} \times 100 = 70\%$

This is a much less impressive figure: although the hotel has sold a good proportion of its rooms, a significant number of the twins and doubles have been let for single occupancy (ie for one person) – *wasting* the potential sale of the other bed.

This picture can be confirmed by calculating the **double or multiple occupancy percentage**:

$$\text{Double occupancy} = \frac{\text{Double/twins let to 2 persons}}{\text{Total number of double/twin rooms}} \times 100$$

In our example: $\frac{45+25}{150} \times 100 = 46.66\%$

So less than half of the double-occupancy rooms are being let accordingly: the other half are wasting the potential sale of the other bed. If the hotel has a 'per room' tariff, rather than a 'per person' tariff, you might not think this matters too much as the hotel isn't losing out on a room charge for the second person. But single occupancy also means a single meal in the restaurant, single bar charges and so on, the hotel *is* missing out on potential revenue overall.

Again, in calculating the total number of sleepers, we tend *not* to make temporary adjustments for additional guests 'squeezed in' by the use of fold-out beds and so on, but stick to a standard figure of the number of 'beds'.

ACTIVITY 4   **20 minutes**

Here's an example from a past Front Office Operations exam! The Miramar Hotel is located in a popular coastal resort town in the South of England. It has two types of rooms:

Type A rooms: rack rate £120. There are 100 of these rooms, all doubles.
Type B rooms: rack rate £95.80. There are 80 of these rooms, all doubles.

The hotel recorded the following occupancy data for Monday 3 May 2004.

	Number of rooms occupied	Single or double occupancy	Rate (£)
Type A	30	Double	120
	25	Double	80
	10	Single	55
Type B	35	Double	60
	8	Single	40

Calculate (a) the room occupancy percentage and (b) the sleeper occupancy percentage.

3.3 Revenue, yield and profit statistics

Now we add monetary values to our occupancy statistics, to see how the hotel is doing **financially**.

Average room rate (ARR) or average daily rate (ADR)

The average room rate (ARR) or average daily rate (ADR) shows how much a room is being sold for across the hotel. Using the mean average:

$$\text{ARR/ADR} = \frac{\text{Total room revenue on a given day (usually excluding VAT and sales tax)}}{\text{Total rooms sold}}$$

Let's say the Hill Town Hotel (from our earlier example) has a simple per-person rate of £50. Its total room income on the day in question would be £50 x 245 guests = £12,250. For this day, the average daily rate (ADR):

$$\text{ARR/ADR} = \frac{12,250}{175} = £75.00$$

Why is this useful?

- It gives a quick indication of how much **single occupancy** and **discounting** (rooms let at less than full rack rate) is taking place, because this lowers the ARR. (If our hotel was fully occupied at the full per-person rate, ARR would be £87.50.)

- ARR can be used to calculate **lost room revenue**, by multiplying the number of *unsold rooms* by the average rate. In our example, 25 unsold rooms x £75.00 = £1,785 in lost revenue. This is a particularly useful measure for motivating marketing and sales staff!

- ARR can be compared with a known **breakeven figure** (the rate at which the hotel is covering its costs on a room), to ascertain whether the rooms division has made a profit on a given night.

One limitation of average rate figures is that they don't really allow you to compare your hotel's performance with that of another hotel, or this year's performance with last year's. Therefore, a number of more sophisticated measures has been developed for this purpose.

Yield (percentage revenue achieved)

Yield percentage – also called '**percentage revenue achieved**' or '**income occupancy percentage**' – expresses the room revenue *actually* earned by the hotel as a percentage of the *maximum possible* revenue it could have earned (by 100% occupancy at full rack rates).

$$Yield = \frac{Total\ room\ revenue\ (rooms\ sold \times rates\ charged)}{Potential\ room\ revenue\ (total\ rooms \times full\ rack\ rates)} \times 100$$

E X A M P L E

Remember, the Hill Town Hotel has the following room breakdown for July.

Rooms			Beds	Occupancy
50	Single rooms	=	50	45 occupied
80	Twin rooms	=	160	45 occupied by two people, 30 occupied by one person
70	Double rooms	=	140	25 occupied by two people, 30 occupied by one person
200	Rooms		350	175 rooms let (245 sleepers)

Let's now give it a slightly more realistic tariff (excluding VAT), as follows:

Single room: £45.00
Twin: £60.00 Single occupancy: £50.00
Double: £75.00 Single occupancy: £60.00

Now we can do the calculations.

Potential revenue = (50 × £45) + (70 × £75) + (80 × £60) = £12,300

Total actual revenue = (45 × £45) + (45 × £60) + (30 × £50) + (25 × £75) + (30 × £60) = £9,900

$$Yield = \frac{£9,900}{£12,300} \times 100 = 80.49\%$$

> Note that in this scenario, we have assumed that all our guests have paid the full rack rate. Obviously, the yield will be lowered if some guests pay discounted rates. Yield is thus affected *both* by rate discounting *and* by occupancy rates.

Yield measures *both* the hotel's success in maximising occupancy *and* in securing rates as close to full rack rate as possible. As we saw earlier, there is a trade-off in the two variables: the hotel may *need* to discount rooms in order to boost occupancy. Yield percentages therefore represent an important management tool, as a guide to how successfully this trade-off is being made.

You can also calculate yield using *average* revenue for a period – if you wanted to compare yield in two different years, say. Average revenue is calculated as average rooms sold (total rooms x occupancy %) multiplied by average room rate (ARR).

RevPAR (Revenue per available room)

Also known as 'rooms yield', RevPAR combines the average room rate and occupancy percentage figures, to determine the contribution each hotel room has made to the financial performance of the hotel in a given period.

In a hotel charging a per-room rate, this could be calculated, simply, as:

$$\frac{\text{Room revenue in a given period}}{\text{Number of available rooms}}$$

The position is a bit more complicated if it charges a per-person rate, however, because of the varying multiple-occupancy percentage. An alternative calculation can therefore be used:

RevPAR = Average room rate x room occupancy % in a given period

On the day illustrated in our example above: RevPAR = £75.00 × 87.55% = £65.63

RevPAR is particularly useful because it provides a standard measure, which can be used to compare the hotel's performance with other hotels; or to compare one season's performance with another; or to compare this year's performance with last year's.

ACTIVITY 5   20 minutes

Let's go back to the Miramar hotel. Remember:

Type A rooms: rack rate £120. There are 100 of these rooms, all doubles.
Type B rooms: rack rate £95.80. There are 80 of these rooms, all doubles.

The hotel recorded the following occupancy data for Monday 3 May 2004.

	Number of rooms occupied	Single or double occupancy	Rate (£)
Type A	30	Double	120
	25	Double	80
	10	Single	55
Type B	35	Double	60
	8	Single	40

This time, calculate:

(a)   The ADR for Monday 3 May.
(b)   The RevPAR for Monday 3 May.
(c)   The yield percentage for Monday 3 May.

GOPPAR (Gross operating profit per available room)

Of course, businesses are interested in the 'top line' of revenue – but they are even more interested in the 'bottom line' of **profit**: that is, how much revenue they earn *over and above* the **costs** of operating the hotel.

DEFINITION

Profit is the difference between costs and revenue: that is, the *surplus* left over for the business, after costs have been covered.

Gross operating profit is the profit of the business *before* the deduction of charges such as bank interest and taxes. In other words, it is the basic difference between revenue and operating costs.

$$GOPPAR = \frac{\text{Gross operating profit (total revenue} - \text{total costs) for a given period}}{\text{Total rooms available}}$$

Gross operating profit figures will be drawn from the hotel's accounts, as prepared by the Finance Manager or hotel accountant.

Let's say the Hill Town Hotel has 200 rooms, and makes a GOP of £70,000 in its May accounting period (31 days). The Sea Bell Hotel has 100 rooms, and reports a GOP of £40,000 in its May accounting period (30 days).

Hill Town's GOPPAR = $\frac{£70,000}{200 \times 31}$ = £11.29. Sea Bell's GOPPAR = $\frac{£40,000}{100 \times 30}$ = £13.33

Despite the different sizes of the hotels, and the different lengths of the accounting periods, we can still see at a glance that the Sea Bell Hotel is a more profitable operation.

4 Front office reports

As we have already seen, a range of information has to be prepared by front office to support management decision-making, and passed from front office to other departments, both to co-ordinate operations efficiently – and to ensure that guests needs are seamlessly met, despite service tasks being allocated to different groups of staff. We will now look at some of these reports and notifications.

4.1 Daily occupancy reports

The various occupancy and revenue statistics discussed so far in this chapter are pretty indigestible in their 'raw' form – as you may have found! They need to be combined and summarised in an easy-to-use format for use by management.

An **occupancy report** is usually prepared daily, either by night audit staff or by the last shift on reception duty. A specimen report form is shown in Figure 6.1, although the exact format and content will depend on the hotel and the computer system used to generate the report (if any).

Note that:

- Different room types are listed separately, to show the occupancy from each type.

- Discounted and complimentary rooms are listed separately, so that managers can ensure that all reductions are justified, and have been authorised.

- The 'room revenue' figure can be cross-checked against the amount posted to guest bills.

- No-show and cancellations are expressed as a percentage of reservations.

4.2   Occupancy forecasts

Having compiled 'historical' data about occupancy rates for each day, month, season and year, the hotel is not only interested in looking *backwards* to analyse its performance, it will also be interested in **projecting** historical patterns and trends *forwards* to help it forecast or estimate future occupancy levels.

As we saw earlier in the chapter, the hotel will seek to forecast future booking levels and patterns, for the purposes of **yield management**, so that it can target its marketing, booking and pricing decisions in such a way as to 'smooth out' fluctuations in demand. A **three-month forecast** is often used for this purpose.

However, there is also a need for more **short-term forecasts**, so that reservations staff can make more immediate booking decisions (whether to hold or release rooms and at what rate), and so that operational departments can plan for estimated levels of occupancy.

- A **monthly general forecast** of occupancy can be made by front office, based on: occupancy in the same month of previous years; the level of advance reservations already made; and any known factors which might be anticipated to increase occupancy (eg a special event in the area) or decrease it (eg a new competitor hotel) compared to the previous year.

- A **five-day forecast** is often produced by front office to cover the next five days, enabling it to take into account more accurate information about current reservation levels, guests' changing plans (eg extended or shortened stays) and so on. The five-day forecast is generally compiled daily, updating it (with the latest reservation data) and extending it one day further ahead. It is posted at the reservations desk – allowing clerks to accept or reject short-notice bookings (and to post 'go slow' notices on the stop/go chart, say) on the basis of the forecast for a given day. It is also circulated to other departments, so that housekeeping can plan work rosters, food and beverages can plan the purchasing of supplies and so on.

DAILY OCCUPANCY REPORT

Day: _____   Date: ___ / ___ /2009

Room type	Total rooms	Out of service	Vacant	Let	Single occupancy	Company rate	Comps
Single							
Twin							
Double							
Suite							
TOTAL							
Revenue							

Analysis

Room occupancy %	
Bed occupancy %	
Double occupancy %	
Occupancy week to date	
Occupancy this night last year	
Cancellations %	
No-shows %	

Total room revenue	£
Average room rate	£
Yield %	

Discounts and complimentary

Rooms	Rate	Name	Affiliation/Explanation

Comments

Prepared by:

Figure 6.1: A simple daily occupancy report form

FIVE DAY FORECAST

Today
Day: _____   Date: _____

Departures

	Vacant overnight	
Plus	Check outs	
Plus	Extra departures	
Equals	Available	

Arrivals

	Reservations	
Minus	No-shows	
Plus	Chance	
Equals	Net arrivals	

VACANT (short)

Next 4 days

Day/date	/	/	/	/
Departures				
Projected check outs				
Plus Extra departures				
Arrivals				
Reservations				
Minus No shows				
Net arrivals				
VACANT (short)				

Prepared by: _____

Figure 6.2: Five-day forecast

FOR DISCUSSION

That's pretty much the last of the numerical or statistical topics covered in this Study Guide! You've had to take in a lot of information, perhaps of an unfamiliar type, in this chapter. Which topic are you least confident about? What might you do to increase your knowledge, skills or confidence in this area?

4.3 Departmental notifications

In a computerised system, the sharing of information between different departments of the hotel is comparatively easy. Each relevant department will have access to the same Hotel Management System, via its own computer terminal(s) and/or hand-held devices, and can call-up a variety of reports and status displays.

When a guest arrives, reception inputs the details in the check-in system – and the arrivals list, housekeeping task lists, guest index (for switchboard) and so on are automatically updated, for the information of other departments. Similarly, if a guest changes rooms, or checks-out, all relevant records and status displays are adjusted accordingly. All relevant records can be printed out (eg to give housekeeping a list of the rooms that require preparation for re-letting on a given day), or interrogated by entry to the data base (eg if housekeeping wants to confirm the status of a particular room).

Many hotels still use manual notifications, however, or keep the system in place as a 'back-up' and, as ever, it helps to know what the underlying procedures are.

Arrivals list

One day in advance, an **arrivals list** is prepared, showing a list of all arrivals expected on the following day: we discussed this in Chapter 3, as part of pre-arrival procedures. In addition to the copy retained by reception, to check off check-ins, the arrivals list will be circulated to:

- The concierge, porter or enquiry desk: in case of messages, mail or visitors for guests who are due to arrive

- The switchboard: in case of telephone calls for, or enquiries about the arrival of, a guest

- Housekeeping: to confirm that rooms will be made up for a new occupant, and any special requests and requirements

- Guest services: to confirm any special requests and requirements (eg flowers in the room for arrival)

- Guest relations: to warn of the arrival of any VIP guests, for whom special arrangements must be made

Change notifications

When guests check-in – or at any other point during their stay – they may request or require:

- A **different room** – eg if the room allocated is not to their liking, or if something is wrong with the room (the air conditioning isn't working, say), or if the room is not available for the whole duration of their stay

- A **different rate or terms** – eg if they request an upgrade part way through their stay, or are given a discount or special terms in compensation for some failure of service

- A **different number of people** in the room – eg if an additional party joins them part way through their stay.

This effectively alters the position previously notified via the arrivals list. As we discussed in Chapter 3, such changes need to be separately notified to departments such as housekeeping (to prepare the new rooms), switchboard and concierge (to change the destination of messages and enquiries), porters (for transferring luggage), restaurant/bar and billing (to change the room/rate for posting charges) etc. In a manual system, these can be done using a single multiple-part **change notification** (which may be called a removal – ie move – slip): Figure 6.3.

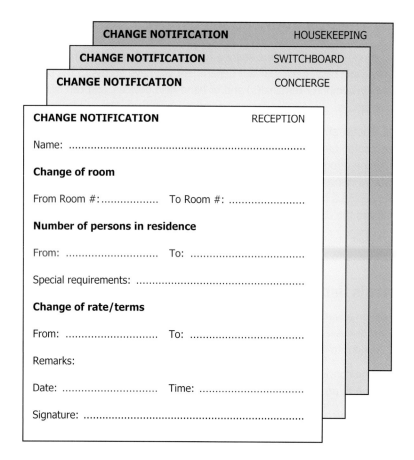

Figure 6.3: A simple change notification slip

Guest list

An alphabetical guest list (also called a **house list** or **guest index**) is generally prepared each evening to reflect the day's *actual* arrivals. This is generally circulated throughout the hotel, so that any department can be aware of (and, if necessary, verify) the identity of *bona fide* guests on the premises. This will be of most use to:

- Reception: eg to quickly locate or verify a guest's room number, if the guest asks for a key

- Switchboard and concierge: eg to quickly locate a guest's room number, if telephone calls, mail or enquiries come in for them

Room list

A list of all the rooms in the hotel, in room number order, may prepared in accordance with room status records and housekeeper's reports, to show the current status of each room.

E X A M P L E

Depending on the particular protocols and terminology used by the hotel, each room may be shown as:

- Vacant

- Vacant dirty (a vacated room that has not yet been serviced by housekeeping)

- Vacant clean (a vacated room that has been serviced by housekeeping)

- Vacant inspected (a vacated room that has been serviced and inspected for readiness)

- Stayover/occupied clean (a currently occupied room that has been serviced for the day)

- Stayover/occupied dirty (a currently occupied room that has not yet been serviced for the day)

- Vacant arrival inspected (a vacant room that has been inspected as ready for re-let)

- Vacant pick-up (a vacated room that only needs partial servicing to be ready for re-let, eg because a guest has changed rooms shortly after occupation)

Groups list (or function list)

Because groups and functions require more preparation, a separate list of expected **groups, tours or functions** will be prepared weekly, to cover the following week or ten-day period. (This is sometimes also called a 'ten-day forecast': remember, it refers only to *anticipated* arrivals, on the basis of bookings – not actual occupancy).

This list aids management in planning staffing levels and allocations (eg if special staff have to be brought in for a large conference), and helps all staff to be aware of projected levels of occupancy and special requirements to be planned for the week head.

VIP/SPATT and service lists

As we saw in Chapter 3, the hotel may make special arrangements for VIPs, CIPs and Special Attention guests, and the list of in-coming guests of these types will be separately notified to all front office and operational departments, stating any special measures to be taken.

The hotel may also offer a range of **additional services** to all guests on check-in, and if guests choose to take advantage of these services, their requests must be notified to the departments concerned.

- A **list/timetable of early morning call requests** will be provided to switchboard (if not programmed into an automated system) the evening before.

- A **list of newspaper requests** (by room number) will be provided to whoever is responsible for their distribution.

- If guests have made requests or reservations though reception for **additional services** (eg the delivery of flowers to a guest's room, or an appointment with the tours/entertainment desk), a schedule of these requests will have to be provided to the relevant departments.

Departures list

As detailed in Chapter 4, a **departure list** will be compiled, usually in room order, to indicate guests due to depart on the following day. This will again be circulated to all departments (perhaps together with the guest/house list), so that they know *not* to provide further services or credit. It will be particularly relevant to:

- Billing: to anticipate the preparation of the guest's final account

- Switchboard/concierge: in the event of messages or enquiries for departed guests

- Housekeeping: to prepare task lists and allocate work, on the basis of which rooms will need to be made ready for re-letting, which rooms are likely to be readily accessible (vacated by standard check-out time) and so on.

5   Operational reports

5.1   Operational reports

A number of reports is required to keep the operations of the hotel running smoothly, and to check that all departments are 'on the same page' as far as requirements are concerned.

Housekeeper's report

The housekeeping department should compile a report on the state (and status) of each room in the hotel, as it checks, services and inspects them during the morning. This will be summarised on a standard form, as shown at Figure 6.4.

HOUSEKEEPER'S REPORT

Fourth (4th) Floor   Date: _____ Time: _____

SUMMARY:

Type	Let	Vacant	Out of service	TOTAL
SB				
TB				
DB				
TOTAL				

BREAKDOWN:

No	Type	Status	Persons	No	Type	Status	Persons	No	Type	Status	Persons
201	SB			209	DB			217	TB		
202	SB			210	DB			218	TB		
203	SB			211	DB			219	TB		
204	SB			212	DB			220	TB		
205	TB			213	DB			221	SB		
206	TB			214	DB			222	SB		
207	TB			215	DB			223	SB		
208	TB			216	DB			224	SB		

Key:	**VAC**	Vacant	**OCC**	Occupied	**GCO**	Guest checked out
	OOS	Out of service			**DND**	Do not disturb (room not accessible)

Figure 6.4: Housekeeper's report

As we saw in Chapter 5, the night auditor should check the housekeeper's report against the front office room status records, to identify any discrepancies that may need investigation or correction.

- There may be more people staying in the room than notified to front office, in which case the hotel may be losing per person revenue.

- If a room is reported as 'vacant', when front office has it listed as occupied, the guest may have changed rooms without the records being properly adjusted – or the guest may have 'skipped out'.

- If a room is reported as 'occupied', when front office has it noted as vacant, the guest may have taken the room, or changed rooms, without the front office records being adjusted accordingly – or the room may have been occupied by an unregistered and perhaps unpaying guest (with or without the co-operation of a member of staff).

Standard room/maintenance report

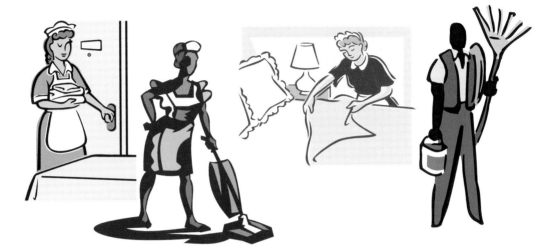

Housekeeping staff may only have 20 minutes allocated per room to clean, service, re-supply and inspect the room, in the course of their daily work. A more thorough and systematic inspection may therefore be required, in order to identify maintenance and redecoration needs which have not otherwise been reported by housekeeping – or by guests.

Rooms may be periodically **inspected** by the duty manager, together with housekeeping and maintenance supervisors, to ensure that their standard of maintenance and decoration is adequate: that the room is clean; that all appliances are working; that upholstery, curtains, fixtures, fittings and paintwork are in good repair and look fresh; and so on. This report will be used as the basis for:

- Maintenance requests;
- Scheduling re-decorating; and
- Reporting back on the performance of housekeeping.

Incident book, handover report or department diary

Each operating department should keep some kind of **log of what has happened** during the shift and the day. The shift leader will record information about actions that have been taken; actions or enquiries that are still in progress; guest requests that have been met (or not yet met); and any 'incidents' that have happened during the shift.

Such a log is useful in the hand-over from one shift to another – especially if there are guest queries or actions still in progress when the shift ends. It is important that *someone* knows what has happened, where the issue is 'up to' and what still has to be done.

The log may also contain useful guest information for the next shift to bear in mind (eg if there has been a complaint, or a guest has been moved, or a staff member has suspicions about a guest).

It may also contain useful information about what has been done or decided during a shift, in the event of subsequent queries or enquiries. Some of this information may also be useful for formulating or adjusting policies and procedures, so that future problems can be avoided; successful actions can be repeated; and incidents can be used as case studies for staff coaching and training.

5.2 Financial reports

A number of financial reports (in addition to the daily occupancy report, discussed earlier) may also be compiled by the night auditor. Examples include:

- A **daily business**, **trading or sales report**, setting out the daily sales/income totals of each revenue-earning department, plus summaries of their activity (eg the occupancy percentage of the rooms division, and the number of persons or 'covers' served by the restaurant at breakfast, lunch and dinner). This is one way of measuring the contribution and performance of each department.

- **Method of payment summary**, setting out the number and value of transactions made by cash, credit card, foreign currency, traveller's cheque and so on. This can be used to help forecast cash float requirements, the cost of transactions etc.

- **Debtor analysis**, setting out payment amounts overdue by various periods (an aged debtor analysis) and/or stating **bad debts** as a percentage of turnover.

- **Budgets** showing target and actual revenue, and target and actual costs, for each department. These are usually prepared by the central accounts department, based on reports from the various departments. They are to monitor and control spending; to measure profitability and performance; and to act as a motivational tool (since departments may have set revenue, cost reduction or profit targets which they will strive to achieve).

6 Guest history information

Guest history information is often compiled and kept by hotels which:

- Want to offer **personalised service** – by being able to 'recognise' guests as returning customers, offer them rooms and amenities according to their previous likes and dislikes and so on.

- Want to pursue **relationship marketing** to guests – by being able to maintain contact with them after their stay, and offer personalised offers and reminders, in order to create repeat business, a growing 'relationship' with the customer, and, ideally, customer loyalty.

- Want to **streamline administration** of reservation and check-in, by retaining previously obtained guest information – so that it doesn't have to be obtained and input again.

- Luxury hotels may compile guest history records as a matter of course, in the anticipation of guests returning, because personalised service is such an important part of their offering. For smaller hotels, and hotels with a high proportion of transient and non-repeat trade, it has traditionally not been worthwhile, other than for known repeat or regular visitors. However, in this – as in most things – computerised systems have put it within reach of the smallest hotel: allowing guest information to be input, stored, updated and retrieved easily and cost-effectively (and without filing space).

6.1 What information should be kept in guest history records?

The first time a guest stays in a hotel, a guest history record will be opened, and it will be updated on all subsequent stays. A **guest history card** will usually contain basic information such as:

- Name, contact and registration details of the guest
- Date of arrival
- Room occupied
- Number of nights
- Room rate
- Amount spent in total during the stay
- Special requests/preferences noted (eg newspaper taken, view requested)

In addition, the hotel may compile a range of other details picked up by the receptionist and other staff: the names of the guest's partner and/or children; the guest's birthday; their stated likes, dislikes and interests; their reason for staying in the area and so on. This enables the hotel to welcome guests by name; ask (without inappropriate familiarity) after the family; send a birthday card, personalised or targeted offers and invitations (eg if there is a special event in the area, in which the guest might be interested); and so on.

In a manual system, this information could be kept on a simple index card, with relevant headings (and space for notes). In a computerised system, it can be entered into relevant fields in guest records – from the first booking enquiry onwards. The following is a basic guest record screen.

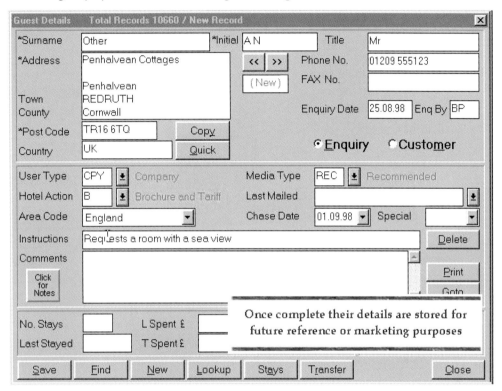

Source: http://intranet.bpc.ac.uk/widecoll/hotel/HotPerAv.html

Figure 6.5: Guest record (in Word Perfect)

Note the additional information that can be stored in the database in such a system. 'Media type', for example, refers to how the guest heard about the hotel (via advertisement, the hotel website, a travel agent or, in this case, recommendation). Statistical reports can be generated from the database to show how effective and cost-effective the hotel's advertising and web site marketing is. Data on amounts spent per stay (and as a cumulative total per customer) can automatically be compiled as revenue statistics.

When the reservation clerk enters a name and details into a computerised reservation/records system, the software will identify matching data and alert the clerk to the existence of a match:

- Enabling the clerk to respond with recognition, if (s)he is speaking to the guest on the telephone

- Supplying the relevant guest record, so that details do not have to be re-input, and appropriate offers (eg of the type of room the guest requested previously) can be made

FOR DISCUSSION

Do you think it is worthwhile for a hotel to keep detailed guest history records?

Justify your view.

SUMMARY

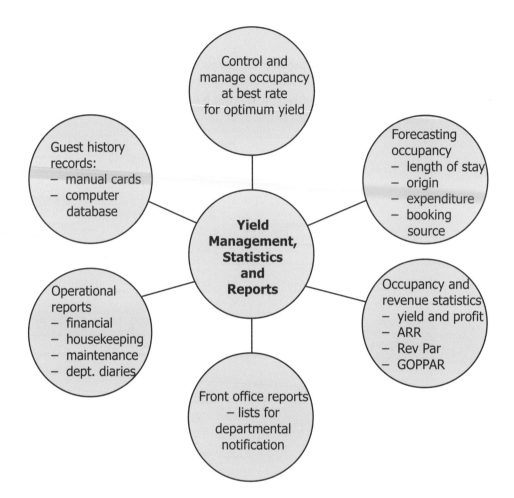

SELF-TEST QUESTIONS

1 Business customers tend to be more price sensitive than leisure customers. True or False?

2 Identify four statistical forecasting methods for forecasting demand.

3 Yield management is only appropriate when overall demand is ....

4 Give the formula for calculating (a) average length of stay and (b) average guest spend.

5 What is ADR?

6 Yield is also known as 'income occupancy percentage'. True or False?

7 What do RevPAR and GOPPAR stand for?

8 The daily occupancy forecast posted at the reservation desk to help clerks make decisions about short-range bookings is the .... forecast.

9 What is a 'house list'?

10 Identify two reports prepared by housekeeping, of particular interest to Front Office.

SELF-TEST ANSWERS

1 False

2 Moving average; weighted average, time series (trend) analysis, regression analysis

3 High

4
$$\frac{\text{Total number of sleeper nights sold}}{\text{Total amount of guest bills}} \qquad \frac{\text{Total amount of guest bills}}{\text{Number of guests}}$$

5 Average Daily Rate (total room revenue *divided by* total rooms sold)

6 True

7 Revenue Per Available Room; Gross Operating Profit Per Available Room

8 Five-day

9 Guest index

10 Housekeeper's Report and Standard Room Report

ANSWERS TO ACTIVITIES

1 No answer is given to this activity, because it requires personal verbal communication. Note, however, that explaining a topic to others is good practice for training or coaching staff – and also helps the person explaining to become more confident.

2 Fluctuations in the level of demand may be caused by a wide range of factors: economic recession, local events and attractions, fluctuations in exchange rates (which may make travel less attractive to overseas customers), security or health scares, competitor offers – and of course, the hotel's own advertising and sales activities.

3 (a)

Length of stay (nights)	Number of guests	Sleeper nights
1	26	26
2	43	86
3	22	66
4	8	32
5	14	70
	113	280

Calculating a mean average, therefore: $^{280}/_{113} = 2.47$.

The mode is 2 nights.

(b)

UK	$^{53}/_{113} \times 100 = 46.9\%$
US	$^{26}/_{113} \times 100 = 23\%$
Japan	$^{13}/_{113} \times 100 = 11.5\%$
France	$^{12}/_{113} \times 100 = 10.6\%$
Other	$^{9}/_{113} \times 100 = 8\%$

You might present this in various ways. One good approach would be a pie chart:

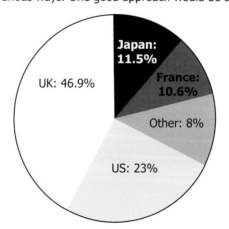

BPP
LEARNING MEDIA

4 First, let's do some preliminary calculations.

	Total number of rooms	Total beds	Number of rooms sold	Occupancy	Actual sleepers
Type A	100 (D)	200	30	x2	60
			25	x2	50
			10	x1	10
Type B	80 (D)	160	35	x2	70
			8	x1	8
Total	180	360	108		198

D = Doubles

(a) Room occupancy = $\dfrac{\text{Rooms sold}}{\text{Rooms available}}$ = $^{108}/_{180} \times 100 = 60\%$

(b) Sleeper occupancy = $\dfrac{\text{Beds sold}}{\text{Beds available}}$ = $^{198}/_{360} \times 100 = 55\%$

5 Again, let's do the preliminary work.

	Total rooms	Rack rate	Potential revenue (£)	Rooms sold	Rate	Actual revenue (£)
Type A	100	× 120	12,000	30	× 120	3,600
				25	× 80	2,000
				10	× 55	550
Type B	80	× 95.80	7,664	35	× 60	2,100
				8	× 40	320
Total	180		19,664	108		8,570

(a) ADR = $\dfrac{\text{Total revenue}}{\text{Rooms sold}} = \dfrac{£8,570}{108} = £79.35$

(b) RevPAR = $\dfrac{\text{Room revenue}}{\text{Available rooms}} = \dfrac{£8,570}{180} = £47.61.$

RevPAR = ADR x occupancy % = £79.35 × 60% = £47.61.

(c) Yield % = $\dfrac{\text{Total revenue}}{\text{potential revenue}} = \dfrac{£8,570}{£19.664} \times 100 = 43.58\%$

CHAPTER 7

SECURITY AND SAFETY RESPONSIBILITIES

Chapter objectives

In this chapter you will learn

- The security and safety aspects of a hotel
- Potential areas of health and safety risk and how they can be managed
- Hotel accident, fire and other emergency procedures
- Potential areas of security risk and how they can be managed
- The Data Protection Act and the hotel's duty to protect guests' personal information
- The use and protection of keys and key cards
- Managing safety deposit boxes and individual room safes for protection of guests' belongings

1 Introduction

Duty of care is a legal concept arguing that people and organisations have a duty to take reasonable care to avoid actions which are likely to cause loss, injury or damage to others. If someone is owed a duty of care, and there is breach of that duty which causes loss or damage, the injured party can take legal action for 'negligence' and seek compensation.

The duty of care is a complex legal principle, and we won't go into its subtleties here. In general, however, you should be aware that a hotel has *invited* guests and visitors (and employees and contractors) onto its premises, by the nature of its business, and in law it, therefore, has a duty to take reasonable care to protect them from loss and injury. This duty of care is increased by the contract between a hotel and its paying guests and employees. The hotel has specific obligations to ensure that the premises are safe, and that people entering those premises receive the protection (for themselves and their belongings) that they are entitled to expect as part of their contract.

Legal obligations aside, safety and security are key issues for any hospitality establishment to:

- Protect people from harm, loss, fear or distress (which we hope goes without saying).

- Protect the property and assets of the hotel.

- Protect the reputation of the hotel: maintaining guest satisfaction, goodwill and positive recommendation to others – or *avoiding* complaints and bad publicity and word-of-mouth about an hotel's lack of hygiene, safety or security.

- Avoid the costs of accidents, fire, theft, fraud, law suits, compensation claims and other consequences of poor safety and security.

- Comply with the relevant law on health and safety, duty of care, hospitality, data protection and so on – and avoid the penalties for non-compliance (eg fines or closures).

General dimensions of safety and security

Is a hotel really such a 'dangerous' place? Think about it. There are the normal hazards of any building environment and the normal hazards of careless behaviour. Add the assumption that there will be a lot of money, cameras and travel documents vulnerable to theft – not to mention all the hotel equipment, fixtures and fittings and the fact that there will be unknown people coming in and out all the time. Multiply by the number of people in one place... Not *necessarily* a recipe for disaster – but a fair amount of vulnerability!

There are four basic types of threat you need to be concerned about, as a member of front office staff.

Threats	Examples
Threats to the health, safety, comfort and well-being of guests: your number one priority	- Fire emergencies - Accidents (due to inadequate maintenance, lighting, signage etc) - Terrorist emergencies (eg bomb threats) - Poor hygiene (particularly in food handling) - Threats to guest privacy (eg via intrusion into rooms, press exposure, breach of confidentiality) - Threats to guest enjoyment (eg as a result of noisy or disruptive behaviour by other guests)
Threats to the property of guests while in the hotel	- Theft, pick-pocketing or mugging - Confidence tricksters/fraud - Accidental or malicious damage to property - Loss of luggage or property left for safekeeping

Threats	Examples
Threats to the premises, fixtures and fittings, financial assets or reputation of the hotel	▪ Damage to furniture, fixtures and fittings (other than by normal wear and tear) ▪ Theft of equipment, fixtures and fittings or cash ▪ Guests leaving without paying ▪ Fraud (by guests or staff) ▪ Immoral or illegal behaviour (eg drug dealing or prostitution) carried out on the premises
Threats to the health, safety and well-being of the hotel's staff (ie 'health and safety at work').	▪ Fire emergencies ▪ Accidents ▪ Terrorist emergencies ▪ Poor work environment, systems or practices (leading to illness, injury or stress) ▪ Abusive behaviour by guests (or fellow staff) ▪ Robbery or attack (especially for night staff)

We'll look at some of these examples as we proceed through this chapter.

FOR DISCUSSION

Pick two or three of the examples listed, and try and find or 'swap' some stories from the experience of fellow students and colleagues in the hotel industry. How common are such 'risk events'?

Let's start by examining the issue of **health and safety**, as it applies to both guests and staff.

2 Health and safety aspects of hotels

As we have just seen, hotels can be surprisingly hazardous environments! As the communications hub of the hotel, both for staff and guests, the front office will naturally be the place where potential **risks** are reported (eg if a guest or member of staff discover faulty wiring or an area of wet floor); where **actual accidents** or cases of ill-health are reported; where **assistance** is requested (eg if a guest or member of staff requires first aid or the calling of a doctor or ambulance); and where people look for **guidance** in case of emergency.

Some of the health and safety aspects of hotels are beyond the immediate scope of this syllabus: food hygiene and safety, for example, will be considered separately and in detail, elsewhere in your studies. However, we will look briefly at some of the hazards that may occur at or around reception – and some of the health and safety issues that reception will be asked to deal with.

2.1 Everyday health and safety hazards in hotels

Staff may be going busily about their duties, and guests may be going busily about their own activities (whether they are in the hotel for business or pleasure): it is easy to be unaware of potential hazards as you move about a familiar area – and even more so, about an *un*-familiar area! Hotel staff, however, are in a better position to identify potential hazards, and they also have a duty of care to guests: either to eliminate the risks, or to inform guests about them before accidents happen.

ACTIVITY 1   10 minutes

Look about you where you are sitting right now, as you read this chapter.

(a)   Before you read on, see if you can identify *ten* things that could potentially cause an accident for an unwary person, or someone behaving in an irresponsible fashion.

(b)   What could you do to minimise the risk from each of these ten things?

EXAMPLE

The following are just a few of the hazards that may be present for guests (and staff) in a hotel setting.

- Tripping hazards such as poorly maintained carpet; trailing wires from electrical appliances; luggage and other items left in hallways or gangways; unmarked steps up or down (especially in poorly lit areas)

- Wet patches on bathroom or other slippery floor surfaces

- Steep stairs (particularly if poorly lit, or with insecure banisters)

- Poorly maintained electrical appliances, power sockets or adaptors (creating risk of electrical shock or fire)

- Glass doors and windows (requiring some form of warning or markings to avoid people walking into them)

- Poorly organised storage areas (with the risk of heavy objects falling onto people, or making people stand on chairs to reach them)

- Poorly stored or labelled chemicals and other substances (eg cleaning fluids)

- Un-emptied litter bins (creating a fire and/or hygiene hazard)

- Blocked or locked escape/emergency routes, inaccessible emergency equipment (like fire extinguishers), or poorly maintained smoke/fire alarms

- Irresponsible or careless behaviour (such as horseplay or running in confined spaces, diving into an unknown swimming pool, carrying overloaded trays of hot liquids)

- Smoking (even in authorised areas) around flammable substances or materials

- Everyday risks such as scalding (from in-room coffee/tea making facilities), cuts (from using scissors or bottle openers), bruises (from banging into table corners in unfamiliar rooms) and so on

- Abuse of alcohol or drugs – making any of the above hazards worse!

What can be done about such things?

- **Awareness** and vigilance. Front office staff should look out for hazards and take note of any reports or comments by guests or other staff that might indicate a potential problem.

- **Removal of hazards**, where possible. If you notice a problem that you can put right yourself (eg moving obstructions from a gangway, or closing an open filing cabinet), do so.

- **Warnings**. If a hazard cannot immediately be dealt with, issue a warning. This may mean placing a 'Warning: wet surface' sign over a spillage, or placing an 'out of order' notice on a piece of equipment. You will find a range of warnings signs in hotels: from safety instructions on equipment, to 'no smoking' signs, to rules about swimming pool safety.

- ■ **Reporting**. Hazards that need authorisation or special skills to deal with should be notified to the appropriate person (eg the duty manager, housekeeping or maintenance staff) as soon as possible.

- ■ **Supervision, training and discipline**. Safety procedures are designed for everyone's protection, and failure to follow them is a serious issue. If you see a fellow member of staff breaking safety rules, you will need to deal with the matter: first, perhaps, by having a quiet word with the person concerned, and then, if necessary, by informing someone in authority. It may be unpleasant to be the 'whistleblower', but safety is your responsibility. Similarly, a guest breaking safety rules (eg by smoking in no-smoking areas or behaving in a boisterous fashion) should be approached politely, and tactfully 'reminded' of the rules, if a guest refuses to comply, the matter may be referred to the duty manager for further handling.

The flow chart, overleaf, offers an overview of the process of **risk management**: Figure 7.1.

2.2 Health and safety at work

In addition to thinking about the safety of guests, every country has laws and regulations setting certain minimum standards for the protection of health and safety of employees in their workplace. In the UK, the **Health and Safety at Work Act 1974** is the main piece of legislation setting out the responsibilities of employers and their employees.

Responsibilities of employers	Responsibilities of employees
■ To provide safe systems (work practices)	■ To take reasonable care of themselves and others affected by their acts or omissions at work
■ To provide a safe and healthy work environment (well-lit, warm, ventilated, hygienic and so on)	
■ To maintain all machinery and equipment to a necessary standard of safety	■ To co-operate with the employer in carrying out their responsibilities (eg by obeying all safety rules)
■ To support safe working practices with information, instruction, training and supervision	■ Not to interfere intentionally or recklessly with any machinery or equipment provided in the interests of health and safety (eg not switching off smoke alarms)
■ To consult with staff safety representatives on issues of concern to staff	
■ To communicate safety policy and measures to all staff, clearly and in writing	

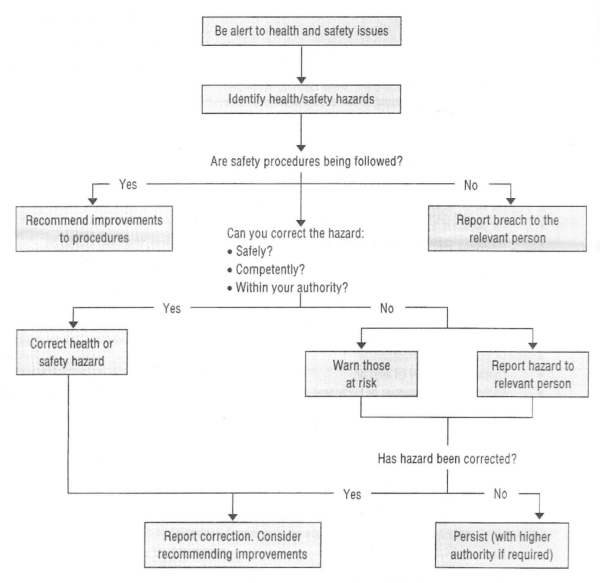

Figure 7.1: Risk management process

Health and safety is thus a shared responsibility of management and staff. As the Act requires, hotels should have their own **health and safety policies**, clearly posted on the staff notice board, in office manuals and so on. There should also be a person specially designated to promote health and safety measures and compliance with regulations. If you work in a hotel environment, you need to make sure you familiarise yourself with the relevant policies, and know who your health and safety officer or representative is.

Different departments of the hotel will be subject to different types of health and safety risks.

- Housekeeping staff may face risks from the storage and handling of cleaning chemicals which may be dangerous if misused. Such matters are covered by separate provisions in the **Control of Substances Hazardous to Health (COSHH) regulations**. Front Office should have on file a **Materials Safety Data Sheet (MSDS)** with information on the storage and handling of all chemicals, and what to do in case of emergency.

- **Maintenance staff** may be at risk when using tools or dealing with electrical wiring.

- **Porters** may be at risk of back injury through heavy lifting (and poor lifting technique).

- **Any staff** may be at risk of falls, slips and trips; misuse of equipment; and so on.

Under the Management of Health and Safety At Work Regulations 1992, department heads may be asked to carry out **risks assessments** to identify the main risks in their own areas of activity. Staff also have a duty under the regulations to inform their employer of any situation which they think may pose a danger.

E X A M P L E

'A Word from the FOM'

Health and safety is vital in a hotel. Everyone must be willing, aware and involved – from wiping up a spill to picking up a piece of rubbish – or, when it's raining outside, putting 'Slippery When Wet' signs out on the floor. The most common accidents we encounter are from slips, trips and falls; manual handling (heavy lifting); and misuse of dangerous substances – and these can affect both guests and staff.

2.3 Fire prevention and fire emergency

Fire is a particularly terrifying prospect in a hotel, because of the number of people housed in what is for them an unfamiliar (and potentially confusing) environment. It is vital that front office staff are fully familiar with, and practised in fire emergency drills; and that they be available to give calm, practical leadership in the event of a fire emergency.

The main causes of fire in a hotel are:

- Electrical fires (eg from overloaded power sockets or poorly maintained wiring)

- Flammable substances (such as chemicals or aerosol cans left in direct sunlight)

- Flammable materials (such as waste paper, chemical-soaked rags, clothing and some furniture materials), particularly where these are likely to come into contact with heaters, electrical sparks, cigarettes or sparks from log fires

- Human error (eg carelessly disposed of cigarettes, fat fires in the kitchen, heaters obstructed with towels or clothes causing overheating)

The **Regulatory Reform (Fire Safety) Order** came into effect in October 2006, replacing a range of other UK legislation (such as the Fire Precautions Act 1971). It places a duty on any person who owns or controls a business or premises to put in place certain fire risk assessment, prevention and emergency procedures:

- Fire risk assessment
- Fire safety policy
- Fire procedures (such as evacuation)
- Staff training
- Fire drills
- Means of escape
- Signs and notices
- Emergency lighting
- Fire alarm
- Fire extinguishers
- Fire doors and compartments

Picture: www.uk-fireprevention.co.uk

All hotels in the UK are also required to qualify for a **Fire Certificate,** which is issued after a rigorous inspection to ensure that such prevention and emergency measures are in place.

EXAMPLE

FIRE SAFETY CHECKLIST

Maintenance

☑ Premises are kept clear of combustible waste and refuse

☑ Points of entry are kept secure against intruders (limiting risk of arson)

☑ Gangways, exit routes and fire doors are clear and in good repair

☑ Electrical equipment is switched off or unplugged when not in use

☑ Access to storage areas is limited to authorised personnel

☑ Flammable substances are stored away from possible sources of ignition

☑ All machinery and equipment is regularly maintained and cleaned

☑ Appropriate safety instructions are issued for all substances, machinery and equipment

Smoking

☑ Smoking is prohibited in all but designated smoking areas, and prohibitions are strictly enforced

☑ Non-combustible receptacles are provided for cigarette ends (separate from waste containers)

Fire doors and exits

☑ Designated fire doors are clearly labelled 'Fire Door: Keep Shut'

☑ Fire doors are kept free for emergency access (never locked or blocked)

☑ External doors (which have to be kept fastened while people are in the building) are fitted with quick release devices, such as a panic latch or release bar

☑ Fire exits are clearly indicated, easy to open in an emergency and kept free of obstruction

Fire and smoke alarms

☑ Smoke alarms are fitted in all rooms and areas of the hotel, maintained and tested regularly

☑ Fire alarm call points are clearly marked, accessible, easy to operate and tested regularly

☑ Alarms may be combined with a voice evacuation system, using the public address or telephone system to issue evacuation instructions

Fire emergency provisions

☑ Sprinkler systems (activated automatically) are maintained regularly

☑ Emergency lighting is provided in public areas, corridors and escape routes

☑ Fire evacuation plans and instructions are clearly posted in all rooms (including details of safe rendezvous points outside the building

Staff training

☑ All new staff are instructed in fire precautions and emergency procedures during induction

☑ Designated 'Fire wardens' or 'Fire marshals' are appointed and trained

☑ Staff are trained in the correct use of fire-fighting equipment (eg fire extinguishers)

2.4 First Aid

DEFINITION

First aid is the immediate help given in an emergency to keep a sick or injured person as safe and as comfortable as possible, until medical aid can be obtained (eg by calling a doctor or ambulance). It should only be administered by a suitably qualified person.

Every hotel should have:

- At least one member of staff who is **qualified to render first aid**. Front office staff, being the first port of call in an emergency, would be good candidates for this kind of training.

- A **telephone directory** of staff members who hold a first aid qualification, for contact in an emergency; and another directory of local doctors, emergency dentists, hospital accident and emergency departments and the ambulance service, for call if first aid is not sufficient to deal with the problem

- A number of **first aid boxes** (one of which will be held at reception), with basic first aid supplies, including bandages, splints, antiseptics and so on, with instructions for their use.

In the area of **health emergency**, it is particularly important to recognise the limits of your authority and expertise – however powerful your desire to be helpful! The most valuable things you can do are as follows.

Step 1   **Attend quickly** – in case time is of the essence. It may be advisable to have another person with you, even if you think you can cope alone, in order to have a witness, assistant or 'crowd controller' to reassure other guests.

Step 2   **Stay calm**, and help the sick or injured person to stay calm as far as possible: listen and reassure.

Step 3   **Assess** the severity and nature of the incident, in order to decide what to do next, whom to call, and how to minimise risk, stress and disruption to other guests.

Step 4   **Do not attempt** to deal with a hazard or injury, unless you are competent and qualified to do so.

- Call for assistance from specialised personnel (eg maintenance) if required to control further risks (eg to deal with broken glass, spillages, electrical hazards etc).

- Keep the injured person quiet, still (do not move an injured person unless absolutely necessary to ensure their safety) and warm; cover any open wounds with a sterile dressing from the first aid box – and call for assistance from a qualified first aider.

Step 5   **Take careful note** of what happened immediately before and during the emergency (what the casualty was doing; how (s)he looked; whether (s)he was unconscious and for how long etc), this may be helpful to medical staff.

Step 6   **Stay with the sick or injured person** until assistance arrives. Follow the instructions of the first aid officer and/or duty manager in regard to calling for further assistance (eg the ambulance service).

Step 7   **Write notes** of what happened, as a preparation for filling out the hotel's accident or incident book, reports to management and/or incident reports required by law (which we discuss later).

2.5 Emergency evacuations

There should be clear procedures for handling major potential incidents such as fire, bomb threats, or the discovery of unsafe structures or substances in the building, which may necessitate the affected area – or the whole premises – being evacuated.

Evacuations are generally notified and managed by a safety or security officer, fire officer or chief warden, who should have some sort of formal training, and are responsible for making sure that everyone known to be in a building at the time of evacuation (a) gets safely out of the building and (b) can be accounted for. Once the decision to evacuate is made:

- The **alarm** should be sounded, to warn all occupants of the building that an emergency has arisen and that evacuation procedures are being put into action. Staff should also make themselves available to issue personal reassurance and instructions to guests in public areas, where possible, and to give assistance to any guests with mobility problems.

- Relevant **emergency services** (eg the fire brigade, policy or terrorist response unit) should be called by the designated person.

- Consistent with safe and swift departure, staff may carry out any **containment** measures (eg closing windows and doors, switching off equipment and machinery) and **security** measures (eg placing cash and valuables in safes). The receptionist or other designated person should secure and remove the current guest list: this will be used to 'call the roll' to ensure that no-one is left behind in the building.

- The area will be **evacuated**, using the quickest and safest routes (eg not using lifts in the event of fire): staff and guests should be clearly advised not to linger or return for personal belongings. There may be a Floor Warden positioned on each floor of the hotel, to check that each floor is 'cleared' – and to note which rooms are *not* cleared (eg if a guest refuses to leave), so that emergency services can be notified.

- Everyone should **assemble** in the designated assembly point(s) outside the hotel, where the roll can be called, and information about persons unaccounted for given to emergency personnel. Only when the fire or safety officer declares an 'all clear' should people return to the building.

It is a legal requirement for staff to undertake **emergency evacuation drills** on a regular basis. Guests will have to be informed of these, and invited to take part if they wish.

2.6 Incident reporting

Employing organisations with more than ten staff must by law keep an **accident book**, in which can be recorded all details of accidents and events which have occurred on the premises, which required treatment or advice. These details could be used as evidence in a legal action (eg for compensation), so details must be noted systematically and accurately when incidents occur, and retained for a period of three years after the date of the last entry in the book.

In the UK, under the **Reporting of Injuries, Diseases and Dangerous Occurrences Regulations (RIDDOR) 1995**, certain accidents, dangerous occurrences and cases of disease must also be notified to the relevant authorities: the environmental health department of the local authority, or the Health and Safety Executive. If an accident results in death or major injury, or the hospitalisation of a member of the public; if there is a 'near miss' that might have caused such injuries (eg a fire or explosion); or if there is a case of poisoning, legionnaires disease or other health emergency; the relevant authority will need to be notified immediately by phone, and a detailed RIDDOR report form completed.

The format of a typical accident book is shown opposite at Figure 7.2.

Accident book

Full name, address and occupation of injured person (1)	Signature of injured person or other person making this entry* (2)	Date when entry made (3)	Date and time of accident (4)	Room/place in which accident happened (5)	Cause and nature of injury † (6)
1					
2		=	=	=	
3					
4					
5					
6		=	=	=	
7					
8					
9					
10					

* If the entry is made by some person acting on behalf of the employee, the address and occupation of that person must also be given
† State clearly the work or process being performed at the time of the accident

Figure 7.2 Accident book

ACTIVITY 2   **10 minutes**

It's 8.15 am on Tuesday 16 June, 2009, at the Hill Town Hotel. The Head Porter, John Knox, is attempting to retrieve a guest's luggage from the storage room in the lobby. You hear a crashing noise, and a shout, and – handing the guest you are dealing with over to a colleague, with an apology – you move swiftly but calmly to investigate. John is sitting on the ground, somewhat dazed. It appears that a set of golf clubs, which had (rather foolishly) been stored on an overhead shelf, has fallen as a result of the shelf being bumped, and has hit John on the head. There is a slight cut on John's head, which is bleeding, but he is conscious and able to answer your questions. You tell him to sit still, and use your walkie-talkie to call a colleague, whom you know is a qualified First Aider.

Fill out the Accident Report Book (Figure 7.2) with an appropriate entry.

3 Security aspects of hotels

DEFINITION

Security embraces a range of precautions that a hotel might take to minimise the risk of damage, theft and loss and other threats:

- To the persons of guests, visitors and employees
- To the property of guests and the property and assets of the hotel
- To the confidentiality or integrity of data and information used and held by the hotel

Security, like health and safety, is important for a number of reasons.

- First of all, to protect **guests**, **employees and others** on the premises from danger, fear or loss

- To protect the **assets of the hotel** (money, fixtures and fittings – and reputation) and save the costs arising from their loss or damage

- To prevent or minimise **disruption** to normal operations and guest service (which may affect guests' experience and/or reflect badly on the hotel)

- To protect **confidential and sensitive information** from unauthorised access and its potential consequences.

FOR DISCUSSION

Think of the various people, processes or items in a typical hotel that might be the focus of attempted theft/fraud, sabotage, disruption or attack. Which people, processes or items might you consider most at risk?

We'll start your list with some examples.

- Cash and cheques
- Keys and key cards (giving access to guest rooms)
- Moveable/saleable items such as laptops, mobile phones, TV/video equipment
- Staff who have direct access to cash, cheques, credit cards and financial records
- Check-out processes (risk of error or fraud in payment, risk of guests 'skipping' without paying...)

Carry on...

3.1 Dimensions of security

As we saw at the beginning of the chapter, security has a number of dimensions.

Security of people

Attention will have to be given to protecting people – staff, guests and visitors – from:

- **Physical harm or threat**: eg from mugging or assault, or terrorist threats

- **Invasion of privacy**: eg from room invasion, having their personal property handled or scrutinised without permission, or having their 'business' examined or publicised. VIP guests in the hotel may be particularly sensitive to invasion of privacy (eg if the hotel fails to protect them from press intrusion), but there may be other sensitive issues: front office staff should not question or divulge any personal details about guests unnecessarily.

- **Stress and fear**: eg from intimidating, abusive or disruptive behaviour by others, or perceived lack of security/safety and so on.

Security of property

Attention will have to be given to protecting:

- The **hotel building** (eg by fire prevention and protocols for handling bomb threats)

- The **fixtures and fittings** of the hotel, which may be subject to theft and/or wilful or accidental damage

- The **belongings of guests and staff**, which may be vulnerable to theft or damage

- **Cash and other financial assets** of the hotel, which may be vulnerable to various forms of theft and fraud

Security of data

Information is an item at risk of security breach. It can be damaged, lost or stolen in the same way that equipment and valuables can. People may seek to sabotage or steal information from organisations for:

- **Fraud or theft**: eg stealing guests credit card or identifying details, in order to perpetrate credit fraud; or stealing security access codes, computer passwords or banking/delivery schedules in order to plan thefts, espionage or robbery.

- **Commercial purposes**: eg stealing confidential reports or plans from the hotel for use by competing hotels (commercial espionage); or stealing guest data for sale to other hotels or marketing agencies

- **Pure nuisance value**: eg a disgruntled employee or computer hacker sabotaging the hotel's computer systems with a virus or inaccurate information.

3.2 General principles of security

Generally speaking, effective security is a combination of delay, checking and alarm.

Delay	*Lines of defence before vulnerable areas and items can be reached.*
	▪ Staffed reception area through which all entrants must pass
	▪ Areas clearly marked 'Staff Only'
	▪ Locked front door if reception is unattended at night
	▪ Lockable or staffed offices (eg where cash, data and valuables are kept)
	▪ Lockable filing cabinets, safes and deposit boxes
	▪ Password-protected computer records
	▪ Advising guests not to leave belongings unattended
Checking	*Procedures for authorised access to vulnerable areas or items*
	▪ Verifying guest identities at check-in and payment
	▪ Checking guest credit-worthiness or ability to pay
	▪ Challenging people who are in unauthorised areas or behaving suspiciously
	▪ Using passwords and key codes for access to computers, rooms
	▪ Checking authorisation for charged expenses etc
Alarm	*Procedures for alerting those responsible for responding to security breaches*
	▪ Electronic security alarms and front desk alarm call buttons
	▪ Protocols for front office to call security officers or police
	▪ Computer warnings of unauthorised data access attempts
	▪ Individual alertness and awareness of security issues

3.3 Who is responsible for security in a hotel?

The answer, really, is: **everyone**. All hotel staff, and guests and visitors, will need to take some responsibility for looking after the security of their own belongings, being vigilant about suspicious packages or behaviour, using security measures and procedures (such as locking room doors at night) and so on.

A large hotel might have dedicated **security staff**, or general responsibility for security may be allocated to the **premises manager** or duty manager. Front office staff need to know exactly whom to call in case of suspicious activity, a report of theft or violence, unauthorised access to data or areas of the hotel and so on.

The security role of front office staff

Front office has a key role in security because:

▪ It is the area through which most people enter the hotel, whether legitimately (as *bona fide* guests and visitors) or otherwise.

▪ It is the area through which most people *leave* the hotel, whether legitimately (eg having paid their bill) or otherwise.

▪ Front office staff are most likely to recognise legitimate guests and visitors by sight, and therefore to be able to identify suspicious people wandering round the hotel.

▪ Front office staff deal directly with guests and other visitors, and may therefore get a 'sense' of the potential for security problems (eg guests intending to skip out without paying; guests operating illegal activity (such as drug dealing or prostitution) in the hotel; potential thieves purporting to be visitors or contractors).

- Front office staff handle cash, credit cards and other payments, accounting records, equipment, room keys, guest valuables and guest and hotel data. They are therefore (a) responsible for their security, (b) vulnerable to robbery, (c) open to temptation to commit theft and fraud themselves and (d) able to contribute significantly to the improvement of general security in the hotel, through vigilance and the following of security procedures.

However, it is also important to recognise the *limits* of your responsibility for the security of the hotel! You will need to find out what your personal responsibilities are – and where they stop.

First of all, **follow the rules that affect your own behaviour** directly.

- If you see doors, windows, filing cabinets or cash boxes **left open** (or unlocked if they are supposed to be locked) when an area is unattended: close or lock them.

- If you have **keys** to a filing cabinet or safe, or the password to a computer, use them responsibly and keep them safe.

- Obey all the hotel's **security warnings, checks and procedures**: these may relate to handling cash and valuables; verifying guest identity; checking the validity of payments; challenging suspicious visitors; notifying security about unidentified luggage or packages and so on. We will discuss these issues further below.

Notify another appropriate person if you become aware of a security problem outside your authority or capability to deal with.

- The **premises manager or maintenance** **staff** may need to be notified of doors, windows or locks that need fixing.

- **Suspected security breaches** or packages, or evidence of theft, be reported to officers with the response measures. The front office anticipated types of incidents and the case: when to inform **internal security** station, and when to dial 999 (or hit the emergency **police assistance**.

  problems (eg suspicious visitors or vandalism or data exposure) should authority to initiate appropriate should maintain a **register** of all action to be followed in each **staff**, when to call the local police emergency alarm button) for

- If **other staff** do not appear to know or adhere to security procedures, you may need to draw their attention to them tactfully. If breaches continue, you may need to approach their supervisor.

Don't be a hero! If you find yourself in a dangerous situation, remember, your safety, and that of guests and other staff, comes before the protection of property!

3.4 General hotel security procedures

It is all too easy for front office staff to have a lapse in concentration: leaving a cash drawer open and turning away, for example, in the presence of an unknown member of the public. It is all too easy to get so used to doing things in a particular way that you stop asking questions: is the person asking for the key to room 102 *really* entitled to it?

E X A M P L E

Each hotel will have its own **security procedures** for a range of front office operations. Some basic ones may be as follows.

- Be vigilant to the *potential* for breaches of security.

- Handle all cash transactions (eg counting cash floats) out of sight of the guest and other unauthorised persons.

- Don't handle cash without some sort of receipt or authorisation to justify and prove the transaction: follow all internal procedures and policies in regard to handling cash.

- Don't accept guests' property for safe keeping, or return lost or deposited property claimed by guests, unless the transactions are properly recorded and countersigned by the guest: follow all internal procedures and policies in such matters.

- Keep your own belongings and valuables secure and out of sight.

- Store keys and room allocation data out of sight of the general public, to prevent thieves from claiming to be a room occupant, or knowing when guests are out of their rooms. Keep all keys, and especially master keys, under close supervision.

- Maintain the confidentiality of all security procedures, routines and controls (eg keys, pass codes) and issues: be aware that you may be overheard discussing such matters.

- Verify the identity of arriving guests prior to issuing keys, and take steps to ensure payment as far as possible (as discussed in Chapter 3).

- If visitors request access to guests, check that they are expected (or put them through to the guest's room by telephone): don't give out room numbers or instructions without checking with the guest.

- Don't allow visitors to enter restricted areas of the premises (unless escorted).

- Challenge suspicious persons in the hotel, especially in restricted areas, where safe to do so. The civil law on 'trespass' in the UK entitles a property owner to stop other people from coming onto his property without permission, or to require them to leave. While *bona fide* guests and visitors are entitled to be on the premises and use designated facilities, they do not have unlimited rights to enter all areas of the hotel, especially other guest rooms and areas marked 'Staff only'. This enables staff to challenge suspicious activity if necessary – although, as ever, this should be done tactfully, in case of genuine mistake ('May I help you? What room were you looking for?')

- Be alert to suspicious behaviour or circumstances: ladders placed next to windows, fire exits left open, unknown people sitting in reception (or in a parked car outside) for a long period of time and so on.

- Know the protocol for dealing with suspicious luggage or packages, which could represent a significant threat in these days of terrorist attacks (see below).

- Know the channels and protocols for notifying the duty manager, internal security staff, police or emergency services in the case of different types of security breach (or suspicions of security breach).

3.5 Suspicious packages or bags

Unfortunately, terrorist threats to public establishments is now a fact of life. In addition to telephoned or mailed **bomb threats** (which may or may not be a hoax, but will need to be handled as a serious risk), front office staff will need to be vigilant about: **unattended and/or 'out of place' items** left in public areas, which may contain some form of incendiary or explosive device; and **suspicious mail packages**.

If you become suspicious about an item, or one is reported to you, the first priority will be to ensure the safety of people.

- Do not attempt to touch, move or check the item – and advise others not to do so.

- Remain calm – and advise others to do so. Panic may be almost as dangerous as the item itself – or more, if your suspicions turn out to be groundless.

- Ask other staff whether the item is recognised and when it was first noticed: it may be possible to identify the owner before the incident escalates further.

- Report the matter to the duty manager or internal security staff immediately: there should be a clear protocol for such notifications. The responsible person should take the decision to call the police.

- If possible, move people away and block off the area, without causing alarm: a pretext (such as closure for maintenance or cleaning) may be used, if necessary.

- The duty manager, security officer or police (if involved) may decide to evacuate the area or building, in which case emergency evacuation procedures (explained earlier) will be applied.

EXAMPLE

'A Word from the FOM'

In our hotel, the duty manager does a 'Floor Walk' once per shift: checking all areas of the premises, to identify anything suspicious, any potential security risks, and any health and safety hazards that may not have been noticed or dealt with.

These days, being in an inner city area, we're particularly aware of parked cars: if a vehicle seems to be in one place too long, or looks abandoned, we will call the police to report a possible stolen vehicle. (One more reason why it's a good idea to get guests' car registration details...)

ACTIVITY 3   10 minutes

What security risk(s) can you identify in the following scenes?

(a) There is one person on the reception desk, and she is dealing with five impatient guests, plus two couriers trying to deliver packages to guests.

(b) It is very hot near the kitchen area, so the back door at the end of the corridor has been propped open to allow air to circulate.

(c) A visitor has been shown into the Front Office Manager's office and asked to wait. He is early for an appointment, and the FOM has not yet returned from lunch. Nobody else knew about the appointment. The visitor says he does not wish to be in the way, and shuts the office door.

4 Data and privacy protection

As we have seen, hotels can gather and retain a great deal of information about guests, some of it perhaps quite personal – and some of it potentially damaging to the guest (eg if they are placed on a circulated 'black list'). In addition, hotels are often places where people 'let their hair down' and get away from their everyday environments: they may be behave in ways, or be in places, or be with other people, that they would not necessarily want other people to know about. Hotels, therefore, have a responsibility to respect people's personal information and privacy.

4.1 The Data Protection Act

Especially with the advent of computerised record-keeping systems, fears have arisen with regard to: access to personal information by unauthorised parties; the likelihood that an individual could be harmed by the existence of data which was inaccurate, misleading or sensitive (eg credit or medical data); and the possibility that personal information could be used for purposes other than those for which it was requested and disclosed (eg sold to marketing agencies).

The **Data Protection Act 1998** addressed these concerns. The law is an attempt to protect individuals (not corporate bodies) in regard to the gathering, storage and use of personal data (information about a living individual, including both facts and expressions of opinion) which are processed in such a way as to enable individual records to be systematically accessed. As you can see, this would apply to hotels, which must register with the Information Commissioner as 'data controllers'.

Data controllers have to comply with eight principles, to ensure that all personal information is:

- Fairly and lawfully obtained and processed

- Processed and held only for one or more specified (registered) purposes

- Adequate, relevant and not excessive in relation to its specified purpose

- Accurate (correct and not misleading as to matters of fact) and up-to-date

- Not kept for longer than is necessary for its specified purpose

- Processed in line with the rights of the individual:

    - To be informed that his or her personal data is being held, and the purpose(s) for which it is being held

    - To have access to personal data on request

    - To have personal data corrected or erased, if they are inaccurate or contain expressions of opinion based on inaccurate information

    - To prevent the use of personal data for unsolicited direct marketing

- Secure from unauthorised access, alteration, disclosure or destruction

- Not transferred to countries outside the European Economic Area, except to countries where the rights of data subjects can be adequately protected.

EXAMPLE

The Information Commissioner's Office offers the following checklist to help hotels (and other data controllers) comply with the Data Protection Act. Being able to answer 'yes' to every question does not guarantee compliance, and you may need more advice in particular areas, but it should mean that you are heading in the right direction.

- Do we really need this information about an individual? Do we know what we're going to use it for?

- Do the people whose information we hold know that we've got it, and are they likely to understand what it will be used for?

- If we're asked to pass on personal information, would the people about whom we hold information expect us to do this?

- Are we satisfied the information is being held securely, whether it's on paper or on computer? Is our web site secure?

- Is access to personal information limited to those with a strict need to know?

- Are we sure the personal information is accurate and up-to-date?

- Do we delete or destroy personal information as soon as we have no more need for it?

- Are staff trained in their duties and responsibilities under the Data Protection Act, and are they putting them into practice?

If you want more information about the Data Protection Act, you can check out the web site of the Information Commissioner's Office (responsible for administering the Act), which has lots of helpful guidelines and tools.

Link: http://www.ico.gov.uk/what_we_cover/data_protection.aspx

Protecting guest information

In addition to the broader framework of the Data Protection Act, front office staff will need to observe internal data security procedures such as:

- Not leaving guest records or correspondence where they can be seen or accessed by unauthorised persons (eg prior to filing, or when being consulted).

- Not giving guest (or staff) details to unauthorised enquirers – including other staff members.

- Using passwords, where advised, to secure computers and data files.

- Not sharing computer passwords (or filing cabinet keys) with unauthorised people.

- Selecting communication methods to protect confidentiality: avoid posting information on notice boards, or discussing it in an open office area, if it should be regarded as private and confidential.

Photo: http://www.surrey.police.uk

Registration details must be produced on request by a police officer or Home Office representative, but records required for other purposes need only be provided after the production of a court order.

4.2 Protecting guest privacy

Privacy may be a major issue for some guests, including VIPs (who may have a particular stake in avoiding the attention of the press or general public) and guests who may be in places or with other people that they don't want others to know about (which, within reason, is entirely their business).

Front office staff should certainly *not* be responsible for '**tipping off'** press or members of the general public to the presence of a VIP guest in the hotel. Any **requests for information** about guests (even as simple as 'do you have a Mr X staying in the hotel?') should be handled with caution, and in no circumstances should room or telephone extension numbers, or details of the guest's whereabouts, be given out without the guest's prior and express permission.

Famous guests may be pestered by press and fans in public areas, and it is part of the hotel's hospitality to prevent this from happening as far as possible: eg by providing private check-in, security escort, private dining rooms and so on.

In general, **tact** will have to be exercised with all guests. Reception staff may suspect that 'Mr Smith' is not the real name of a registering guest: this may be generally accepted, but if there is any suspicion that a false name is being used with intent to defraud (eg using a stolen credit card), or that the person may be wanted by police under their real name, proof of identity may be requested. Reception staff may equally suspect that 'Mr and Mrs Smith' are not really married – but this is nobody's business but their own. Confidentiality is part of the hotel's duty of care.

Guests' **requests for privacy** – for example, putting a 'Do Not Disturb' notice on the door of their room, or requesting switchboard to hold all telephone calls – should be respected by hotel staff where possible.

5 Protection of guest belongings

According to the **Hotel Proprietors Act 1956**, a hotel proprietor may be liable for loss or damage to a guest's property while on the premises (not including cars or their contents). This liability can be limited to £50 in respect of any single article and £100 for any one guest – provided that a special notice has been displayed, warning guests of the limited liability and advising them to use the safe deposit provision for items of value. However, if the property was deposited (or offered for deposit) for **safe custody** by the hotel – or if the loss or damage was caused by negligence or actions of the hotel – then the hotel is fully liable.

What this means in practice is that:

- The hotel is directly responsible for the safekeeping of articles *offered* for **safe deposit** by guests: it is bound to accept them for safekeeping, or shoulder the risk of their loss or damage. Most hotels, therefore, have a safe or deposit box installed in the front or back office area, in addition to in-room safes for the independent use of guests.

- The hotel is directly responsible for the safekeeping of articles *deposited* by guests: proper procedures must be operated by trained and trustworthy staff, in order to maintain adequate security.

- The hotel needs to post the statutory notices, warning guests of their rights and the limited liability of the hotel, in each room.

5.1 Hotel safe

A small hotel may simply offer guests the facility to place their documents or valuables in the hotel safe, usually in the cashier's office. In such a case:

- The guest is generally given a **deposit envelope**, into which they seal their property and write their signature across the seal (so that any attempt at tampering will be evident).

- The cashier writes the guest's name and room number on the envelope, and issues the guest with a **receipt** for 'one sealed envelope' (the cashier doesn't need to make a detailed inventory of the contents). The receipt is signed by both the cashier and the guest.

- The receipt number is written on the envelope, and the envelope is deposited in the safe.

When the guest wants the property back:

- (S)he presents the receipt, and the cashier withdraws the relevant envelope from the safe.

- The guest **verifies** that the envelope has been returned with the seal intact, and **signs** the receipt book, allowing the cashier to verify the guest's signature – and leaving a record of the completed transaction.

The problem with this system is that it requires fresh envelopes and receipts every time a guest wants access to valuables (eg jewellery, which may be deposited after each wearing), but it does offer reasonable protection for both the guest and the hotel.

5.2 Safety-deposit boxes

Larger hotels may offer individual safety-deposit boxes (as in a bank), which are locked and unlocked only by using two keys, simultaneously. One key, specific to a particular box, is issued to the guest and the other is a master key held by the cashier.

A **safe deposit index card** is usually filled out with the guest's name, address and room number, and the number of the box. On issuing of the guest key, and each time the contents of the box are accessed, the date and time is logged, and the guest's signature is obtained (allowing it to be verified), with the countersignature of the cashier. Both parties are then present, as both keys are used to unlock the box.

When the guest finally takes the contents of the box back into his possession, he signs a receipt (often part of the safe deposit index card), acknowledging that the has received the contents of the box and released possession of the box and key.

5.3 Individual room safes

As an alternative to guests' giving the hotel custody of their valuables, guests may be provided with an in-room safe (often located in a cabinet or wardrobe, out of immediate sight).

Most modern guest safes are operated using a numerical touch pad and small display screen. The machine instructs the guest to close the safe door, and use the key pad to programme in his or her own access code: the safe door locks. The same access code must then be entered to unlock the safe. This means that a new code can be entered each time the safe is used: secure, easy and flexible.

Most systems have an emergency facility to open

Photo: http://www.horizon.bc.ca

the safe if a guest forgets the access code: hotel management may have access to a default code, or the safe manufacturer may have to be contacted for one. But, basically, it is the guest's responsibility to remember the code.

ACTIVITY 4   5 minutes

Draw up a table comparing the advantages and disadvantages of (a) a hotel safe or safe deposit box and (b) an in-room safe, as a way of protecting guests' valuables.

5.4   Lost property

Despite any or all of the above security measures, guests still lose valuables and other items of property: often leaving them behind in various areas of the hotel. It is usually the responsibility of security to store lost property and to liaise with front office to manage its return to the guest. There should be standard procedures for:

- **Holding** lost property items in a secure place. Articles found in guest rooms after their departure may be kept in a dedicated lost property area. Articles found in other areas in reception or the cashier's office may be held at reception (where guests are most likely to enquire about them) for 24 hours, before unclaimed articles are sent to the lost property area.

- **Reporting** lost/found property items to the supervisor.

- **Recording** details of the articles found (usually in a book or dedicated computer record): a complete description of the article; the time, date and place of its finding; and the name of the finder.

- **Returning** the property to the owner, if possible. If the article is left in a room, the hotel may be able to contact the last known guest. If someone enquires after an article, steps will have to be taken to verify that the person is in fact the owner: they should be able to describe the item fairly accurately before it is handed over, and they should sign a receipt for its return (a copy of which will be kept by the hotel).

Special procedures may be in place for:

- **Urgent, identifiable items** – such as guests' passports, drivers' licences, travel documents or wallets. In such cases, every effort should be made to contact the guest (eg if they have left a mobile number, or it is known which airport they are due to depart from).

- **Valuable articles**, for which special security arrangements may be required: eg held in safety deposit boxes, and subject to rigorous (through polite) verification before being handed to claimants.

- **Suspicious articles**, including unidentified bags, parcels or electronic devices. Because these pose a safety risk (as discussed earlier), they should not be touched or moved, and their presence should be notified to security or management.

6 Keys and key cards

6.1 Different types of keys

Traditional keys

Some hotels use traditional room keys, attached to some kind of 'tab' which:

- Identifies the hotel and the number of the room for guests, and

- Is large and heavy enough to act as a reminder to the guest to leave the key at reception when (s)he goes out – and, more especially, when (s)he leaves the hotel!

The trouble with traditional keys is that they are all too easy to lose – and if they fall into the wrong hands, it is obvious which door they belong to, giving thieves easy access. Meanwhile, getting the guest into the room involves spares and pass keys – and, ultimately, blocking use of the lost or stolen key involves changing the lock.

Photo: http://farm1.static.flickr.com

Key cards

The other problem with traditional keys is that a particularly confident thief could simply walk up to a busy reception in a large hotel and ask for the key to a room. In order to prevent this, some hotels issue 'key cards' to guests on check-in. These consist of a card or small booklet with the guest's name, room number and room rate or terms entered on it, together with pre-printed details of the hotel's services and facilities for the information of guests.

Guests are requested to show their key card at reception whenever they ask for their keys, to verify their right to take them. They may also be used as a general proof of identity in the hotel, or to indicate the guest's right to charge expenses incurred within the hotel (and partner establishments) to his or her account.

Electronic keys

The ultimate solution to the security (and convenience) issues of traditional keys, however, is the use of magnetic-strip electronic key cards, which look similar to credit cards. An electronic card acts as an entry key to the guest's room, by insertion in, or swiping through, a reading device attached to the door locking mechanism. It can also be used:

- To activate power in the guest's room, by insertion in a door-side device. This ensures that lights and air-conditioning are turned off when the guest leaves the room, saving the hotel the costs of utilities – and improving its carbon footprint and 'green' credentials!

- As a 'charge chard' for use within the hotel: authorising the charging of services to the guest's account (eg by verifying the guest's account status and terms) and/or posting charges directly to the guest's account by swiping through electronic point-of-sale devices in the restaurant, bar and so on.

In pure security terms, the electronic key has several advantages over traditional keys.

The room number is not written on the card, reducing the risk that it can be used for unauthorised entry to the guest's room. Instead, the key card is usually presented to the guest in a small cardboard sleeve, on which the receptionist writes the allocated room number (ie a traditional key card).

Cards are not specific to particular rooms: they are 'attached' to a particular room by insertion or swiping through an activation device – which programmes both the card and the room door with an access code. Cards are *de*-activated or 'cleared' on the guest's departure. This means that:

- Use of the card can be 'blocked' if it is lost, stolen or retained by a departed guest: the room /key code is simply changed, and the old code invalidated.

- Spare and replacement keys can be activated and allocated as required.

- Un-activated keys can be stored space-efficiently and in no particular order with minimal risk of theft (because they do not give access).

FOR DISCUSSION

What ways can you think of for an unauthorised person to gain access to a guest's room? (Be as creative as you like!) What would the hotel do to minimise the risk of this happening?

6.2 Storage and handling of keys

One of the benefits of electronic keys is that there is much less need for guests to hand their key into reception each time they leave the premises: there is much less security risk and hassle if the key is lost or stolen, and the electronic key fits neatly into a wallet.

With traditional keys, however, it is common for guests to be asked to leave their keys with reception when going out, and to pick them up from reception on return to the hotel. In a busy reception, this can amount to quite a lot of to-ing and fro-ing!

Traditional keys are often stored on room-numbered hooks in **key racks**, enabling reception staff to store and retrieve them easily on request. Electronic keys, being smaller, can be stored in room-numbered racks or index-tabbed filing boxes.

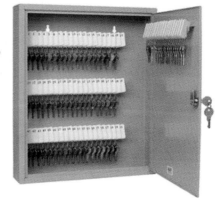

It is important for all traditional keys and activated key cards to be stored safely, and ideally out of sight of guests and general public:

- So that the means of entry to guest rooms are not vulnerable to theft

- So that people cannot see who is in or out of their rooms, since this also increases the risk of burglary in unattended rooms.

6.3 Loss of keys

The loss, theft or inadvertent 'taking away' of traditional keys is a problem for the hotel for several reasons, even if it has back-up or spare copies to allow the room to be re-let.

- There will be no remaining spare key in case of emergency.

- A replacement key will have to be made.

- More importantly, the situation poses a security risk, as the person with the key can enter the room at any time (exposing subsequent guests in that room to the risk of theft, attack or disturbance).

Some hotels put their postal address on key tabs, with the request that guests who find they have inadvertently walked out with a key post it back to the hotel. However, this does not remove the risk that a copy has been made. The lock should ideally be replaced, and the costs of doing this may be charged to guests who have lost keys (if it is considered that this can be done without loss of goodwill).

As we have seen, electronic keys are much less vulnerable to theft – and in any case, can be easily blocked and replaced: much less of an issue.

6.4 Master and sub-master keys

DEFINITION

Master keys are keys which open all the rooms in a hotel which are not subject to a special lock. **Sub-master keys** are keys which open all the rooms on a floor or block of the hotel.

The purpose of master keys is:

- To facilitate access to guest rooms by staff responsible for their upkeep (eg housekeeping and maintenance), in the absence of the guest – without their having to carry around a full set of single-room keys. Sub-masters are usually used for this purposes: signed out at the beginning of a shift and signed back in at the end, so that their whereabouts (and responsibility for their security) can be clearly identified.

- To allow emergency access to locked rooms and areas for which the key is not available. The key may have been lost or stolen, or someone may have locked themselves into the room (and been taken ill, say).

Master keys are usually strictly controlled, allocated to the duty manager and/or heads of department.

SUMMARY

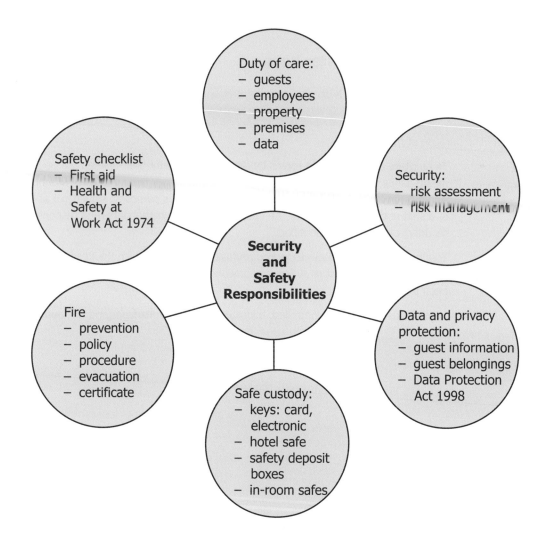

SELF-TEST QUESTIONS

1 What are the regulations covering the handling of chemicals called?

2 Under the Health and Safety at Work Act, employers have sole responsibility for health and safety. True or False?

3 All hotels in the UK are required to qualify for a Fire ....

4 Who is responsible for managing emergency evacuations from a hotel?

5 Give three reasons why someone might want to access information without authorisation.

6 A hotel is not entitled to require people to leave its premises. True or False?

7 What is the legislation protecting the rights of individuals to access information held about them?

8 To whom must guests' registration details be disclosed on request?

9 To what amount is a hotel's liability for loss or damage to guests' property generally limited, provided that statutory notice has been given?

10 What is a 'key card'?

SELF-TEST ANSWERS

1 Control of Substances Hazardous to Health (COSHH)

2 False

3 Certificate

4 The chief warden, safety/security office or fire officer

5 Fraud/theft, commercial purposes, or nuisance value.

6 False: it can eject 'trespassers'

7 Data Protection Act 1998

8 A police officer or Home Office representative

9 £50 in respect of any single article; or £100 for any one guest.

10 A card or booklet with the guest's name, room number and room rate on it, which guests must show at reception in order to collect a key.

ANSWERS TO ACTIVITIES

1 No answer is given to this activity, as it involves your own observation and reflection – but if you need help, some ideas are provided in the text following the activity.

2 No answer is given to this activity: we have already described the incident. You merely have to demonstrate your skill in selecting and summarising the information on the form.

3 (a) The receptionist's attention is overloaded. It would be easy, in the general to-and-fro, for an unauthorised person to get past him or her, and into the guest areas of the hotel. It might also be a temptation to let the couriers deliver direct to the guest rooms – which may also be a risk. The receptionist should be able to call on a 'back-up' person to help in busy periods.

(b) It is surprisingly quick work to slip through an open door, gather a bag or armful of valuable items, and slip out again. In this case, there is an added risk since the door may be out of the way of 'normal' traffic. A further risk exists of the door being forgotten over night, if it is not usually left unlocked. The only way to minimise this risk is *not* to open the back door, or to allow it to be opened on a security chain or with a security gate or grille.

(c) The risk is that the visitor is not *bona fide* – nobody has checked – and has been left alone and unobserved in the office, where he has unchallenged access to anything left lying about. Ways of minimising such a risk include: vetting visitors at reception; requiring visitors to wait at reception until the manager is available; requiring people who are expecting visitors to warn others in the office; and having someone escort and stay with a visitor at all times, tactfully. As a last resort, the receptionist should ensure that the door to the FOM's office is kept open, and the visitor is visible to staff at all times.

4

	Advantages	Disadvantages
Hotel safe/ Deposit box	▪ Limits hotel liability for loss of guest valuables ▪ Protects guest valuables from theft ▪ Protects hotel from accusation of theft/loss of valuables	▪ Inconvenience of multiple withdrawals ▪ Space constraints ▪ Lack of flexibility/control for guest ▪ Extra work for cashier
In-room safes	▪ As for hotel safe/deposit box, plus ▪ Flexible, frequent, easy access to valuable for guest, without going to reception ▪ Guest retains control of valuables and privacy of contents ▪ Less work for hotel staff	▪ Slightly less secure (eg if access code known or guessable) ▪ Safe is left unattended (and could theoretically be tampered with) ▪ Guest may forget access code.

CHAPTER 8

GUEST SERVICES AND COMMUNICATIONS

Chapter objectives

In this chapter you will learn

- Communication systems used in and by hotels
- How to manage a hotel switchboard and take guest messages
- How to handle incoming and out-going mail for guests
- What facilities are required to attract business guests
- Facilities offered in a guest business centre
- How to offer communication assistance for foreign guests
- How to respond to guest information requests

Topic list

Hotel communication systems
Telephone services
Mail services
Business services
Information services

1 Hotel communication systems

In this chapter, we will look at a range of 'miscellaneous' services offered to guests, which generally come under the heading of communications: handling mail and telephone calls for guests; giving information to guests; providing access to business communication services (such as Internet and e-mail facilities); and so on.

In a large hotel, these services may be provided by a separate front-of-house switchboard, concierge, enquiries or mail-and-information desk, and perhaps a hotel 'business centre'. In a small hotel, they may come under the heading of 'miscellaneous guest services' provided by reception staff.

1.1 Communication in hotels

Communication is one of the key tasks of Front Office staff – and one of the key skill sets that you will need to develop, in order to work successfully in the field.

FOR DISCUSSION

Brainstorm a list of all the different scenarios in which a member of Front Office staff may have to communicate with other people. (Think about communication with management, team members, other departments – and, of course, guests.) What methods of communication (face-to-face, telephone, written or electronic) might be most appropriate for these messages or exchanges of information, and why?

We have already considered a wide range of written and verbal (person-to-person or telephone) messages that need to 'flow' between Front Office and management; Front Office and other departments; and between Front Office and guests.

What we *haven't* yet considered is the flow of communication between guests and other guests, and between guests and the 'outside world' beyond the hotel. Access to such communication facilities is part of the service offered by the hotel, and for some customers (such as business travellers) it may be an important and valuable one.

We will start by briefly surveying some of the main communication systems used by hotels.

1.2 Telephone systems

The telephone is now the most common system for most immediate communication applications, both within the hotel and with the outside world. The telephone is fast, interactive (allowing for convenient

exchange of information and question-and-answer) and personal. It allows direct person-to-person contact and the use of social skills (which makes it particularly good for customer service, selling and the handling of awkward situations like complaints or giving bad news). At the same time, it allows *remote* communication – whether from office to office or room to room, or across the world!

A wide range of telephone equipment, and related services and facilities, is now available to cater for different sized establishments, with communication needs of varying complexity. Because of the need to control calls, a hotel would typically operate on a **switchboard** system, either routing *all* calls through a central operator, or handling *incoming external calls* only, in which case individual extensions will be able to dial each other and connect to outside lines.

The most common system nowadays is a private automatic branch exchange **(PABX) system**. This allows direct dialling between internal extensions (ie from department to department and room to room); direct dialling out from extensions; and access to the switchboard operator or telephonist if required. A large **PABX system** would have a centralised switchboard with one or more operators. Nowadays, however, the system can also be **computerised**, or linked into the Hotel Management System, for automatic facilities such as: taking voice mail messages; programming in automated early morning alarm calls; logging of guest telephone calls and call charges; and so on.

Source: http://img.alibaba.com/photo

Figure 8.1: PABX system

In addition, a range of other telecommunications facilities may be used in a hotel, such as:

- **Mobile telecommunications**: cordless phones, **mobile telephones**, 'walky-talkies' and pagers, so that staff members can keep in contact with each other while 'on the move' or contact 'mobile' staff (such as housekeepers, porters and drivers). Guests' in-room phones may also be cordless, so that they can move around the room while making or taking a call.

- **Answering and messaging services**: answer machines, voice mail, SMS messaging and mobile e-mail, for example, may be used to take enquiries, pass on messages for guests, or send quick requests and reminders to mobile staff.

- **Telephone conferencing**: from basic 'speaker phones' to multiple-party calls, allowing virtual telephone 'meetings' between different departments or offices, when required.

The whole telecommunications network of a large hotel might therefore look more like the following: Figure 8.2. (PSTN and ISDN refer to the type of digital telecommunications network used by the system.)

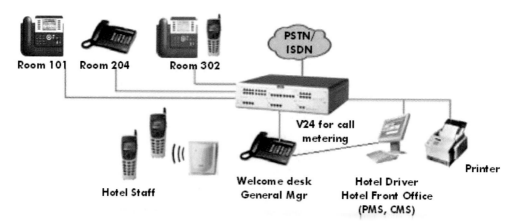

Figure 8.2: Hotel telecommunications system

1.3 Facsimile transfer (fax)

DEFINITION

Facsimile transfer (fax) is a system which uses telecommunications links to transmit hard-copy documents from one fax machine (or computer) to another.

A fax machine is like a cross between a scanner and a telephone. You feed documents into the machine, which scans them, transmits the data down the telecommunications link, and reproduces them on a similar machine at the other end. Faxes can also be sent from computer terminals.

Fax is very useful in business settings, because it enables you to send hard-copy written or printed documents more or less instantly to remote locations – where before you might have had to send them by mail. This can be used to send urgent booking forms, confirmation letters, maps and other information to guests, for example. Similarly, prospective guests and agencies will often use fax to send booking confirmations and rooming lists to a hotel swiftly.

We can't go into detail about how to use fax machines here: you will need to become familiar with whatever equipment is used in your own workplace – and its instructions! Basically, you prepare the documents (with a fax cover/header sheet); dial the recipient's fax number on the 'phone' part of the machine, wait for a connection, and then feed the pages into the machine (which should mark them in some way, or otherwise notify the user that the page has 'gone through'). The machine will generally then print out a report showing date/time, duration of call and number of pages successfully sent (or an error report).

Perhaps the most important point to note is the use of a **fax cover/header sheet**, as a kind of 'covering letter' for whatever is being sent. This should contain: the hotel's letter head; the name and fax number of the person to whom the fax is being sent; the name and contact details of the person sending the fax; a note of the number of pages being faxed (so that the recipient can check that they have all arrived); and an appropriate message (personal greetings, explanation of the attached documents, or the content of the main message, eg a booking confirmation).

1.4 Internet and e-mail

DEFINITION

The **Internet** is a worldwide computer network, using telecommunications links to connect individual computer terminals, and giving access to websites, e-mail and other communication tools.

E-mail (electronic mail) is the term for sending data, messages and documents electronically from computer to computer.

Many hotels will create a 'virtual' communications hub on the Internet by having their own **website**. The site may be used simply to advertise the hotel – although this can be done in very creative ways, eg by allowing 'virtual tours' of the hotel. It may also allow prospective guests and enquirers to download brochures and forms; to send e-mails to the hotel; and perhaps also to access the Hotel Reservations System, to check room availability and make reservations.

ACTIVITY 1   20 – 30 minutes

If you have access to the Internet, check out some interesting hotel web sites. Consider the role of each web site you look at (a) in selling the hotel, and (b) in providing a 'hub' for communication. Consider how effective each site is: how interesting, interactive, up-to-date and helpful is it for prospective guests?

You might either use a search engine (such as Google) to find hotels you know about or are interested in, otherwise you might like to check out the following sites.

- http://www.londonbridgehotel.com (Do click on the 'virtual tours' link, and see what you think of this feature)

- http://www.napilikai.com

- http://www.marriott.com

E-mail has replaced letters, memos, faxes and even telephone calls as the swiftest, cheapest, most flexible and convenient method of communication both within hotels and between hotels and the outside world – at least in countries where the Internet is available. E-mail messages are typed into the sender's computer, using special software programmes, and are then sent to the recipient's 'e-mail address' where they await collection in a electronic mail box or 'in box':

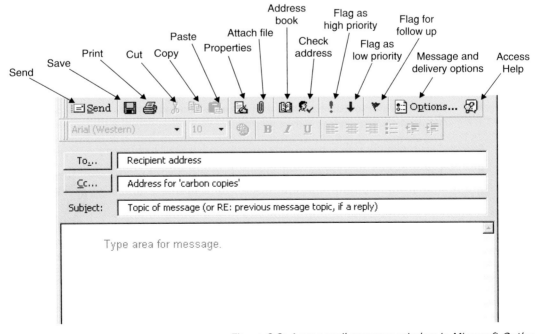

Figure 8.3: A new mail message window in Microsoft Outlook

LEARNING MEDIA

E-mail offers many advantages for internal and external communication.

- Messages can be sent and received very fast, worldwide, and regardless of time zones and office hours (since the systems works 24/7, and messages await collection at the recipient's convenience).

- E-mail is highly economical (estimated 20 times cheaper than fax); often allowing worldwide transmission for the cost of a local telephone call (connecting to the local service point of the Internet Service Provider).

- The recipient can print out a hard copy of the message (and/or documents 'attached' to the message), and the sender has documentary evidence of having sent the message (and, where requested, of the recipient having received it), in case of subsequent queries or disputes.

- E-mail message management software (such as Outlook Express) has convenient features such as: message copying (to multiple recipients); integration with an 'address book' (database of contacts); stationery (allowing the hotel's letterhead to be used); facilities for mail organisation and filing etc.

Again, we can't really teach you how to use e-mail here: you will need to become familiar with the software used in your workplace. Most organisations also have **guidelines** for the use of e-mail, to ensure that the system is not abused, and that all messages uphold the reputation of the organisation.

1.5 Paper-based written communication

Hotels will also, as we have seen in previous chapters, use a variety of more 'old fashioned' paper-based communications, sent via the internal mail delivery system (eg forms, reports and messages) or via the external postal system (eg brochures, confirmation letters, reservation forms, vouchers, copies of accounts, feedback forms and other documentation exchanged with guests).

In order to be effective in a Front Office role, you will need to become familiar with – and proficient and professional in the use of – a range of written formats. Each hotel will have its own standard forms, documents and 'house style' of communication.

1.6 Face-to-face communication

In addition, hotels will use a variety of 'face-to-face' communication mechanisms, such as:

- **Meetings** (eg staff meetings, shift handover meetings, management meetings)
- **Interviews** (eg staff selection, appraisal or disciplinary interviews)
- **Presentations** (eg for staff training or for selling the hotel to travel agencies or corporate clients)
- **Person-to-person discussions and information exchanges** of all kinds – especially Front Office service interactions with guests!

Face-to-face communication is particularly effective in hospitality situations.

- It allows **non-verbal cues**, both audible (eg tone of voice) and visual (body language) to be used to enhance understanding, communication and persuasion.

- It allows for **immediate interaction**: on-the-spot exchange of questions and answers, for example.

- It **humanises** communication, allowing personal rapport to be established and social skills to be used: this is particularly helpful for managing sensitive or awkward situations – but it is also a key ingredient in providing hospitality and personal service to guests.

1.7 Communication services for guests

A hotel's guests may be far from family, friends and business networks, and they will often want to maintain these connections while they travel. In addition, they may need access to communication facilities in order to organise travel and entertainment, arrange to meet people, use the Internet and so on. Communication services are thus an important part of a hotel's total 'package of benefits' for guests.

We will now look at some of the main communication services provided through Front Office:

- Guest telephone services
- Guest mail services
- Business services
- Information services

2 Telephone services

One of the most important duties of Front Office is to answer the phone on behalf of the hotel, and either deal with the enquiries or issues raised by the caller (eg give information or take a reservation); or transfer the call to the person or extension requested (whether a staff member or a guest); or transfer the call to the most appropriate person or department to help the caller; or take messages if required.

In a larger hotel, there will usually be a separate **switchboard operator** or **telephonist** to perform all these tasks. In smaller hotels, the receptionist may answer the phone alongside her other duties – and particular care will have to be taken to avoid *sounding* irritated or confused by the interruption! As with guests calling in person at the front desk, every telephone caller will expect to be greeted courteously and professionally, and given the telephonist's full and undivided attention for the duration of the call.

A C T I V I T Y   2   **5   m i n u t e s**

Why is the role of telephonist so important for a hotel?

_____

2.1 Managing the switchboard

Staff should be trained in handling incoming and outgoing calls using the hotel's switchboard system. However, there are certain basic requirements and techniques that should be observed.

- **Every incoming telephone call** should be answered promptly and with an appropriate greeting: 'Good morning. The Hill Town Hotel. You're speaking to Joe: how can I help you?'

- The switchboard operator should have immediate access to a **directory** of in-house extensions, to transfer calls to other departments or individuals; a **guest index** (an alphabetical list of guests, by name, showing their room numbers, extensions and dates of stay), in order to put calls through to guest rooms; and **arrivals and departure lists,** in order to deal with calls for guests who have not yet arrived or already checked out.

- The switchboard operator should be **familiar with the procedures** for dealing with different types of calls: to whom different types of enquiries should be transferred; what information about guests can be given out to callers (if any); how to deal with common switchboard problems (eg disconnected calls, unobtainable numbers, engaged numbers); how to provide particular switchboard services (eg directory enquiries or reverse-charges or 'collect' calls); and how to take messages or connect callers to voice mail facilities.

- Callers should not be **left on hold** indefinitely, if the extension to which a call has been put through is not being answered, or if the switchboard operator puts a caller on hold while making enquiries or handling other calls. The operator should return regularly to an on-hold caller, keeping him informed of progress ('I'm sorry, there's no answer on that extension', or 'I'm sorry to keep you waiting, I'm just looking up the records now: can you hold for another moment?') and offering options where possible ('Would you like to leave a message?', or 'Can I get Ms X to call you back when she becomes available?').

- When **transferring a call** to another department, the switchboard operator should ascertain the caller's name and purpose for calling, and pass this on to the target recipient, so that callers don't have to repeat themselves.

2.2 Incoming calls for guests

In the past, before mobile phones, the only way guests could be contacted by phone was for them to give out the telephone number of the hotel, and have calls put through by the hotel switchboard to a telephone in their room, or courtesy phones in the public areas of the hotel. These days, people are much more likely to receive calls on their **personal mobile phones** – but the hotel will still need to plan for incoming guest calls, where people do not have mobiles, or where they do not get mobile coverage, or where they have chosen not to travel with their phone.

The first requirement for putting incoming calls through to guests is for switchboard to be able to locate the guests' room numbers swiftly and efficiently. In a manual system, this requires a printed **guest index**. In a computerised system, the operator can simply type in the guest's name, and the room number will come up on screen.

If a guest does not answer the incoming call, (s)he may be out of the hotel, or elsewhere in the hotel, or simply not taking calls. In such a case, the switchboard operator should inform the caller that the guest does not appear to be in their room, and may offer a number of options.

- If the call is urgent, it may be possible to try and **locate the guest and inform him of the call**, by 'paging'. A member of uniformed staff may be sent round the public areas of the hotel calling 'Paging Mr X', or the hotel might have a public address system for this purpose – or a message could be sent through to the restaurant or bar, asking them to enquire after the guest in their areas. Some hotels offer personal 'pagers' (messaging devices) to guests who are expecting an important call, or the guest may simply keep reception informed of his whereabouts, so that he can be notified when the call comes in.

- The caller may be offered the option of **leaving a message** for the guest, either in person with the switchboard operator (who writes down the message to be passed on to the guest), or via a recorded 'voice mail' option on the telephone system.

2.3 Taking guest messages

There may be a variety of options for taking messages for guests.

- In a manual system, the telephonist may take a **hand-written message**, perhaps on a pre-printed telephone message pad. The message should clearly state: the date and time of the call; the name and room number of the recipient; the name and telephone number of the caller; and the substance of the message (if any). Message pads often include a range of 'tick boxes' with common message options such as 'Called', or 'Returned your call' or 'Please call back': Figure 8.4. The message should be placed in the guest's key pigeon hole, or held at Front Office. The telephone system of the hotel may also allow a 'message waiting' alert to be left on the guest's in-room telephone (eg a flashing light or message).

- The telephone system of the hotel may offer individual **voice-mail**, which allows callers to leave recorded messages. A 'message waiting' alert is shown on the in-room phone, and the guest can dial in his or her extension (or a pre-allocated access code) to retrieve the message.

- In a **computerised system**, the switchboard operator may type messages into the 'Message' area of the system, for subsequent printing out or transmission to the guest: Figure 8.5.

Attention: _____

From: _____

Of: _____

TELEPHONED	PLEASE PHONE
CALLED TO SEE YOU	WILL CALL AGAIN
WANTS TO SEE YOU	URGENT

Phone No: _____ Date: _____

Message: _____

_____

_____

_____

_____

_____

Taken by: _____

Figure 8.4: Standard telephone message page

ACTIVITY 3   **5 minutes**

You are on switchboard one afternoon, and have the following conversation with a caller.

You: Good afternoon, Hill Town Hotel. [Your Name] speaking. How can I help you?

Caller: Yes, hello, I'd like to speak to E J Jones, please. I believe he's staying at your hotel.

You: Mr E J Jones? Just a moment, please, while I check for you... I'm afraid Mr Jones has not yet checked into the hotel, Sir. Can I take a message for you, or - ?

Caller: Oh. Just tell him John N'tabele called, and I'm in town this evening and would like to meet up with him at about 8 pm if possible – but I'll call him again at about 6 pm.

You: Just a moment, Sir. Can you spell your name for me?

Caller: Oh, yes. It's N-apostrophe-T-A-B-E-L-E. N'tabele, from MinCorp. I'm on my mobile: xxxx-yyy-zzz.

You: Thank you.... I'll just read the message back to you, Mr N'Tabele, if I may? You would like to meet up with Mr Jones at about 8 pm, but will call him again at about 6 pm. You are from MinCorp and your contact number is xxxx-yyy-zzz. Is that correct?

Caller: That's right. Thank you.

You: Thank you, Mr N'Tabele. Goodbye.

Write the message you will leave at reception for Mr Jones on the message pad as shown in Figure 8.4.

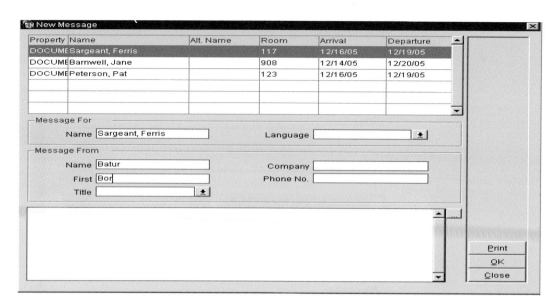

Figure 8.5: Computerised message screen (in Fidelio)

Whether manual or computerised, the system should also include some kind of **message log**, enabling Front Office staff to monitor the status of messages: that is, whether they have been successfully passed on or not. This will be particularly helpful when one shift hands over to another, to avoid messages being 'forgotten'. An example of a computerised message log is as Figure 8.6.

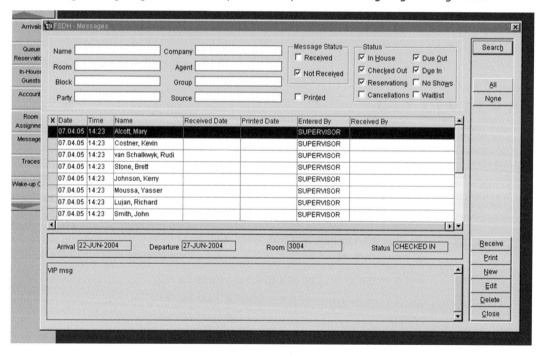

Figure 8.6: Message log screen (in Fidelio)

2.4 Outgoing calls by guests

Outgoing calls are somewhat different to incoming calls. In the past, outgoing calls had to be 'placed' on the guest's behalf by a switchboard operator, nearly all hotels will now have PABX systems which allow guests to dial out directly from their in-room telephone extensions, for room-to-room, outside line and even international calls. Thus the telephonist may not be involved at all, in the way that (s)he often is for incoming calls.

While incoming calls are generally 'free' to the guest (paid for by the caller), outgoing calls cost the hotel money. The costs of calls must be recovered by charging guests, and – since the ability to make calls is a service provided by the hotel – the hotel will often take a profit margin (or 'mark-up') on the call charge. This can be a significant source of extra revenue, but it does raise several issues.

- The **cost of calls** from hotel phones is often a cause of surprise and resentment to guests: the basis on which calls are charged should be clearly stated, as part of in-room information (and ideally, together with instructions for making outgoing calls).

- Guests may need **information and assistance** about how to obtain outside lines from the hotel system; information on area and international dialling codes; and so on. Instructions are often provided in in-room information packages, but even so, some guests may ask switchboard for assistance.

- There needs to be a system for **logging calls** (time/date, duration of call, number dialled), so that appropriate charges can be made, verified by the guest, and proved in case of billing queries. Most PABX systems now include facilities for call logging, and a **Hotel Management System** may include facilities for call logging and automatic posting of telephone charges to guest bills.

- If guests have limited credit facilities within the hotel, there needs to be some system for **barring extensions** from making calls, or expensive types of call (eg national or international calls). This can be done automatically in a PABX or computerised system.

Outgoing call services are now much less a part of switchboard's workload, since many travellers are equipped with personal **mobile phones**, the call charges from which may be considerably cheaper than hotel call rates. Mobile phones are also more confidential, since the numbers dialled from the hotel system are generally logged.

E X A M P L E

A range of other guest services may be provided via the telephone system, depending on the technology and procedures used by the hotel.

Early morning calls and **appointment reminders** may be offered by the switchboard operator. The operator would keep a log of requested alarm/reminder calls may be kept, and telephone the guest's room at the requested time. ('Good morning, this is your early morning call.') Alternatively, this may be done by the telephone system itself, with a recorded or digital voice message transmitted to the guest's phone at a pre-programmed time. Even in hotels with computerised systems, however, reception may choose to make the calls personally, as a mark of personal service.

Message-waiting alerts may similarly be made personally, working through the message log ('Mr X? You have a message waiting for you at reception.'), or by the telephone system.

Direct dialling to room service, restaurant, housekeeping, laundry and other departments, to access services without going through reception.

In addition, **Front Office staff** may need to call out from the hotel for a range of purposes: to return calls by enquirers or travel agencies after gathering information; to re-confirm bookings or notify guests of changes (eg the need to re-locate a guest because of over-booking); to make calls on behalf of guests (eg to call a taxi or doctor, or to make travel, entertainment or restaurant bookings). Basic telephone technique will apply to these calls.

- Make them as efficient as possible (because they cost the hotel money). Have all necessary information to hand before you dial!

- Record the call: what information has been given, what has been agreed or promised etc. This is especially important for bookings, negotiated rates, notified changes and so on, which may be queried or disputed later.

- If you promise to call someone back with information or a decision: do so within the promised time; or take steps to ensure that someone else will do so (eg by leaving a note on the shift hand-over log).

A C T I V I T Y   4   **5   m i n u t e s**

Telephone technique is very important in making a good impression, and handling a call efficiently.

What phrases might you use instead of the following (inappropriate) words and phrases, when dealing with a telephone caller?

- 'OK'
- 'Hang on a sec'
- 'I'm sorry: (s)he's out'
- 'Mr who?'
- 'What did you say?'

3   Mail services

In the past, mail handling was one of the Front Office's most important and time-consuming responsibilities, as written communication sent by post was the main form of communication to the hotel and to hotel guests.

In recent decades, however, **telephone and e-mail** communication has taken the place of much written communication. Meanwhile, transport schedules and travel patterns mean that guests tend to stay a **shorter time** in any one place, meaning that they tend not to arrange for postal mail to be sent to them at a hotel: e-mail is much more convenient, as it can be picked up from an electronic 'mail box' from any computer terminal at any time.

Even so, guests may arrange for mail or courier deliveries to be **sent to them at a hotel** – and the fact that there may be a narrow window of opportunity for it to reach them means that all such mail must be handled efficiently and promptly.

Photo: www.rcofficeconcepts.com

Guests may also ask Front Office staff to **arrange for out-going mail**, and receptionists will need to be familiar with the requirements, speed, security and cost of different types of service available: ordinary post; special delivery; registered post; recorded delivery; courier services etc.

A large hotel will potentially have a high volume of incoming and outgoing mail to be sorted and processed. In such a case, there will probably be a dedicated back-office **mail room**, where all the various operations can be handled discreetly and efficiently.

3.1 Handling incoming mail and messages

Incoming mail will be sorted and divided into three basic categories: **hotel mail** (which needs to be distributed to the relevant departments or individuals direct from the mail desk or mail room); **staff mail** (which may distributed via departments or staffroom mail racks); and **guest mail** (which needs to be processed for distribution to guests).

All incoming mail should be **date/time stamped** on arrival and sorting, so that there is no possibility of dispute about when mail arrived (eg in the case of a reservation or cancellation notice), or how long it took the hotel to pass mail on to a guest, in case of problems resulting from any delay.

The next step is to **distribute** mail and messages to the target recipient. Let's focus on guest mail.

If the guest is listed in the guest index as 'currently resident', mail or messages may be:

- **Delivered** directly to the guest's room (eg if the hotel has pages available for this purpose) – especially if the item is marked urgent, or cannot be received by a third party (ie it requires the recipient's signature and proof of identity before it is handed over).

- Placed in key pigeon-holes or mail racks. In an old-fashioned system, there may be a rack of **'pigeon holes'** at reception to hold both mail/messages and keys for each room. Whenever the receptionist takes charge of a guest's keys, or hands them out, there is the opportunity to check for mail and messages and give them to the guest.

- Held at Front Office (eg if the item is too large to fit in a key/mail rack). A note (or special **'mail advice** slip') may placed in the key rack to alert the receptionist to the fact that the item is awaiting collection. The receptionist may telephone (or leave a 'message alert' on the phone), to notify the guest that there is a message or mail awaiting collection.

If mail arrives for guests whose names are **not on the current guest index**, the mail handler will check the arrivals list and/or the reservation records.

- If the guest is **expected**, but has not yet arrived, the mail can be held at Front Office, with a 'mail advice' slip or message added to the guest's reservation file, to alert front desk that mail is awaiting the guest when (s)he checks in.

- If the guest has **already left** the hotel, mail can be forwarded to the guest's address (as found on the registration card). If a departing guest expects mail, (s)he may be asked to fill out a 'mail forwarding' form, with a forwarding address, a request to forward mail for a specified period, and perhaps an authorisation for the hotel to charge any costs incurred. A log should be kept of all mail forwarded to guests, in case of subsequent queries and disputes.

Secured mail

Secured mail (such as **registered mail** or **courier deliveries**) may be urgent or contain valuable items or documents: it will generally require a signature upon receipt, and in some circumstances may only be signed for by the target recipient, on proof of identity. If a Front Office staff member signs for a piece of mail, its safe delivery becomes the responsibility of the hotel, so:

- Only trustworthy staff members should be authorised to sign for, and take custody of, such deliveries.

- The hotel should keep a log of secure mail received, including the registration number, date/time received, addressee, date collected and guest signature (to confirm receipt).

- Secure mail should be regarded as valuable and placed in the hotel safe or a locked drawer.

- A mail advice message should be immediately left or sent to the guest.

- Guests should be asked to sign for the item on collection, showing proof of identity.

Photo: http://www.bicyclecouriers.com

If secured mail arrives for a departed guest, the hotel should attempt to contact the guest by telephone or e-mail and ask for forwarding instructions.

ACTIVITY 5   5 – 2 0   m i n u t e s

Find out what the size requirements, delivery times, guarantees, postal charges and procedures are for various types of secured and unsecured mail in the country where you work.

3.2 Handling outgoing mail

Front desk may have the responsibility of collecting all mail being sent out from the various departments of the hotel, arranging for delivery to the post office, and recording postage charges. This may involve:

- Mail sorting

- Weighing (since postage is calculated by weight)

- Affixing stamps or using a **'franking' machine** [illustrated] to stamp envelopes as 'postage paid' (by prior arrangement with the post office)

- Delivering mail to the post office (or arranging for its collection)

- Recording the quantity and cost of mail sent out

As with all other such procedures, each hotel will have a standard way of doing things, and staff will need to 'learn the ropes' and follow the protocols laid down.

Source: www.neopost.ie

FOR DISCUSSION

'Mail handling is so routine: why spend so much time talking about it?'

What are the arguments for taking mail handling seriously, as part of the responsibilities of Front Office?

4 Business services

As we have noted elsewhere in this Study Guide, many hotels get a high proportion of their occupancy and revenue from **corporate or business travellers** – or would like to do so!

Business travellers have particular needs when it comes to communication: being away from the facilities of their offices, they need to stay connected. They may need to access data from their offices, or send data back, update records or make reports. They may need to keep in touch with colleagues, staff members or clients. They may need to prepare and print reports; make or change arrangements for meetings; or have professional-looking spaces to hold meetings in. And so on.

Hotels can, therefore, attract and retain corporate clients and business customers by the range and quality of communication and 'office' services they offer.

4.1 The executive floor or executive lounge

A hotel with a high proportion of corporate/business customers may offer a dedicated floor, block or area of the hotel specifically to suit their needs.

- The executive floor may include **accommodation** specially customised for business travellers, with extra space for work (eg desk areas), in-room internet access (for guests using their own laptop computers) and extra power points (for equipment).

- **Executive-grade rooms** may also offer extra amenities for personal grooming (eg clothes pressing, hair dryers, extra coat hangers), and perhaps also after-work relaxation and 'pampering' (eg in-room movies, bathrobe and slippers, up-graded toiletries).

- **Client entertainment** and **business networking** areas may be provided (eg in an executive lounge), for the exclusive use of guests of the executive floor. A lounge may offer clusters of chairs, all-day refreshments (eg tea and coffee) and snacks. The refreshments area may also offer continental breakfast for executive-floor guests in the morning, and evening bar service.

- Executive facilities may also offer **special services** such as private check-in and check-out (at a separate reception desk or in the executive lounge) and dedicated concierge service, to facilitate service for corporate travellers.

- The executive floor may also house the hotel's **business centre**, with conference and meeting rooms, office equipment (phones, fax machine, photocopier, internet-linked computer terminals) and even secretarial services, where required.

E X A M P L E

The following is drawn from the web site of the Hilton Hotel, Sofia – as an idea of business facilities – and how they are marketed!

A unique combination of facilities and services for the discerning business traveller

Why do more business people return to Hilton hotels than to any other hotel group? One of the reasons is because we offer you the Executive Floor Experience. It means that wherever you travel, you are always guaranteed a special welcome.

*On our **Executive Floors**, your room and bathroom have extra facilities, with plenty of space to work and relax. You will notice the difference from the moment you take advantage of the exclusive check-in/check-out, speeding you past any queues at reception.*

*And then there is the **Executive Lounge** where you can enjoy complimentary breakfast, plus all-day snacks and beverages. Just ask the Executive Lounge Manager if there is anything else you need. It adds up to an atmosphere that is designed to help make your business trip as productive and stress-free as possible. You will see how we have taken care of every detail, leaving you free to concentrate on your business.*

*That is why our **Executive Floor benefits** typically feature:*

- *Complimentary round trip airport transfer by shuttle bus*

- *Complimentary premium mineral water*

- *Private check-in & check-out, early arrival and late departure*

- *Complimentary Executive Lounge access with breakfast in the morning, snacks, drinks, cocktails and hors d'oeuvres throughout the day*

- *Daily complimentary newspaper delivered to your room*

- *In-room fax for Park Executive Suites and private fax service from Executive Floor Reception*

- *Modem connections and additional power points giving you direct e-mail and internet access*

- *Handy extension leads and a complete range of adaptors so you can stay connected at all times*

- *International and satellite TV channels*

- *Tea and coffee making facilities*

- *Dedicated reading/work lamp*

*In the **Executive Lounge**: space to feel comfortable and relax, space to eat and meet, refreshment bar in the afternoon, full range of concierge services, business services (faxing, PC with internet access), CD music system, TV in sitting area, newspapers and magazines, reference library, selection of books and games; stationery pack.*

Link: http://www.hilton.bg/id-51/hilton-sofia-executive-floor.html

4.2 The guest business centre

Whether or not such extensive facilities are made available, on an exclusive basis, to designated executive travellers, the hotel may offer business centre facilities which are accessible to all guests on request.

Photo: www.deluxehotel.com.au   *Photo:* http://static.roomex.com

A hotel business centre might offer services and facilities including:

- Desks or workstations

- Photocopying services or self-service photocopiers

- Incoming and out-going fax services or self-service fax machines

- Binders, laminators and other document preparation services/equipment

- Hire of a data projector (for presentations)

- Access to computer terminals with fast Internet access and peripherals such as scanners and printers

- Courier booking service (for sending urgent and valuable documents and parcels)

- Business stationery

- Meeting rooms and meeting areas

- Secretarial support services (eg dictation, typing, document preparation, copying and so on).

Equipment may be made available on a self-service basis, or with the assistance of business centre staff, or on a full-service basis (eg photocopying and faxing done for the guest by business centre staff). Whereas these amenities may be included in the tariff for an executive floor or executive lounge, in a guest business centre (open to all guests) charges may be incurred for use.

In many hotels, the business centre would only be open during certain hours. Outside these hours, guests may request reception staff to send an urgent fax, or take a photocopy, on their behalf – and the staff member will have to follow the hotel's rules and procedures about such requests.

4.3 Guest internet access and e-mail facilities

It is worth noting that, these days, it is not just business travellers who want access to the Internet and e-mail facilities. Many guests will want to use the Internet to stay in touch with friends and family; view and share digital holiday photographs; confirm flights; search for travel and local information; make travel and entertainment bookings; or simply supplement the in-room entertainment provided by the hotel.

Many larger hotels, especially those with a high proportion of business trade, therefore, offer Internet access and e-mail facilities in one way or another, even if they do not have business centres.

Photo: https://static.roomex.com/photos

Photo: http://www.venere.com/img/hotel

- There may be **Internet desks or 'kiosks'** in the reception or lounge area of the hotel, allowing guests to use computer terminals at an advertised rate per block of time. This may be paid for with a credit card, inserted or swiped on logging on to the terminal, or may be logged and charged to the guest's account, by arrangement with reception.

- There may be **in-room Internet access**, with telecommunications points into which guests can 'plug' their laptop computers. Use of this system may be automatically logged and charged to guests, in the same way as telephone calls using the hotel's system, on an advertised cost-per-minute basis.

Nowadays, even these kinds of arrangements may not be required for some users, as they have mobile wireless modem devices which they can simply plug into their laptops, to give them fully independent, wireless Internet access in areas wherever their Internet provider has coverage.

EXAMPLE

'A Word from the FOM'

Many hotels currently charge for in-room Internet access for guests: the hotel may own the network, or use a contractor, but if they charge guests per minute or block of time, it represents a good revenue stream for the hotel.

But my feeling is that it will become a free guest service within the next five years, as standard. Free, unlimited access is in such high demand by business travellers: hotels that don't provide it will start losing corporate accounts.

5 Information services

We have repeatedly noted, throughout this Study Guide, that Front Office is the 'communications hub' of the hotel. One of the most important responsibilities of the front desk, enquiries desk and/or concierge of the hotel is the provision of information to guests: about the hotel and its facilities and services; functions and events taking place in the hotel; the local area, its amenities and attractions; available transport and activities; and so on.

5.1 Types of information provided by Front Office

It should go without saying that Front Office staff will need a good level of knowledge about the **hotel**, **its services**, **amenities**, **policies and charges**. If guests want to know how to go about depositing articles in the hotel safe, or what time the restaurant opens, or where to find a courtesy phone, this information should be readily available.

Information about the **local area**, **tourist attractions**, **activities and venues** is often made available for guests at the enquiries desk, or via information displays in the reception area. Guests may be offered maps, tourist guides, brochures and so on, or referred to the information on display (although *not* in such a way as to imply: 'Why ask me? The information's over there.')

Photo: http://www.niagarafallshowardjohnsons.com

Some information may not be quite so straightforward. Guests may want to know how long it will take to get to the nearest airport by taxi; or may ask for a restaurant recommendation in the local area; or want directions to a sporting or entertainment venue. Front Office staff should anticipate these kinds of questions, and be prepared to give appropriate answers.

In some cultures, service staff tend to give enquirers the answer they think they want to hear – even if the information is inaccurate or incorrect. Hotel Front Office staff should always think carefully about what will **serve the interests of the guest** best – and **protect the hotel**. Obviously you can't guarantee that a taxi will get to the airport in a certain time, or that a particular restaurant will be a good experience. Be honest if you don't know, are expressing an opinion, or can't guarantee your information – but offer information where you think it will be helpful.

Front Office staff will not know the answer to all queries 'off the bat'. A guest may want to know the times of services at a particular place of worship, or how to find a specialist shop or activity in the area, or the phone number of an emergency dentist. In such cases, the staff member should offer to **look up or find out** the information for the guest: in Front Office directories; on the Internet; or by telephone enquiry.

5.2 Looking up information for guests

Common information requests and reference resources may include the following.

Topic	Information source
Transport	▪ Printed timetables/schedules for buses, trains and airlines
	▪ Telephone directory for bus, train, airline and taxi providers
	▪ Direct telephone link to local/preferred taxi companies
Entertainment and tourism	▪ Directory of restaurants, cafes, clubs, entertainment venues (cinemas, theatres, sports venues), sporting facilities (golf/tennis clubs, water sport providers) etc
	▪ Directory of local travel agents and tour operators
	▪ 'What's On?' guides provided by local tourism offices, destination marketers, newspapers and so on
	▪ Programmes for local cinemas and theatres
	▪ Brochures provided by entertainment venues, tour companies etc
	▪ Directory and/or brochures of sister hotels and other hotels (for onward travel arrangements)
	▪ AA and RAC handbooks (covering UK regions, towns and cities; hotels, restaurants and entertainment venues; transport service; road maps) and their equivalents in other countries
Local facilities and amenities	▪ Directory of local hairdressers, chemists/pharmacies, doctors, dentists, banks, shopping centres
	▪ Street maps of the town/city and local area
General information	▪ Directory of the embassies, consulates and passport offices of different nations
	▪ Listings of selected local places of worship, with contact numbers and service times
	▪ Local telephone directories and business directories (eg the White Pages and Yellow Pages)
	▪ Local, national and international newspapers (available for reference or purchase)
	▪ The Post Office Guide (to postal services, rates and regulations)

We have listed 'paper' sources, which will be compiled, added to and updated on a regular basis – but of course, there are online/Internet equivalents for all of these, plus a wide range of helpful information search websites. Reception should compile a directory of useful web sites and their addresses.

5.3 Communication assistance for foreign guests

Before we leave the subject of communication and information services, we should note that some hotels make special efforts to assist foreign guests who may not speak the local language.

- The hotel may seek to employ **multi-lingual staff** in Front Office roles: that is, who speak more than one language. Hotels in non-English speaking countries, for example, often seek to employ staff who can speak English (since this will be the first or second language of a high proportion of guests from various countries).

- If the hotel has identified a high proportion of its guests as being of a particular origin, it may seek to employ staff who can communicate in their language. It may also have key documents and welcome packs prepared in their language, to assist them through the main procedures of the guest cycle. In Sydney, Australia, for example, many large hotels cater for Japanese travellers in this way, because of the high proportion of Japanese corporate and leisure trade.

- The hotel may be able to offer translation and interpretation services, by arrangement with specialist outside agencies, for conferences, business meetings, special functions (eg weddings) or VIP guests.

SUMMARY

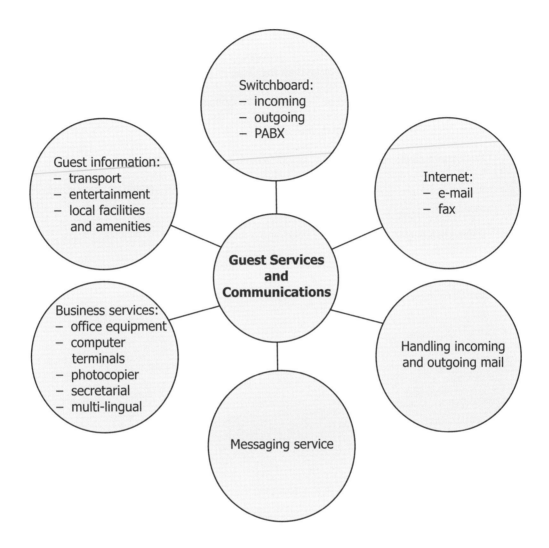

SELF-TEST QUESTIONS

1 What does PABX stand for?

2 What should go on a fax header sheet?

3 E-mail is generally more expensive than fax. True or False?

4 What four documents should be held by a switchboard operator to help locate numbers?

5 What does 'extension barring' mean?

6 What three categories should mail be sorted into?

7 A ....machine may be used instead of affixing postage stamps to outgoing mail.

8 Distinguish between an 'executive floor' and a 'business centre'.

9 List three ways of providing guests with Internet access.

10 Identify three types of information that guests may want from reception.

SELF-TEST ANSWERS

1   Private Automatic Branch Exchange

2   Letterhead of the hotel; name and fax number of target recipient; number of pages in the fax; message.

3   False

4   Directory of numbers; guest list/index; arrivals list; departures list

5   Preventing telephone extensions from making dial-out calls or expensive types of call (eg international)

6   Guest, staff and hotel

7   Franking

8   Executive floors include accommodation and are for the exclusive use of guests of that floor. A business centre offers office/communication facilities only, and is open to all guests on request.

9   Business centre, lobby terminals or kiosks, in-room access.

10   Any three of: transport, entertainment and tourism, local facilities, general information and hotel services and facilities.

ANSWERS TO ACTIVITIES

1 No answer is given to this activity, as it involves your own Internet research.

2 Why is the role of telephonist important? First, because of the need to provide a professional service which meets the needs of the caller and intended recipient of the call. Second, because of the need to create a good impression of the hotel, especially since this may be the *first* (and only) contact with a prospective guest before (s)he decides where to stay! Third, because of the potentially serious consequences of mishandling calls or messages. And last, because of the need to use the telephone system efficiently – without wasting the money and time of the caller *or* the hotel.

3 No answer is given to this activity, as the information has already been given. The question merely tests your ability to select and summarise the relevant information on the stationery provided.

4 Some suggestions are as follows:

'OK': 'Certainly, Mr/Ms/Mrs....'

'Hang on a sec': 'One moment, please' or 'Will you hold the line, please, Mr.....'

'I'm sorry, (s)he's out': 'I'm sorry, but Mr/Mrs.... is not in the office at the moment. Can someone else help you, or can I take a message?'

'Mr who?': 'I'm sorry, this is a rather bad line: could you give me your name again, please?'

'What did you say?': 'I'm sorry, can you repeat that, please?'

5 No answer is provided for this activity, as it requires you to do your own inquiry. This is useful practice for the following section of this chapter, which deals with being able to research information when you need to. If a guest asks about 'registered mail', for example, or 'how do I send a package securely overseas?', you will know where to find the information.

CHAPTER 9

INTERPERSONAL AND SELLING SKILLS

Chapter objectives

In this chapter you will learn

- The importance of Front Office roles in 'selling' the hotel
- Personal qualities and social skills that can be used by Front Office staff to support guest satisfaction and maximum occupancy
- Selling skills and techniques
- What attributes and facilities attract guests to a hotel: needs and wants of different guests
- Problems that may inconvenience guests, and how to deal with them
- How to encourage and utilise guest feedback
- How to handle guest complaints in a constructive manner
- Staff training and induction for Front Office roles

Topic list

The importance of Front Office roles in 'selling' the hotel
The hotel 'product'
Personal and social skills for Front Office roles
Selling skills and techniques
Handling guest problems, feedback and complaints
Staff development and management

1 The importance of Front Office roles in 'selling' the hotel

As the hospitality and travel market continues to expand, and as the Internet makes more and more information available to travellers, competition between hotels is growing increasingly intense. Travellers have a much wider choice of options – and easy access to detailed comparisons (and user reviews) of hotel facilities, prices and service, worldwide.

It is the responsibility of the hotel's **sales and marketing department** to plan hotel services and amenities that will appeal to a target audience; to implement advertising and public relations activities to raise awareness and attract customers; to ensure that the hotel is promoted by various sales or 'distribution' channels such as travel agencies, tour operators and internet booking sites and, over all, to maximise room revenue.

In a deeper sense, however, '**marketing**' is the responsibility of *all* staff, because every contact with members of the public and potential guests (eg at the point of enquiry) may influence their impression of the hotel, and whether they will be attracted to stay there. Every contact with guests staying in the hotel may influence their satisfaction with their stay, and whether they recommend the hotel to others, and whether they intend to return in future. All staff are 'ambassadors' for – and 'promoters' of – the hotel.

Even so, Front Office has a particularly important part to play in the promoting and selling of the hotel.

- Front Office staff have a key role in **converting enquiries** into actual sales, that is, in convincing a prospective customer to decide in favour of buying the 'product' offered by the hotel.

- Front Office staff are an essential part of the **first impression** made by the hotel (whether by phone, in writing or in person at front desk), which may be important in converting enquiries – and also in reassuring arriving guests that they have made the right choice, contributing to customer satisfaction, and perhaps predisposing guests to further purchases with the hotel.

- Front Office staff have ideal **opportunities to sell** additional services to guests at various points in the guest cycle, by virtue of dealing directly with guests at these points. At the reservation stage, for example, the clerk can offer options to help the enquirer to make the decision to stay at the hotel – closing the sale. On arrival, the receptionist can inform the guest of additional services or options which

Photo: www.lda.gov.uk

might be purchased: a better grade of room, perhaps, or the use of the hotel restaurant. On check-out, the receptionist may offer help with future bookings, or suggest that the guest join the hotel's loyalty programme – and so on.

- Front Office staff have the most direct **customer service** role in the hotel, being the focal point of guest queries and access to services. Guests' impression of – and satisfaction with – hotel service will largely be shaped by the conduct of the people they deal with at the front desk and on the switchboard.

1.1 Basic principles of marketing

Marketing has been defined as 'the management process wich identifies, anticipates and supplies customer requirements efficiently and profitably'.

You may have identified marketing with advertising and selling – but as our definition shows, these are only part of the marketing task! Marketing is beyond the scope of this Study Guide, but it is worth bearing the following points in mind, as relevant to the Front Office task.

- **Know your target market**. The guest statistics we discussed in Chapter 6 are gathered specifically to help the hotel identify its main customers, where they come from and what 'types' of traveller they are: travel agency, tour operator, business house and independent travellers; business or leisure; domestic or overseas; transient or long-stay. The hotel can target its marketing and selling efforts accordingly.

- **Identify the needs and wants of the target market**, and develop and promote the product accordingly. Long-stay customers will probably require a more varied range of facilities, more comfortable accommodation and more catering options than transients. Business travellers will require a different range of services (office and communication services, conference/meeting facilities etc) to leisure/tourism travellers (entertainment, transport – perhaps on a limited self-funded budget). Front Office staff will need to match the offer of services and facilities:

  - To the needs of each **market segment** (eg highlighting services of most interest to the type of traveller), in order to present them with the most attractive 'package of benefits' for their needs.

  - To the hotel's **preferred/targeted segments**: those which are most profitable for the hotel (eg repeat, high-volume and full-rack rate business) and which fit its desired image. (Package tours and groups may not fit the hotel's image, for example, or may alienate private clients paying the full rack rate.)

  - The hotel's **yield management** requirements (eg maximising occupancy by offering special promotions for tourist business on weekends, while catering for business travellers during the week).

- **Strive to satisfy or delight the customer**, by meeting – and if possible, exceeding, their expectations. Disappointed customers represent, at best, one-off sales. Satisfied customers are more likely to represent repeat sales, high-value and/or additional sales (through positive word-of-mouth promotion and recommendation).

- **Develop the potential for relationship with the customer**. 'Relationship marketing' is based on developing long-term, mutually beneficial relationships with customers, by offering personalised service; maintaining contact with the customer after an initial sales transaction; listening to the customer, in order to provide tailored offers and improved service; and building repeat business and customer loyalty over time.

FOR DISCUSSION

Why might a relationship marketing approach work well for a hotel? What would make it *possible* (eg in terms of the hotel's ability to gather and use information about guests to build on-going relationships)? How would it help the hotel to give a better service to guests? How might it support the competitive success and profitability of the hotel?

In this chapter, we will look at two basic aspects of the marketing role of Front Office:

- **Customer service**: the interpersonal or social skills and attributes required to deal with customers in a way that is likely to enhance and maintain their satisfaction with the hotel.

- **Selling**: the techniques required to persuade prospective customers to buy the hotel 'product', to buy more, and to buy repeatedly – all of which adds to the revenue, yield and profitability of the hotel.

1.2   Customer service

Excellent customer service is an essential part of selling – as well as of Front Office operations in general – because it is a key component in the total hospitality 'product' offered to guests.

It is a powerful contributing factor to guests' **satisfaction** with the hotel and with their stay: perhaps more so than the standard of the rooms and amenities. It is also a powerful factor in **differentiating** one hotel from another in the minds of prospective guests. Hotel rooms often look the same; hotels of a similar grade generally offer similar facilities. But customer service sets a hotel apart: the quality, style and consistency of service cannot be separated from the particular people employed to deliver it, how they are trained and supervised and the general 'culture' of the hotel.

Satisfying and retaining customers depends on a hotel's ability consistently to fulfil guests' expectations, and to create a positive experience at every encounter with customer service staff. A single disappointing, unsatisfactory or frustrating **service encounter** – and/or the hotel's subsequent poor response to handling the problem – may be sufficient to spoil guests' positive impression, lose their trust, and make them less likely to use the hotel in future (particularly in the face of marketing efforts from competing locations and establishments). It may also induce them to share their negative impressions with others, and if this means giving negative feedback to a travel agent or tour operator, or reporting the problem to a corporate travel buyer – or leaving negative comments on an online hotel review site – can cause significant damage to the hotel's reputation.

On the positive side of this equation, as we have seen, particularly satisfying service encounters are an important source of added value for customers, a part of the package of benefits that helps to attract and retain them, and potentially a key differentiating factor between the hotel and its competitors.

EXAMPLE

'An example of how to handle [potential customer service crises] can be found in the case of Thomas Cook, the UK travel agency and tour operator. An electrical fault on an aircraft… meant that 220 passengers were delayed at Funchal airport for two hours… Towards the end of this period, passengers were directed to the cafeteria to receive a free drink and snack.

When it became clear that the flight would not take place that day, a Thomas Cook representative announced that all passengers would stay the night in a five-star hotel and would receive free dinner with drinks. After 30 minutes, passengers boarded coaches and were seamlessly transferred to the hotel. While at the hotel, passengers were kept fully informed of the situation and given the time to meet the following morning. Representatives were on hand to answer queries…

When passengers met to take the early-morning trip to the airport, they were served coffee and biscuits. Coaches were waiting outside the hotel ready for departure.

Despite the inconvenience of arriving a day late, passengers appreciated the smoothness of the service recovery operation. Clearly, Thomas Cook and its airport representative Serviceair had excellent service processes in place.'   *(David Jobber, Principles & Practice of Marketing)*

1.3   The sales role of Front Office staff

With increasing competition and focus on yield management, the **selling** function has become an increasingly important part of the Front Office role – a fact that has been strongly reflected in the selecting, training, appraisal and reward of reservations and reception staff. Indeed, the success of the Front Office team is often measured according to its success in selling: on increasing the occupancy and revenue of the hotel – or in other words, as discussed in Chapter 6, on **yield**.

You might associate 'selling' with 'hard-sell' techniques, persuading people to buy things they may not really need, or to pay more for them than they are really worth. This is *not* how it works in the hotel industry.

For one thing, the 'product' offered by a hotel is **hospitality** – and badgering guests to spend money is not welcoming or relaxing for them!

More importantly, from a business point of view, the hotel will earn more revenue and profit by creating a long-term, **mutually satisfying relationship** with guests: having them return repeatedly, spend more while they stay, and provide 'free' promotion of the hotel to other people. This depends on making guests feel that they are receiving genuine service, hospitality and value for money. Which in turn depends on selling being done in an **intelligent** and **guest-focused** way: giving guests information, and options, and access to additional services and facilities which are relevant to their needs and will enhance their stay. If handled skilfully, therefore, selling can add value for the guest, as well as for the hotel.

FOR DISCUSSION

'You can always get away with selling an inadequate product or service. Once.'

What do you think this statement implies for the selling of hotel services?

1.4 Aims and benefits of Front Office selling

The dual purpose of selling is therefore:

- To maximise room revenue, in order to support the hotel's profitability. This can be done *either* by increasing occupancy (bringing in more customers), or increasing guest spend (persuading guests to pay more) – and ideally, both!

- To achieve customer satisfaction.

Let's look at this in more detail.

Increased occupancy

Selling by Front Office staff may tip the balance of decision-making in favour of the hotel, increasing occupancy by: offering extra nights; filling rooms which might otherwise have been unoccupied; offering options (eg on dates or room types) to secure a reservation which might otherwise have been lost; reducing the risk of no-shows by securing deposits; and so on. We will look at this in more detail later in the chapter.

Meanwhile, satisfied customers are more likely to return to the hotel. They are more likely to make an advance reservation (because they have a definite preference). They may also be more likely to stay for longer (now that they *know* they are going to enjoy the experience). These factors all contribute to increased occupancy, and to the hotel's ability to manage occupancy.

Maximised revenue

The aim of selling is to get the maximum revenue from a limited number of rooms.

As we saw in Chapter 6, accommodation is a **service**. When you sell a hotel room, you are not transferring 'ownership' of anything tangible to the customer (as with a physical product): you are merely selling an entitlement to enjoy certain facilities and services *for a certain period of time*.

The time factor is very important. Services are said to be '**perishable**': customers can't buy hotel rooms (or an airline reservation, or theatre tickets) and store them for their own use. They have to consume the service within a specified window of opportunity – or they've missed their chance. Similarly, a hotel has to sell a room for a given night, or the opportunity is lost, the 'sell by' date of a room is always 'tonight'! This means that:

- You have a **fixed number of rooms** for any given night: you can't 'produce more' rooms to match periods of increased demand, or 'produce less' rooms to match lower demand. Your aim is to sell as many as possible of the rooms you have.

- If you don't sell a room for a particular night, you **lose the potential revenue** from that room.

- If you get more enquiries than you have rooms, you **can't sell rooms twice**: you will have to turn away some enquirers (or sell them a room on another night).

- The principles of **yield management** (as discussed in Chapter 6) suggest that you will try to secure the best possible rate for a room – consistent with maximising occupancy. You may have to discount the full rack rate in order to attract customers for vacant rooms – because discounted revenue is better than no revenue at all (as long as the hotel covers the cost of letting the room, so that it makes some profit on the sale). You may have to prioritise higher-paying customers than lower-paying ones competing for the same room at the same time.

Customer retention and loyalty

Customers who experience a product or service which meets – or exceeds – their expectations are more likely to feel positively about the organisation providing the product or service, and more likely to use it again, when a similar need arises.

> **Customer retention** means 'keeping' customers, by creating a preference for your organisation's product, service or brand, and making it more likely that the customer will use it next time they have a need – rather than switch to a competitor.
>
> **Customer loyalty** means that a customer has built-up an emotional attachment to an organisation, product or service, and is willing to use it – in preference to competitors – at every opportunity.

DEFINITION

A C T I V I T Y   1   **1 0   m i n u t e s**

Customer retention (and even more, customer loyalty) is important to a business. See how many reasons you can come up with, why this might be so.

E X A M P L E

'A Word from the FOM'

Repeat business is highly desirable for a hotel. The returning guest is known to the hotel, which minimises the risk – and information gathering. Returning guests tend to be predisposed to be satisfied with the hotel: they already expect a good experience, and aren't looking for problems. They normally book direct – which saves the hotel commission. And some of them can be a pleasure to deal with!

New business

Front Office selling (and positive first impressions) may secure new business by 'converting' undecided enquirers about the hotel; asking guests for referrals to others who might be interested in the hotel's services (eg through 'introduce a friend' schemes); following up on referrals and sales leads; and so on.

New business may also be secured for the hotel by the recommendations and referrals of satisfied and loyal customers. Customers tell other people about their experiences (particularly when it comes to experiences which lend themselves to 'swapping stories', like holidays). In the past, they would just tell the people they knew, even so, word would get around. Nowadays, there are major travel web sites devoted to guest reviews of destinations and hotels, guest 'blogs' (online travel diaries) and so on: a satisfied – or dissatisfied – customer can tell thousands of other people about his experience! So turning out happy guests is one way of increasing occupancy by securing 'free advertising' through positive word of mouth promotion (and avoiding reputational and business damage through *negative* word of mouth).

Staff satisfaction and retention

We should note that high-quality customer service and successful sales are satisfying not just for customers – but for Front Office staff! For one thing, you have the satisfaction of having done a good job, both for the customer and for the hotel. You are also likely to be acknowledged, valued and/or rewarded, since Front Office performance is directly measured by sales figures and customer satisfaction ratings. (As a side benefit, you may also have to deal with fewer unpleasant incidents and customer complaints!)

Staff who enjoy this kind of job satisfaction are more likely to stay with their employer for longer – which is a benefit to the hotel: better continuity of service; better continuity of staff learning and improvement; less wasted investment in staff induction and training; less cost and disruption of hiring and training replacement staff.

2 The hotel 'product'

A **product** has been defined as 'a bundle of benefits' offered to customers. In other words, it is not just a physical item, but a whole 'package' of attributes valued by customers, and benefits which satisfy their needs and wants. In the case of a hotel this might include not just accommodation and facilities, but customer service, a relaxing atmosphere, convenient location, helpful service, prestige, value for money and so on. All these benefits can be sold to guests and prospective guests by Front Office staff.

A broad understanding of what constitutes the hotel 'product' will help Front Office staff to sell intelligently and successfully, by anticipating (or finding out) the needs and wants of customers – and providing them with facilities, and informing them about facilities, which will satisfy them (as well as earning revenue for the hotel).

Again, note that this isn't 'hard' selling, but **value-adding selling**: selling as service. A guest who has been travelling for days will be delighted to hear that the hotel offers laundry and dry cleaning services. Guests arriving in a strange town will be happy to know that the hotel has its own restaurant (and that reception will be happy to make a reservation) – or, if they are tired or travelling alone, that room service can be provided. Many travellers, out of touch with their offices or families, will be glad to be informed that internet access is available. As we will see later, 'product knowledge' is the first ingredient in successful selling, you need to know not just **what customers want** – but what the **hotel can offer** to satisfy them.

2.1 Why customers choose a hotel

Of course, different customers – and different types of customer – may want quite different things from a hotel, depending on budget, circumstances and temperament. The needs of a conference organiser will be quite different from those of a luxury leisure traveller, or chance guest who has been travelling all day and merely wants a bed for the night, or a family looking for a budget holiday break. However, some of the attributes or benefits a hotel might promote to attract customers to the hotel, include the following.

- Accommodation style and quality (eg room size, furnishings, en-suite bathrooms, in-room facilities)

- Hotel facilities and amenities (eg car parking, swimming pool or spa, laundry/dry cleaning services, business/conference facilities, restaurant/bar)

- Location (eg convenience for transport or events, proximity to local attractions, remoteness)

- Value for money (eg budget options, added value at higher rates)

- Cleanliness and comfort (or luxury, depending on taste and budget) of rooms and public areas

- Security/safety or privacy (eg for females travelling alone, families with children and VIP guests, and particularly in dangerous locations)

- Relaxation, pleasure and entertainment (supported by the service, entertainment facilities and atmosphere of the hotel)

- Prestige and fashion (eg for perceived high-class or highly-regarded hotels, recently publicised hotels, or hotels which attract celebrity clientele)

- Familiarity (eg of a hotel chain, or through returning to the same hotel)

- Availability (eg if it is late in the day and a chance guest is worried that (s)he may not be able to find a room)

- Customer service and hospitality (prompt response, problem-solving, assistance, warm welcome)

2.2 Anticipating and meeting guest needs

We have already suggested that effective selling of the hotel product means relating it to the needs and wants of guests. But what do guests 'need'? In general terms, all people 'need' the same kinds of things. Psychologist *Abraham Maslow* identified five innate human needs, and suggested that they can be arranged in a **'hierarchy of needs':** Figure 9.1. Each level of need is uppermost in a person's mind until it is satisfied – and only then does the next highest level of need become a factor.

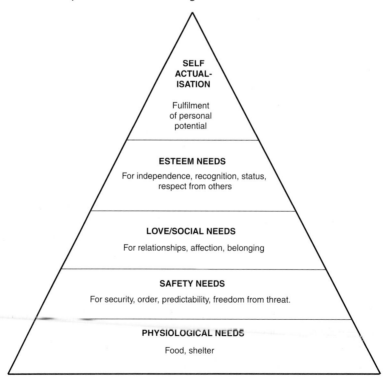

Figure 9.1: The hierarchy of needs

If you think about the hierarchy, it makes sense. Guests are unlikely to worry about social activities, status, or seeking out mind-broadening experiences like sightseeing, if they are hungry or feeling unsafe, for example. But can a hotel really satisfy any of these basic needs?

- Fulfilling **physiological needs** is one of the basic functions of a hotel. Guests who are tired and hungry, or anxious about finding food and accommodation at the end of the day, will be satisfied first of all by knowing that the hotel does, in fact, have a bed for the night, and an open food service.

- Providing **safety** or security, both physical and psychological, is another key requirement. Guests need to *be* safe (eg by being offered secure accommodation) and to *feel* safe (eg by being offered welcome and assistance in an unfamiliar environment, and privacy when desired).

- Once a guest has been provided with these basic requirements, and begun to relax, (s)he may feel the need for **companionship** or **belonging**. This may be satisfied by the 'social' areas and services of the hotel (eg a lounge, bar or meeting area, or entertainments), but also by personal service from Front Office staff, so that the guest feels welcomed and recognised.

- **Esteem** needs can be met by the courtesy and respect shown to guests, the assistance and service offered to them (as if they were 'VIPs'), and perhaps also the perceived quality or 'exclusiveness' of the hotel, or a 'superior' or 'deluxe' room, or a 'Members Club' card.

- **Self-actualisation** is, arguably, a feature of travel, since it broadens the guest's horizons. A hotel can offer guests opportunities to 'improve' themselves physically (eg with exercise facilities), mentally (eg with local information) and experientially (eg with local cultural experiences and sightseeing tours), if they wish to do so.

E X A M P L E

Abbott & Lewry (Front Office, p. 82*)* argue that it is not difficult to contribute to the satisfaction of guests' needs on all levels.

'When a receptionist says: 'Hello, Mr Jenkinson, nice to see you again. How have you been? We've put you into Room 402 as usual', she may well be satisfying several of Mr Jenkinson's needs at once: reassuring him that he is expected (security), initiating a friendly conversation (belongingness), and making it clear that he is welcome (esteem). Satisfying three out of five basic human needs in one short exchange isn't bad: no wonder this kind of approach wins repeat business!'

More specifically, different guests – and different 'types' of guest – may have **specific needs and wants**, which the hotel can anticipate and plan to satisfy.

For example:

- **VIP guests** have needs and wants in areas such as: protection of privacy; heightened personal security; suites of rooms or inter-connecting rooms for security personnel and *entourage;* fast/private check-in and check-out; space for private entertaining; and 'special-status' treatment.

- **Business guests** have needs and wants in areas such as: space and facilities for working in their rooms; swift/efficient check-in and check-out; access to communications and office facilities; the ability to charge expenses to their company; access to meeting rooms; and perhaps extra facilities for relaxation. Some hotels will, as we have seen, have an 'Executive Floor', for all these reasons.

- **Single female travellers** have special needs in areas such as: security and safety; privacy and non-disclosure of their status and room number; freedom from harassment by males (a regrettable fact of life); room-service dining; the opportunity to socialise with other women; facilities for personal grooming (eg in-room hair dryers); and perhaps a bit of extra 'pampering' (eg spa and luxury toiletries). Some hotels will have all-female floors, for all these reasons.

ACTIVITY 2   15 minutes

A specimen question from a past Front Office Operations exam!

All customers have different needs and wants and it is important that hotel employees understand these to make their stay more enjoyable. Below is a list of different types of guests. List some of the different needs and wants of these guests that can be provided by a city centre hotel.

(a)   An elderly couple on a weekend away.

(b)   A family with two teenage children and a three-year old child.

(c)   A single female business traveller.

(d)   An American CEO who is on business but would also like to do some local sightseeing.

3   Personal and social skills for Front Office roles

DEFINITION

Skills are learned patterns of behaviour which enable you to perform complex tasks confidently, competently and successfully.

Personal skills involve behaviour *within* people: they may include self-awareness, time management, stress management, problem-solving and decision-making.

Interpersonal (or social) skills involve behaviour *between* people: communication, persuasion, negotiation, conflict management, team-working.

Of course, we all exercise personal and interpersonal skills in the course of our daily lives: why would we have to *learn* to dress appropriately or to talk to people, in order to be successful in a Front Office role?

The essence of personal and interpersonal skills is that we have **goals or purposes** that we want see fulfilled from our actions, and from our interactions with other people. We use our skills to make them happen. If the outcome isn't what we expected or hoped for, we may need to adjust our behaviour – or improve our skills – so that we get a better outcome next time. Our purpose in dealing with guests in a hotel Front Office, for example, may be to create a positive impression, or to persuade guests to use more of the facilities of the hotel, or to get an agitated guest to calm down. This is where social skills come in.

As with many types of skills, **social skills** can't be taught in a book! You have to develop them through practice; through trial and error; and through watching and imitating people who are good at them (modelling). However, we can at least raise your **awareness** of the effect of your behaviour, and appearance, and communication styles. Are they likely to get the outcomes you want? What behaviours, appearance and communications styles *are* likely to get the outcomes you want?

FOR DISCUSSION

What do you think 'makes' a good Front Office person? What should (s)he be like, and what should (s)he be able to do? What should (s)he look like, in terms of dress and grooming?

EXAMPLE

'A Word from the FOM'

I'd say the most important qualities in a Front Office staff member are: general intelligence, friendliness, energy, openness, decision-making ability, flexibility – and a thick skin! You need to be welcoming. You need to be able to talk to people and help them feel at ease. And you need to be able to handle emotional and stressful situations.

Let's look briefly at some personal and social skills for Front Office roles.

3.1 Personal skills and attributes

What should an effective Front Office person be 'like' – and what should (s)he be able to do? Here are just a few ideas.

- **Time management**. The hotel day will have its own 'rhythm', and there will be procedures and patterns for getting through the day's workload: when to open the mail, when to prepare guest bills and so on. Even so, there will be quiet periods, and it is essential for staff to be methodical and organised in utilising the time to get the most work done – while still remaining flexible and available to meet the needs of guests. Time management is a skill: learn to plan your day; use 'To Do' lists and checklists; batch similar tasks so you can do them together; have the information and equipment you need conveniently to hand; keep a tidy desk; and so on.

- **Stress management**. Front Office can be stressful, with hectic periods, demanding guests and awkward situations. Learn to recognise when you are stressed, and how to de-stress between hectic periods: it may be as simple as a short break, a cup of tea, some deep breathing, or talking to a sympathetic colleague (away from the hearing of guests!).

- **Flexibility and resilience**. Front Office poses ever-changing demands, and your best-laid plans will often be disrupted by unexpected events and guests' changing their minds (probably at short notice). Learn to recognise which rules/procedures are 'non-negotiable' (such as safety protocols) and which are flexible. Practise finding and offering options and alternatives. Learn to adjust with a positive 'can do' attitude and a smile.

- **Willingness and ability to learn**. This may be the most essential skill of all! Learn to learn: from everything you do (but could do better or differently), from every mistake you make, from everything more skilled/experienced people tell you – and from every error or successful behaviour you observe.

3.2 Self-presentation (or impressions management)

You cannot *not* communicate. Even if you say nothing to a guest at all, your dress, hygiene, posture and grooming 'speak' for you – and for the hotel. Front Office staff are the 'face' of the hotel, and are frequently in close personal contact with guests and visitors. So these issues are important.

Element	Comments
Dress and **grooming**	Front Office staff should look neat, well-groomed and professional, and should attempt to *stay* that way, no matter how busy the day is! Most hotels will have a dress code, and some may also provide a clothing or dry cleaning allowance to help staff maintain high standards. Some hotels provide a staff uniform, to promote a professional, standardised and recognisable appearance: identifying staff clearly, so that guests need not hesitate to approach them.  The point is not to draw attention to your dress, make-up (where relevant) or hairstyle, but to create a business-like impression and to reinforce guests' perception that they have come to a clean, well-maintained, high-quality establishment. How you dress is an expression of your pride in your role and workplace: it also helps you to feel more confident and professional – and, therefore, to behave more professionally. (It is also worth thinking about comfort: if you are on your feet all day, for example, flat shoes are a must!)

Element	Comments
Personal hygiene	This may seem like rather intimate territory, but it is extremely important for staff who have close contact with guests. Perspiration stains, body odour and poor dental hygiene are seriously bad 'public relations'! Learn routines to stay clean and 'fresh' – and give tactful feedback to colleagues who may not be self-aware in this area...
Posture	Posture refers to how you sit and stand, and this is very important not just in conveying an impression, but in how you feel. If you sit or stand up straight, with your head up, and your arms relaxed, you convey confidence, alertness, attention and professionalism to others – and are more likely to feel like this yourself.
Position	Position refers to things such as: how close or far away you are from people; whether you face them directly; whether you are separated from them by a desk or counter. It can be used to create a mood and make people feel comfortable: don't invade their 'personal space'; turn to them directly to show that they have your attention; come out from behind the counter if you need to reassure or calm someone.

3.3 First-order social skills

'First-order' social or communication skills (like listening, questioning, verbal and writing skills and using body language) are the **building blocks** of more complex skills (welcoming, persuading, selling, conflict management and team working).

Again, let's look at each element in turn, briefly. It is worth noting that such skills vary from culture to culture: be aware and flexible when dealing with people from different cultures than your own.

'Micro' skill	Comments
Listening	A key role of Front Office is (a) listening to guests to gather information about their needs and wants and (b) listening to guests to make them feel 'heard'! There is a difference between 'passive listening' (letting information wash over you) and **'active listening'** (listening attentively and co-operatively). Active listening techniques include: • Using attentive posture (leaning forward, maintaining appropriate eye contact, nodding, focusing) • Showing that you listen and understand by giving encouraging feedback (nodding, 'yes', 'I understand') • Summarising or reflecting back key points (demonstrating 'empathy') • Taking notes and asking intelligent questions
Questioning	Use appropriate question types to extract the information you need. • **'Closed' questions** (which allow one-word answers) are good for pinning down facts: 'What is your room number?'. • **'Open' questions** (which require longer answers) are good for helping guests to express themselves and feel heard. 'How can I help you?'. Questions can make people feel 'interrogated', so they may need to be softened: 'Would you like tell me what happened?' 'May I take your name/room number?'

'Micro' skill	Comments
Verbal communication skills	Clear articulation and pronunciation of words is vital, because you want to be understood by other people – who may not be familiar with your language or accent. Speak slowly and clearly – but not in an exaggerated (patronising) way.
	Identify, and learn to use, phrases that sound courteous and professional (but not too clichéd): 'Good, evening, sir, how can I help you?', 'Did you enjoy your stay with us, Mr X?', 'Excuse me, I won't keep you a moment.'
	'Pitch' your voice appropriately: avoid speaking too softly (for the person to hear) or too loudly (for comfort or confidentiality). Inject warmth, courtesy, respect and interest into your tone of voice – and *don't* allow yourself to sound bored, irritated or uninterested (even if you are!).
Written communication skills	Learn to use a range of written formats for internal and external communication, such as letters (for confirmations, replies to complaints, guest follow-up), messages, e-mail, various forms and internal memoranda and reports. Follow the 'house style', format and content guidelines.
Non-verbal communication (body language) skills	Learn to control your own **body language**, to convey the impressions you want (and avoid undermining your messages with contradictory 'signals') – learn to observe and interpret the body language of others (to gauge what they are feeling and how you will need to respond to them). Body language includes:
	Eye contact: maintaining steady eye contact demonstrates attention and interest – but too much can be intrusive (especially in some cultures)
	Gestures: avoid fidgeting, distracting hand gestures, and negative gestures (like crossing your arms, which looks defensive, or resting your chin on your hand, which looks bored)
	Facial expressions: never underestimate the power of a smile and an interested look! Check guests' faces for frowns, tiredness, confused expressions: this is good 'feedback' on what the guest is feeling.
	Posture: discussed earlier.

A C T I V I T Y   3   **1 5   m i n u t e s**

OK, we know they're only cartoons, but what might you interpret as the emotional state of a guest who turned up at the front desk with the facial expressions and gestures shown in the 'emoticons' above?

Consciously observe the non-verbal behaviours of people interacting at work, or where you study, or in the street. Consider what you might infer from their behaviour about their mood and relationships with each other – and what you might have to be cautious about inferring, because of lack of information or cultural differences.

3.4 Second-order social skills

Second-order interpersonal and social skills are what you get when you put all the first-order communication skills together in particular contexts: how they are *used* to achieve particular aims and purposes. So here's one more table to take on board!

Social skill	Comments
Greeting/welcoming	**Welcoming** and serving guests involve a whole 'package' of skills, including: ■ Smiling and making appropriate eye contact ■ Addressing the guest respectfully as 'Sir' or 'Madam' initially, and then by correct title and surname ('Doctor Patel', 'Major Smith', 'Ms Dubois') ■ Immediately acknowledging the presence of a guest at the desk (even if you are unable to attend to them immediately) ■ An efficient manner, and proactively offering help ('How can I help you?') ■ Keeping a guest informed of what you are doing (if they are waiting)
Establishing 'rapport'	**Rapport** is a feeling of 'connection' or of 'getting on with' another person. Establishing rapport is a great foundation for persuasion, negotiation, selling, managing complaints and conflicts – and generally making guests feel comfortable. Friendliness (without inappropriate familiarity) is a rapport builder. Other techniques include: ■ Using the guest's name whenever possible ■ Referring to points of interest, or points of common interest ■ 'Mirroring' the other person's terminology and body language (subtly) to show that you are 'like them' ■ Using an open, interested and attentive posture ■ Using gestures which signal positive attitude and co-operation, such as nods and smiles, and appropriate eye contact
Persuading/selling and negotiating	We will discuss selling techniques later in the chapter, but any form of persuasion or negotiation requires behaviours such as: ■ Building rapport: a foundation for positive communication and co-operation ■ Tailoring your questions, offers and proposals to the interests of the other party. (What needs and wants are they likely to have that you can offer to satisfy? What are the benefits to *them* of what you are proposing?) ■ Monitoring the other party's body language for signs of resistance, reluctance, disinterest, lack of understanding – and adjusting accordingly ■ Anticipating objections and having answers prepared

Social skill	Comments
Managing complaints, conflicts and potential problems	We will discuss handling complaints later in the chapter, but special social skills are required in this situation to: • Maintain calm, confident, non-threatening, non-defensive body language • Control one's own emotions (keeping your head when others are losing theirs) • Avoid impact on other guests (eg by drawing the complainer to one side) • Help manage the complainer's emotions (eg by using a moderate tone of voice; accurately but calmly summarising the issue/feelings; assuring the guest that the matter will be dealt with positively) • Use active listening to help the other person feel heard • Being tactful and diplomatic: avoiding criticism, blame, giving offence or causing the guest to 'lose face' (be embarrassed) in front of others.

Of course, these skills may be required in an almost infinite range and combination of situations. Some guest problems or requests may *seem* to be purely 'technical' in nature: a lost reservation form, or a complaint about a room; or even a simple check-in procedure. But social skills will *always* be involved.

The guest whose reservation has been temporarily 'mislaid' will have to be reassured that there is not a problem by the tone and behaviour, as much as the words, of the receptionist. The complainer may have to be calmed down, reassured and attended to in such a way that satisfaction is restored. Even the simple check-in procedure needs to be handled in a welcoming and rapport-building way.

E X A M P L E

Front Office staff must also be constantly alert to potential issues and circumstances – **'reading' situations and body language** – which may make a 'routine' interaction or task into one that needs sensitive handling.

If the guest checking-in is tired and frustrated after a long journey, for example, the receptionist may need to exert herself more than usual to show understanding and empathy, and to offer solutions (from showing efficiency to informing the guest of the comforts in the room).

If a single female traveller is checking-in at the same time as a group of male travellers, she may appreciate the receptionist *not* stating her name and room number in front of them. The receptionist may offer to deal with the male group first, or get someone else to do so, or move them a bit further down the counter to register while the female guest is dealt with – without being obvious or offensive about it.

A disabled traveller will not want attention called to his or her disability, or to be treated 'differently' from others, but at the same time, his or her special needs will need to be identified and catered for.

If a guest appears to be embarrassed about making a request or complaint, the receptionist should be sensitive to the need to reassure and protect confidentiality.

3.5 Working in a team

It is worth noting that Front Office staff don't only have to exercise social skills in dealing with guests – but in working with each other!

It makes a huge difference to the efficiency and effectiveness of a team, and to the working life of its members, if everyone is willing to be co-operative, professional, courteous, friendly and supportive with one another!

Bad atmosphere and relationships in the team spill over into work behaviour, and may well be visible to guests – creating a poor impression (and perhaps poor service). **Positive team working**, and being a 'good colleague', may involve a willingness to:

- **'Pull your weight'**: be reliable in doing your own job and share of the work: not letting others down or expecting them to do your work for you

- **Co-operate** with others in a positive and constructive way (since you have shared goals and tasks)

- **Support your colleagues**: giving help, information, advice or a listening ear when required; refraining from criticism and gossip

- Maintain **courtesy, respect and fairness** at all times

- Recognise where an **interpersonal problem or conflict** exists, and deal with it openly and constructively (and with the person concerned) where possible.

4 Selling skills and techniques

The first thing to remember is that selling is selling – regardless of whether it is carried out in person, by telephone or in writing. *Every* time you answer a guest enquiry; inform a guest about the attributes, services and facilities of the hotel; suggest options for a guest to consider; invite a guest to contact you if they require any further help or information; or ask if you can help a guest with anything else today – you are selling.

4.1 When is the best time to sell facilities and services?

Any encounter with a guest is, in a sense, an opportunity for selling or promoting the hotel, but there are certain key stages in the guest cycle which lend themselves best to the selling of facilities and services.

- **On initial enquiry**: ascertaining the requirements and preferences of the prospective guest and offering/highlighting the facilities and services which will be most relevant and appealing.

- **On booking**: discovering the requirements and preferences of the prospective guest, and perhaps offering alternative or additional options that might meet their needs better; or suggesting options if the guest's requirements cannot immediately be met (eg if a particularly date or room type isn't available), rather than simply letting the guest take his request elsewhere.

- **On check-in**: informing the arriving guest of facilities and services likely to be useful and appealing during his or her stay; and perhaps taking the opportunity to offer an upgrade to superior (higher rate) accommodation or terms.

- **On request**: at any time during the guest's stay, if (s)he asks about particular facilities or services, or for recommendations about dining or entertainment options.

- **On check-out**: asking the guest if the hotel can help with onward bookings (to sister hotels in a chain), or future return bookings.

4.2 Product knowledge

Earlier, we discussed the wide range of reasons customers may have for choosing a hotel, and the wide range of needs that they may want to have met during their stay.

Knowledge of the hotel's product *starts* with comprehensive knowledge of the hotel's rooms (types, sizes, locations, rates, furnishings, fixtures and amenities) – but it doesn't end there. Successful selling requires knowledge of all the additional benefits, services and facilities the hotel can offer or access: car parking, conference facilities, laundry facilities, restaurant, bar, room service, swimming pool, spa or sports facilities, theatre ticket bookings and so on.

Details of all these services may be kept handy in a **product factsheet**, if required for reference. Reception and switchboard should also keep a directory of facilities and services provided by **other sales outlets** and departments of the hotel, with telephone extension numbers or names of persons to whom any guest queries or reservation enquiries should be referred. Banqueting and conferencing enquiries, for example, are often handled by specialist reservations staff.

A similar directory may be compiled of facilities and services provided **outside the hotel**, as a value-adding information service for guests. If the hotel doesn't have restaurant or sporting facilities, it may be able to recommend providers in the local area, and make enquiries and bookings on a guest's behalf. The hotel may even set up special arrangements with such providers, so that guests can obtain priority bookings, or charge activities to their hotel account: in effect, making 'partner' businesses an extension of the hotel's offering (and enjoying reciprocal recommendations and referrals).

In addition to the facilities and services themselves, Front Office staff should determine the hotel's selling proposition – ideally a '**unique selling proposition**' or **USP**. What are the most important attributes or benefits of the hotel, that set it apart from the competition and make it particularly attractive to prospective guests? Is it the under-cover parking? The 24-hour room service? The award-winning restaurant? The free in-room Internet access? Know your hotel's USPs – and use them when describing the hotel to prospective guests!

F O R   D I S C U S S I O N

Think about some hotels that you know about or have visited – or browse some hotel web sites next time you are online. What are these hotels' Unique Selling Propositions?

4.3 Sales support materials

Not all guests will want to receive information about services and facilities 'on the spot', or directly from sales staff (from whom they may feel under pressure). Selling therefore also involves the effective use of **sales support** materials: promotional and informational literature which supports personal selling by offering guests information, advertising benefits, showing illustrative pictures – and giving contact details for follow-up.

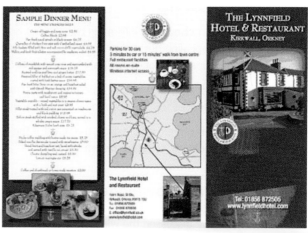

Source: http://www.seabridge.org/images/lynnfield.jpg

Brochures, and lists of hotel services and amenities, are often available and offered to customers to take away and peruse at their leisure. Service/sales staff may also attach or offer their hotel business cards, facilitating the prospective customer in following-up the enquiry, and emphasising personal service.

4.4 Selling techniques

Whole books are written on selling techniques. We're not going to attempt to get too complicated or subtle here – remembering that our focus is on guest-focused selling, not psychological manipulation. The following are some simple approaches for intelligent selling of hotel services and facilities.

- **Start with rapport**. There is an influencing technique called 'pace and lead' which means that you have to 'draw alongside' someone (make them feel understood and secure) before you 'draw ahead' of them and lead them in the direction you want them to go. Make guests feel welcome and secure first: they will then **trust** you to suggest options/alternatives, or to advise them well and in their best interests.

- **Sell the whole 'package'**. As we saw earlier, customers are not just buying rooms – they are buying hospitality, security, status, comfort and so on. Your **manner**, and your ability to build rapport, are a powerful sample of the total service and hospitality package. In addition, you can **describe** services and facilities in terms that appeal directly to what you anticipate the guest to be interested in. Use appealing descriptive phrases when referring to rooms: 'an air-conditioned room', 'a comfortable/spacious room with beautiful city views'.

- **Pace the transaction**. Selling has a natural 'shape' or rhythm to it that supports your aims. In Chapter 2, for example, we mentioned the acronym **QQI: Qualify, Quote, Invite**. Having found out what the guest needs and wants (qualifying), you offer a package to meet those needs (quoting). It is then natural to ask the guest whether he wants to purchase or make a booking (inviting): you have already *made it easy to say 'yes'*, by putting together an offer that meets his stated needs.

  Another simple framework for selling discussions is **ODD: Opening, Development, Dealing with hesitation**. If someone calls to make a reservation enquiry, you can start by simply informing them of the room types you have, and their prices *(opening)*. This leads naturally to questions about the rooms and their facilities, which provides a lead-in to describe them further, stressing the attributes most likely to appeal to the guest *(development)*. By this stage, the guest may be half persuaded, but reluctant to commit for some reason: the price may be too high, or the facilities not quite right. Armed with this information, you can take action to get over the potential objection *(dealing with hesitation)*: for example, you might offer the opportunity to inspect the room (answering doubts as to its suitability); or might offer alternative options; or might stress the value for money represented by the 'best available rate'.

- **Emphasise value for money**. If you are trying to persuade a guest to upgrade to a superior grade (higher-rate) room, you need to justify the extra expense, by explaining or demonstrating the benefits gained for the extra money. (Know *why* the 'superior' is more desirable/expensive than the 'standard', or why a double may be more comfortable for the guest than a single.)

- **Use 'good news'**. You may have 'bad news' for an enquirer: eg the only available room is a twin not a double, or you can only offer full rack rate for that period. You want to cushion this fact and major on 'good news' that will attract a sale. Start with some good news (eg 'Well, Sir, you're in luck: we do have a room available.'); then deliver the bad news ('It is only a *twin* room...'); and finish with the bright side ('... but it is more spacious than the double, with fine views over the city').

- **Use price psychology**. If you offer a guest the 'best available rate', it will sound like a competitive price or a bargain (even if the best available rate is rack rate). You might also quote a very high priced option alongside the alternatives, to make those prices 'look better': people will often go for the second-highest price, because they feel they are getting superior quality, but at a reasonable (not the highest) price. Rooms may already be priced on a psychological basis: eg £99 looks less expensive than £100!

- **Offer 'lead in' rooms**: also called 'selling high' or **'top down'** selling. Say someone rings up to enquire about a double room, and the hotel has standard doubles for £80 and superior doubles for £95. Start by quoting the higher-rate option first ('We have some lovely double rooms available for £95'): if the guest goes for it, you have made a higher-value sale. It is easy to come down to lower-rate options if the guest *isn't* willing to pay that much ('of course, we also have some slightly smaller rooms for £80, without quite as many amenities, but just as comfortable'). It is *less* easy to convince the guest to consider the superior, once (s)he has already settled on a standard: far more conspicuous selling!

- If guests are clearly budget-conscious, however, a **'bottom-up'** selling (or 'selling low') technique may be more effective, quoting high may put them off straight away. Instead, you could start with the cheapest grade/rate of room, to secure the sale – and then inform the guest that for a small amount extra, they could have more space or amenities: emphasising the upgrade as a value for money option.

- **Encourage sight/trial**. Experience is the most powerful convincer. If a guest isn't sure that a more expensive room is better, offer to show him – whether in a photograph/brochure, or by referral (of a phone enquiry) to a virtual tour on the web site, or by showing a walk-in guest the room. Similarly, the hotel may offer incentives to try the hotel restaurant (eg a free drink or voucher), in order to get guests in the door.

- **'Lead' the decision**. An uncommitted enquirer can be subtly steered towards a purchase decision by the sales person's 'assuming' that such a decision is being made. For example, having offered a room, you might ask 'Is that acceptable?' (rather than 'would you like to make a reservation now?'). If the prospective guest says 'yes' (because the room is broadly what he was after), you can start to ask questions about anticipated arrival times, the guest's contact telephone number, how the guest would like to pay for the room and so on. By this time, the reservation is well on the way to being made – and you have been so friendly and helpful, that the guest may not mind being 'nudged' to a decision in this way.

FOR DISCUSSION

Do you feel uncomfortable about any of these selling techniques? If so, why? What could you do to improve your confidence and skill in this area?

Note that, while some of these techniques are subtle and based on psychology, none of them is unethical or dishonest: the guest is not being pressured or manipulated into doing anything.

Let's now look at some of the broader selling approaches that can be used in different contexts.

4.5 Increasing occupancy

Although the main business of attracting guests to the hotel is carried out by the marketing department, as we noted earlier, there are a number of ways in which Front Office staff can help bring in business.

- **Juggling bookings** to maximise occupancy. Skilled reservation staff can 'fit' bookings into the available space on the conventional chart – as can computer reservations programmes – by allocating or re-allocating rooms in such a way as to open up space for additional reservations. In some cases, for example, guests booked into single accommodation may be persuaded to 'double up' or share a twin room (eg within tour groups or conference bookings), in order to free up additional singles.

- **Offering alternatives when taking enquiries**. As we saw in Chapter 2, a reservation clerk need not turn away business because the requested room type or date is unavailable. (S)he may well be able to offer a different type of room (perhaps a twin or two singles instead of a double, at a discounted rate if necessary); different dates (if the guest is flexible); or a referral to a sister hotel (still good marketing, because of the goodwill created by the assistance).

- **Minimising 'no shows'** by 'chasing' unconfirmed bookings, reconfirming the day before, charging non-refundable deposits on reservation, or accepting credit card bookings. Minimising the impact of no shows by planned overbooking, waiting lists, advertised release times and so on, as discussed in Chapter 3.

- **Converting enquiries into sales**, using the various selling techniques discussed above.

4.6 Increasing average room rates and guest spend

The second way of increasing the hotel's revenue, as we suggested earlier, is by getting guests to spend more in the hotel. This can be done in two basic ways: up-selling and cross-selling.

Up-selling

Up-selling (or '**bettered sales**') means persuading guests to upgrade their reservation or purchase, and therefore to spend more – an important way of increasing average rates and yield.

Just as a McDonalds crew member routinely asks 'Do you want fries with that?', a reservations clerk or receptionist may offer a guest the opportunity to upgrade to a higher standard and/or rate of room; higher-range terms (eg from bed and breakfast to fully inclusive); from *table d'hôte* (set menu) to *à la carte* (customer choice) meals in the restaurant; from two nights to three; and so on.

The ideal time for up-selling is **reservation** and/or **check-in** (maximising the added revenue – and avoiding mid-stay changes).

A guest intending to book a standard room may be informed that the hotel also has a 'superior' room available for that period, offering a better view, or more amenities – or whatever the justification of the higher classification and room rate is, whichever is likely to appeal most to the prospective guest. A guest may be willing to upgrade and pay the extra amount for a variety of reasons. If a guest is planning a long stay, (s)he may upgrade for the promise of more wardrobe space; a family may upgrade for more room; a well-off guest, or a guest whose expenses are being paid by a company, may be inclined to upgrade for more status and amenities.

A skilled receptionist should also be able to ascertain from guests on arrival – by questioning and observation – when they might appreciate the offer of larger, superior or more conveniently located accommodation. Again, this should be put to the guest as a value-adding opportunity, not as an attempt to get more money: 'Ms X, I know you booked a single room, but a double room has just become available, and it's quite a bit larger, with a nice view over the grounds. I wonder if you might prefer that to the room we've held for you?'

ACTIVITY 4   2 minutes

What kinds of 'signals' might you look for, to identify guests who might not be too budget-sensitive, or who might have special needs, that might make them open to an offer to upgrade?

Cross-selling

Cross-selling means selling **related or additional products** to the ones the guest has initially purchased. Guests will have already purchased a room and breakfast, but perhaps no 'extras'. Cross-selling persuades them to add the 'extras' that they might not previously have thought of or intended to buy, but which – since they are already in the hotel – they are willing to consider.

Cross-selling involves **informing guests** about the availability of added-value facilities and services of the hotel: the bar and restaurant facilities; spa, gym and sports facilities; laundry and dry cleaning; executive lounge and business facilities; special entertainments (eg a guest cocktail party or dinner show); in-house hairdressing or shopping facilities; tour and entertainment booking service; and so on.

This kind of sales opportunity may occur at **any time** during the guest's stay.

Photo: http://www.amsterdamcityhotels.nl/pics

Remember, cross-selling in a hotel setting is about providing information and options to guests – not being pushy! In order to be most effective, the information should be targeted to the guest's enquiries or anticipated needs. A guest who arrives travel stained after an adventure tour might be informed about the hotel's laundry service. A guest attending a formal evening function may be informed of valet or hair-dressing services. A guest arriving too late for lunch or dinner service may be informed that snacks are available all day from the bar. Business travellers will want to know about communication and office services.

4.7   Repeat business

We have already noted that it is easier and more cost-effective to **retain an existing guest** than to win a new one. Existing guests know the hotel – and are (hopefully) predisposed to like it, having had a satisfying experience. They may well be open to the prospect of a return visit, particularly if they are regular travellers in the area.

The ideal opportunity for boosting repeat business is on **check-out**. A receptionist may ask: 'Have you enjoyed your stay with us?' If the answer is yes, (s)he could go on: 'Might you be returning this way some time in the future?' If guests are intending to return, or state that they regularly travel to or through the location, the receptionist can offer to make a provisional reservation for them. If guests aren't prepared to do this (perhaps being uncertain of dates), the receptionist can furnish them with a brochure and business card, and assure them that they can easily make a reservation at any time: paving the way for a repeat sale by making it clear that the returning guest will be made welcome.

Alternatively, the receptionist may be able to offer the guest the opportunity to join the hotel's **loyalty scheme** or 'membership club'. Such a scheme may simply enable the hotel to keep in touch with the guest, by sending printed or e-mail newsletters, special offers and invitations to particular events). It may also create incentives for return visits: select offers for other hotels in the chain; discounts on future stays, or meals in the hotel restaurant; member privileges (eg pre-arrival room allocation, free newspapers or a fruit basket) on future stays; or a 'points scheme' whereby points are accumulated with each stay (or amount spent in the hotel), towards discount vouchers, free nights or gifts.

E X A M P L E

If you have access to the Internet, you might like to check out some of hotel loyalty programmes, and the rewards they offer to 'frequent stayers'. For example:

- The Hyatt Gold Passport membership: http://goldpassport.hyatt.com/gp/en
- The Marriott Rewards programme: http://www.marriott.com/rewards/rewards-program.mi
- The InterContinental Priority Club: http://www.ichotelsgroup.com/h/d/pc/1/en/home

4.8 Referred sales

Sales may be referred or directed to the hotel, by:

- **Travel agents**, **hotel booking agents** and **tourist information** *bureaux*, as discussed in Chapter 2: such referrals are usually reward by the payment of **commission** on the sale.

- The **central reservation office** or central booking office of a hotel group, also discussed in Chapter 2.

- **Satisfied guests**, who recommend the hotel to friends, relatives or business associates. In such a case, of course, commission would not be paid for the referral – but the referral should be noted on the guest history card, and some acknowledgement may be made on the guest's next visit.

5 Handling guest problems, feedback and complaints

Most guests aren't 'difficult'. They come to the hotel with a legitimate set of expectations (wanting a safe and pleasant stay in the type and standard of accommodation they have booked) – and as long as they are broadly satisfied, things will go smoothly. However, there will inevitably be some guests who have unrealistic expectations; demand the impossible; feel the need to 'throw their weight around' (perhaps because they are stressed or insecure in unfamiliar surroundings and circumstances, or frustrated at not being able to speak the language); are aggressive and rude in making demands or complaints; or perhaps just enjoy fault-finding and complaining. It's a hazard of the job.

Nevertheless, the most unpleasant guest may have a genuine problem, there may be a kernel of truth to an exaggerated complaint – something the hotel can put right or learn from. And just because a guest is aggressive or rude, it does not give hotel staff licence to be the same! This is not an easy area to learn, or to put into practice, but it is crucial to maintaining a pleasant atmosphere and guest satisfaction.

F O R   D I S C U S S I O N

- "There is no such thing as a 'problem guest': only 'a guest with a problem'."
- "The customer may not always be right – but (s)he always has a choice."

Do you agree with these statements? How would you explain the fine distinctions made by each one?

What difference would it make to customer service, if Front Office staff tried to remember these sayings and put them into practice?

5.1 Problems that may inconvenience guests

A range of problems may cause guests inconvenience, or lessen their enjoyment. Some of these will be created by the hotel, or directly within the control of the hotel – and some won't. Front Office staff may, nevertheless, have to handle a complaint about either sort of problem, and do their best to assist the guest in a range of circumstances.

Baker, Bradley & Huyton (Principles of Hotel Front Office Operations) list the following examples of problems that may inconvenience guests.

Cause of problem	Examples
Guests' lack of familiarity with hotel policy or terminology	▪ A guest arrives before check-out time: no room is available until midday ▪ A guest arrives after 6 pm release time: the room has been re-let ▪ A guest has booked a double room, but expects two single beds
Fully booked hotel	▪ A guest refuses to believe that no room is available
Lack of service from front desk staff	▪ A guest is ignored on arrival at front desk ▪ A guest telephoning front desk is kept on hold for a long time
Errors made by the hotel	▪ A guest books a twin room and is given a double ▪ A guest is overcharged ▪ A guest receives slow (or discourteous) service ▪ A guest does not receive a requested early morning call
External factors (outside the hotel's control)	▪ A guest's luggage has been lost by an airline ▪ A guest has mislaid their safe deposit key ▪ A guest has misplaced prescription medication

A C T I V I T Y   5   5   m i n u t e s

Come up with *two* more examples of potential problems inconveniencing guests under each of the headings given in the table above.

In addition to the problems mentioned by *Baker et al*, two of the key causes of problems resulting in a complaint include:

- **Something 'wrong' with the room**. This may be a matter of the expectations or perceptions of the guest: (s)he doesn't like the view, or the décor, or the room is smaller than expected. However, there may also be genuine faults: the room hasn't been adequately cleaned; the air-conditioning or heating doesn't work properly; the window doesn't open; the television doesn't work; the room is noisy because it overlooks the bar; and so on.

- **Disruptive behaviour by other guests**. Many hotels post notices, or statements in their in-room information packs, requesting guests to respect the comfort of other guests, by reducing noise to acceptable levels after 11.00 pm at night. However, not all guests will notice or heed these requests, and their neighbours may be unable to enjoy the peace, relaxation and sleep they are entitled to.

From our lists of potential problems, you should be able to see that some are definitely the responsibility or 'fault' of the hotel. If a guest complains, Front Office staff will need to acknowledge the fact and try to put the matter right. With other issues, however, the hotel may well feel that the *guest* is responsible and has no legitimate right either to complain or to expect the hotel to do something about his problem. Even so, it is the responsibility of Front Office to make each guest's stay as successful as possible, and to create a positive impression of the hotel's willingness to look after its guests' needs.

5.2 Handling guest complaints

Reception will often be the first port of call for guest complaints.

The first point to remember is that the hotel *wants* and *welcomes* guest feedback – including negative feedback – as a tool for improving service and satisfaction in future. It needs to **encourage complaints**, by making it clear to guests that they can come to reception with any needs or problems they may have – and by handling each complaint positively, calmly and constructively (whether or not the customer is 'right').

Minor complaints can often be dealt with by the front desk.

- If there has been an error in the posting of charges, for example, the receptionist can show prompt willingness to investigate; acknowledge any error which is confirmed (while stating that it doesn't happen often); apologise for the inconvenience; and **correct** the room account.

- If something is wrong with the **room**, the receptionist can either have the guest moved to a new room (where required and available), or ensure that housekeeping or maintenance are alerted to fix the problem. (The room may lack soap or towels, say, or an appliance may need replacing.)

- If there has been a failure of service in some way, the receptionist may be authorised by management to offer some specific type and level of **recompense**: a discount on the room or meal, perhaps, or a voucher for an extra service (which has the virtue of not *losing* the hotel revenue).

- If the guest has a problem **unrelated to the hotel** (eg has left personal belongings in a taxi or had luggage mislaid by the airline), the front desk may provide a listening ear, empathy, guidance and assistance where possible – without taking on responsibility for the problem.

If minor complaints are handled efficiently and with good grace, the guest will often leave feeling both heard and well served – and with no lingering worries or negative feelings about the hotel.

In some circumstances, however, a guest may be **angry, aggressive or upset** – or the problem may be more **serious** or **complicated**, requiring in-depth explanation and investigation: the hotel may have lost a guest's luggage or laundry, say. These situations require more sensitive handling.

- If possible, the receptionist should seek to **handle the matter away from other guests**, who may be disrupted or upset by the 'scene' or the complaint. The complaining guest may be invited to draw aside, or to enter a back office or lounge area. If necessary, (s)he may be asked to wait a moment while the duty manager is called to deal with the matter, or the problem is investigated, or while the receptionist finds someone else to cover the front desk while (s)he deals with the issue.

- The receptionist, guest relations officer or duty manager must first of all **hear the details of the complaint**: showing that (s)he is listening attentively; and refraining from interrupting or commenting until the guest is finished. (S)he can then ask supportive questions, to gather details and make sure that (s)he has understood the substance of the complaint, taking notes if required.

- It may also help to **summarise** briefly the main points of the guest's complaint and how (s)he feels about it ('You weren't able to sleep last night because of the noise in the room next door, and I understand that that was very stressful and upsetting for you.') This helps the guest to feel genuinely heard and understood – and may also help to eliminate some of emotion.

BPP
LEARNING MEDIA

- The person handling the complaint should give a **short**, **clear apology** for the upset, frustration or inconvenience experienced by the guest – without being drawn into any explanations, excuses, implied (or direct) criticism of the hotel or blaming of others. The apology is intended to demonstrate understanding of the guest's situation, *not* an admission of guilt or responsibility. ('I am sorry you have been inconvenienced.' ... 'I am sorry to have kept you waiting.')

- The next step is to **reassure the guest** that the complaint will be fairly and constructively handled: explaining what action will be taken (even if, initially, this is just an investigation into the problem) and within what time frame.

- The complaint handler should then **initiate action** to investigate or resolve the problem, or to offer recompense – seeking whatever information, assistance or authorisation may be required. If the process takes time, the guest should be kept informed as to what is going on.

- Finally, the complaint handler should **inform the guest** what has been done or decided. If a receptionist has been handling the matter so far, this final task may be referred to a duty manager or guest relations person – especially if the outcome is not likely to satisfy the guest (eg nothing can be done, or the guest has been found to be in the wrong).

- As follow-up, the Front Office person may need to **check** that the promised action has indeed been taken by other parties (eg maintenance has fixed the guest's TV). (S)he should also re-contact the guest, after everything has 'cooled off', to ensure that the guest is satisfied.

- The incident should be recorded in an **incident log**, for later analysis: there may need to be a change of policy for handling the complaint – or for preventing the problem from recurring. In addition, an incoming shift may need to be made aware of the issue.

FOR DISCUSSION

Suggest what can be *done* to solve each of the potential guest problems listed in section 5.1 above, in such a way as to give the best possible outcome for the guest and for the hotel.

5.3 Interpersonal skills for handling complaints

Particularly well-developed interpersonal skills are required for handling complaints and other 'awkward' situations. A person handling a complaint needs to be able to:

- **Control his or her emotions**, in order to remain calm – especially since the guest may *not* be calm! – and to avoid taking the complaint personally.

- **Control his or her body language**: maintaining a confident and attentive posture; calm gestures; appropriate facial expressions (without annoyance or disbelief); and a firm, steady tone of voice.

- **Listen attentively** (so that the guest feels genuinely heard) but at the same time critically (so that the problem can be properly analysed).

- **Demonstrate empathy**: an ability to understand the guest's position. This can be shown by reflecting back or summarising the guest's complaint – not merely repeating the words, but summing up the issue and the guest's underlying feelings about it.

- **Demonstrate tact and discretion**: respecting guest privacy and confidentiality; not exposing the guest to 'loss of face' (eg if they are in the wrong).

- **Communicate assertively**: that is, communicating calmly but firmly, balancing respect for the rights of the other person with respect for one's own rights. **Assertiveness** *isn't* the same as aggressiveness. It means avoiding aggressiveness or defensiveness on the one hand – and 'grovelling' or 'victimhood' on the other. If a guest is being abusive, you have a right to request that he moderate his tone and language. If a guest has made an error, or failed to observe the policy of the hotel, you can calmly but firmly state this fact.

- **Service orientation**. Perhaps the most important attribute in handling a guest complaint constructively is *willingness* to do so, a professional 'can do' attitude and the awareness that Front Office is the 'hub' for guest issues. (If a guest has a complaint about the room, the answer is *not*: 'That's not my problem: you'll have to talk to maintenance/housekeeping'.)

5.4 Gathering and using guest feedback

We noted earlier that it is in the hotel's interests to get feedback from guests – whether positive or negative in order to:

- Improve the hotel's marketing and selling, by identifying factors that guests particularly value and enjoy about the hotel.

- Improve the hotel's service to guests, by identifying strengths and weaknesses, areas for learning and improvement, and areas for staff training.

- Maintain dialogue with guests: making them feel valued and heard, and encouraging them to develop loyalty to the hotel (eg through follow-up messages asking for feedback after their stay).

The hotel may gather feedback from guests in various ways.

- **Guest and occupancy statistics** will provide indirect indicators of whether guests are satisfied or not: repeat stays, for example, will generally indicate satisfied guests, where one-off stays (and even worse, the withdrawal of repeat business) will generally indicate dissatisfaction.

- **Informal comments** made by guests at reception, or directly to Front Office staff, are an excellent source of informal feedback. Staff should keep their ears open for such responses, and invite it where possible: 'Are you enjoying your stay with us?', 'Is there anything we can do to make your stay more enjoyable?', or 'Have you enjoyed your stay with us – and can we hope to see you again?' This may also be the particular responsibility of the Guest Relations Officer, if any.

- **Unsolicited feedback** may be provided by guests who have had particularly positive or negative experiences with the hotel: writing a letter or e-mail of thanks or complaint after their stay, for example. This is a particularly valuable form of review, because it reflects strong and genuine feelings (with the guest having had time to think about the matter), and because it highlights 'critical incidents' that may not have been picked up by management. Critical incidents offer excellent case studies of what the hotel has done right – or wrong – for analysis and training purposes.

- **Online hotel review sites and traveller 'blogs'**. Many travellers now record their experiences (positive and negative) of hotels on Internet sites such as tripadvisor.com, or on their own 'blog' (web log, or online diary). Hotels can monitor these (by doing a search on their own name). Large hotels may employ a media monitoring agency to check reviews and media mentions (online and in newspapers, magazines and travel journals) for them.

- **Feedback questionnaires** may be left in guest rooms, included in departure packs, or forwarded to them after their stay (by e-mail or mail). This is a systematic way of gathering information about how the guest experienced the various elements of the hotel 'package', as well as information for marketing purposes (such as how the guest 'heard about' the hotel). Such surveys make it optional for guests to give their names: comments are likely to be more honest if they are confidential. (This is perhaps why comments in the 'Visitor's book' of old-fashioned guest houses are so often bland and non-committal...)

EXAMPLE

'A Word from the FOM'

In our hotel we gather guest feedback in a number of ways. We get housekeeping to leave what we call 'Pillow Talk' forms on guests' pillows: a simple form inviting them to tell us how they have enjoyed their stay and what we could do better. On departure, reception staff ask 'How was your stay'? We also send guests a feedback form by e-mail after their stay. And we monitor travel review sites like Trip Advisor.

We discuss any significant feedback received at our staff meetings, and review 'critical incidents'. Guests may alert us to the need for maintenance and refurbishment of certain rooms. And of course, we share complimentary feedback with staff – because they deserve the recognition.

ACTIVITY 6   20 minutes

If you have access to the Internet, you may like to browse:

(a)   The online feedback forms sent to guests by hotels for their comments. For example:

   (i)   http://www.anabellahotel.com/comments.htm
   (ii)   http://www.balidynasty.com/hotel/guest-feed-back

(b)   Third-party web sites on which travellers can review their hotel experiences (and which should, therefore, be monitored by hotels, to see what guests are saying 'behind their backs', as it were!). For example:

   http://www.tripadvisor.com

6   Staff development and management

6.1   Induction or orientation of new staff

DEFINITION

Induction is the process whereby a new member of staff is formally introduced and integrated into an organisation, and begins the process of orientation, settling in and training.

The main **purposes of induction** are:

- To help new recruits to find their bearings in a new job and environment
- To help new recruits begin to 'fit in' to the culture and norms of the team and hotel
- To support recruits in beginning to do the job
- To identify on-going training and development needs.

A **general plan for induction**, which may be formulated by the Front Office manager, and carried out by the duty manager or shift supervisor, will therefore include:

- Pinpointing the areas that the recruit will have to learn about in order to start work in the job. Some more complex tasks or skills may be identified as areas for later study or training.

- Showing the recruit round the hotel premises and facilities, so that (s)he can get her bearings.

- Briefing the recruit on relevant employment policies and procedures: conditions of employment, sickness and holiday absences, shift arrangements, health and safety rules, etc.

- Introduction to key people in the hotel: Front Office managers, co-workers, the heads of food and beverage, housekeeping, maintenance and security and so on.

- Appointing a particular colleague or supervisor as a 'mentor', to observe and assist, answer queries, start training/coaching and generally 'show the recruit the ropes'

- Introducing hotel procedures, policies and systems (perhaps at first by observing or 'shadowing' an experienced employee).

- Planning and implementing appropriate training programmes to familiarise the recruit with the hotel product, procedures, documentation and systems (especially if a Premises Management System is used), and related skills.

- Monitoring initial progress, as demonstrated by performance, and as reported by the recruit's coach, mentor or supervisor. This is the beginning of an on-going cycle of feedback, review, problem-solving and learning/training planning...

ACTIVITY 7   20 minutes

Select any Front Office role that you are familiar with, or that interests you, and draw up a list of items for inclusion in the induction course of a new recruit to that role or department. Use the following grid as a framework. (You might like to photocopy this grid and attempt the exercise for more than one role: good practice for exam questions...)

ROLE/DEPARTMENT: ....

Knowledge/skill area	Items to be covered in training
Hotel personnel and structures	
Hotel procedures	
Documentation, forms, 'house style'	
Personal and social skills	
Technical skills	

Selling skills (where relevant)	
Health, safety and security	

6.2 Staff training and development

Note that induction is only the beginning of an on-going process of training and development.

DEFINITION

Training is a formal learning experience designed to enhance a person's job performance.

Development includes a wider range of learning activities and experience to enhance employees' portfolio of competence, experience and capability, with a view to personal, professional or career progression.

In order to ensure that training meets the real needs of the hotel, the training manager, Front Office manager or other person responsible for staff development should adopt a systematic approach.

STEP 1   Identify and define staff members' **learning or training needs**, based on (a) what they *need* to be able to do to perform their job competently and (b) what they can *currently* do.

STEP 2   **Define the learning required** – in other words, specify the knowledge, skills or competences that have to be acquired. (For technical training, this is not difficult: for example, all Front Office staff must be conversant with the use of the Fidelio Hotel Management System. It may be more difficult for social skills…)

STEP 3   **Define training objectives** – what must be learned and what trainees must be able to do after the training exercise.

STEP 4   **Plan training programmes**:

- Who provides the training
- Where the training takes place
- What training approaches, techniques, styles and technologies will be used.

STEP 5   **Implement the training programme**

STEP 6   **Monitor**, **review and evaluate** training. Has it been successful in achieving the learning objectives? (If not, go back to Step 1 in a continuous cycle…)

Training methods

There is a wide variety of training methods, both: 'off the job' training (classroom lectures and instruction, computer-based training and e-learning); and '**on the job' training** (learning while doing the work itself). While a hotel may send staff on 'courses' of various kinds from time-to-time, they mostly use on-the-job training methods, including the following.

Training method	Explanation
Demonstration/ instruction	A more experienced employee tells trainees what to do, shows them how it is done, and then lets them try it for themselves, giving guidance and correction as required. This works well for learning computerised systems, for example.
Coaching	Trainees are put under the guidance of an experienced employee who shows them how to perform tasks and works with them to plan and implement learning activities. The coach gives advice, instruction, demonstration and supervised practice. In a Front Office setting, (s)he may use case studies, role plays and other simulated work tasks – especially for training in social skills and problem-solving (which are 'risky' to practise in real life situations...) The coach can also act as a role model and guide to the kinds of attitudes and values that underlie effective social skills and behaviours.
Job rotation	Trainees may be moved from one role to another, to allow them to gain experience of a range of areas. A cashier might start out in guest accounting, for example, or a receptionist in reservations, to give them a good grounding in procedures prior to more challenging guest contact. In some hotels, staff rotate through all Front Office roles, for greater variety and skill development.
'Assistant to' or work shadowing	A staff member may be appointed as assistant to a more senior or experienced person, to gain experience of a new or more demanding role. A receptionist may 'shadow' the Senior Receptionist, for example, while a senior receptionist may be an 'assistant duty manager'.

The **advantage of on-the-job training** is that it takes immediate account of job context: you don't have to learn something in a classroom and then *transfer* it to the systems, people and settings of your job (which isn't always easy). It particularly suits people who prefer 'hands on' learning (though it is more difficult for those who prefer to get theory under their belts *before* the practical). And it is excellent for developing social skills and working relationships, since they are built into the training from the start.

The **advantage of off-the-job training** (like using this Study Guide!) is that it suits theoretical/ reflective learners; gives a strong understanding of the underlying principles; and ensures that people learn 'best practice' – rather than the 'short cuts' that an on-the-job coach might teach them. In addition, it avoids the risk of throwing trainees in at the deep end, where their errors ('learning opportunities'!) may have serious consequences – such as a dissatisfied guest. And it gives them focused learning time, without the thousand-and-one distractions and demands of a busy Front Office working day.

FOR DISCUSSION

What methods have been used in your own hospitality and tourism studies and training? How effective are they? What further learning opportunities might you be able to access, in order to improve your knowledge, skills and confidence?

6.3 Managing Front Office quality

Having talked about the importance of Front Office roles in selling and promoting the hotel, it is worth emphasising that the hotel will need to monitor and control the quality of Front Office performance. It can't afford to have surly, lazy or unco-operative staff alienating customers!

Briefly, therefore, there are a number of mechanisms by which the Front Office manager (and/or the management of the hotel) can monitor, control and maintain staff performance.

- **Policies**, **rules and standards**. The Front Office should have policy and procedures manuals setting out detailed rules and protocols for the conduct of staff, and how they should go about their roles. This is important, because people need to know exactly what is expected of them, in order to monitor and manage their own performance standards, and for any correction or discipline (if they fall below the expected standard) to be fair and reasonable.

- **Supervision**. Front Office staff will be monitored and supervised by shift supervisors or other senior members of staff, to ensure (a) that they are performing correctly and to standard and (b) to offer help, guidance and assistance if necessary. This is particularly important because of the money-handling role of Front Office personnel: supervision (and authorisations and counter-signatures and so on) is required to ensure that protocols are followed, and that the hotel is protected from theft and fraud (and from unfounded allegations of theft and fraud).

- **Performance management**. The performance of staff will regularly be reviewed and appraised by each staff member's supervisor or manager (a process known as performance **appraisal** or staff appraisal). The purpose of this should not just be the critical evaluation of past performance, but the identification and solving of performance problems; the identification of learning and improvement needs; and planning of future training and development. At the same time, 'performance management' also includes '**discipline**': that is, the investigation of any performance shortfalls, poor conduct or attitude, with a view to planning for improvement, and warning the staff member of the potential consequences of failing to improve. This process, after several warnings, may eventually result in the dismissal of a staff member who is unable or unwilling to improve.

- **Motivation**. Front Office staff need to be fairly rewarded for their work. At the same time, the reward system of the hotel should allow for incentives to *extra* levels of performance and positive attitude. Supervisors and managers should not hesitate to offer praise and recognition for good performance – and 'heroic' service to guests. However, the hotel may also offer more tangible rewards: Staff Member of the Month awards, with prizes for the staff member most nominated for praise by guests, for example; or 'up-sell' points awarded to staff members who sell upgrades, towards vouchers or gifts.

- **Empowering and equipping staff**. Staff need to be supported in quality performance by management. They need to be given the discretion to be flexible and take the initiative where required to meet guests' needs – without being 'punished' for breaking overly tight procedures. (This is sometimes called '**empowerment**': giving staff authority, within guidelines, for the decisions they need to take to serve guests better.) They need to be provided with adequate resources (including staffing) and technology (eg efficient systems) to do the work that is expected of them. The hotel management can't expect them to work miracles on their own.

S U M M A R Y

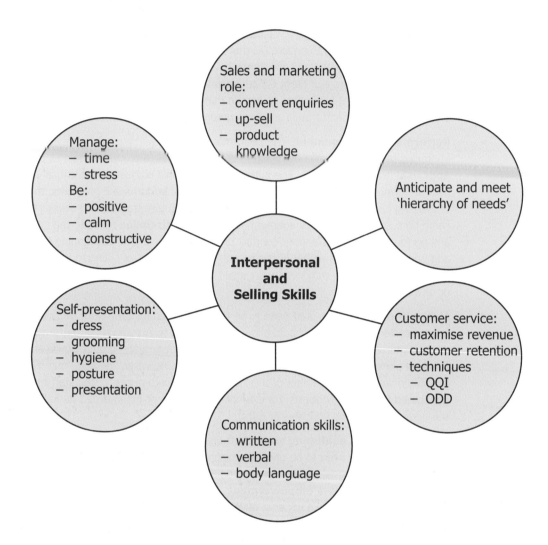

SELF-TEST QUESTIONS

1 What is 'relationship marketing'?

2 Identify five benefits of Front Office selling.

3 List *Maslow's* five human needs.

4 What is 'personal hygiene' and why is it important in Front Office roles?

5 'Have you made a reservation?' is an example of what kind of question?

6 What is (a) rapport and (b) empathy?

7 What is (a) a USP and (b) QQI, in the context of selling?

8 Persuading a guest to upgrade is called cross-selling. True or False?

9 List five ways of gathering guest feedback.

10 Identify four approaches to on-the-job training.

SELF-TEST ANSWERS

1 Relationship marketing is establishing a long-term mutually-satisfying relationship with customers, rather than just a one-off sales transaction

2 Increased occupancy; maximised revenue; customer retention/loyalty; new business; and staff satisfaction/retention.

3 Physiological, safety, love/social, esteem, self-actualisation

4 Personal hygiene is cleanliness: avoiding perspiration stains, body odour, bad breath, unclean hair and so on. It is important to create a positive impression of the hotel, and to avoid unpleasantness for guests.

5 Closed

6 Rapport is a sense of connection, or 'getting on with' someone. Empathy is demonstrating that you can appreciate the other person's viewpoint, eg by reflecting back or summarising what they say/feel.

7 Unique Selling Proposition; Quality, Quote, Invite

8 False. Upgrading is 'up-selling' (or 'bottom-up' selling).

9 Statistics; informal comments; unsolicited feedback; online reviews; feedback questionnaires.

10 Demonstration and instruction; coaching; job rotation; and assistant-to positions.

ANSWERS TO ACTIVITIES

1   Customer retention and loyalty are important for a number of reasons.

- It costs the hotel less to retain an existing satisfied customer (who already knows about the hotel, is open to marketing information about it and is already predisposed to choose it) than to win a new customer (by 'cold' advertising and information, in competition with lots of other providers). Customer retention is a highly profitable way of maintaining occupancy.

- Returning customers are often more amenable to the idea of spending more, staying longer, trying a higher grade of room, consuming more services (especially if given the incentive of special offers as part of a loyalty rewards scheme).

- Returning customers have known details, needs and preferences, which streamlines Front Office procedures (eg the need for credit checking) and makes it easier to provide personalised service (which may in turn contribute to even greater loyalty).

- Loyal customers are a significant source of positive word-of-mouth promotion, recommendations and referrals (especially if given the incentive of 'introduce a friend' offers and rewards).

- Loyal customers are more likely to support the hotel in various ways: providing feedback information; continuing to support the hotel following a crisis or bad publicity; and so on.

2   Some ideas may be as follows.

(a)   Elderly couple: room on the ground floor; quiet room; ability to dine in restaurant; security; assistance with luggage; assistance organising sightseeing activities.

(b)   Teenagers plus three-year old: family room or adjoining rooms; access to baby-sitting; organised activities for kids; cot and/or high chair for the baby; supervised swimming pool; assistance with car hire.

(c)   Single female business traveller: separate floor; safety/security; freedom from 'hassle' by men; room-service; in-room hairdryer and toiletries; clothes pressing service; credit facility; business facilities.

(d)   American CEO: ability to use/exchange US dollars; access to business facilities (executive floor); assistance with organising sight-seeing, car hire.

3   You might have gathered that the emotions convey (from left to right): hard of hearing (and frustrated by it); upset, sad or homesick; anxious about the time (perhaps about to miss a transport connection if the receptionist doesn't hurry up); relaxed and happy; on holiday and determined to have a good time; and happy and satisfied with the service.

The second part of the activity does not have an answer: your observations and reflections will, however, be a good learning opportunity.

4   Signals of being willing and able to upgrade may include: driving an expensive car (or arriving in a limousine); having expensive luggage or clothes; possessing a lot of luggage (need for extra wardrobe space); looking tired and in need of pampering; indicating that the company will be paying for the room.

5 You should have come up with your own examples, but here are some more:

Lack of familiarity with policy or terminology: guest checking-out late; guest expecting meals to be included when they aren't.

Fully booked hotel: guest objecting to being 'booked out' or re-located; group guests objecting to sharing.

Lack of service: guest is kept in a queue at front desk; no porter is available to help with luggage.

Errors by the hotel: a guest receives the wrong newspaper; a guest is disturbed by late-night noise and the hotel does nothing about it.

External factors: a guest has left belongings in a bus or taxi; a guest's sightseeing tour has been cancelled.

6 No answer is given for this activity, as it involves your own research.

7 No answer is given for this activity, as it involves your own choice of role on which to focus. There is plenty of material, in relation to the roles and requirements of the different jobs, from what you have learned so far in this Study Guide. The activity doesn't require you to have an in-depth knowledge of induction or training: merely to know what a given role involves, and the kinds of skills and attributes that a new recruit will need.

PRACTICE EXAMINATION

This is a real past CTH examination. Once you have completed your studies, you should attempt this under exam conditions. That means allowing yourself the full time available of 2½ hours. Do not look at the suggested answers until you have finished.

QUESTION PRACTICE

CTH diploma courses are all assessed by examination. This method of assessment is used as it is considered to be the fairest method to ensure that students have learnt the things they have been taught.

On the following pages you will find a practice exam for this subject. When you have worked through this study guide and answered the self-test questions you should make a full attempt at the practice exam, preferably under exam conditions. This will give you the opportunity to practise questions in the CTH exam format.

The exam questions in this paper are examples of this subject's questions. The answers provided are notes used by the examiners when marking the exam papers. They are not complete specimen answers but are of the type and style expected. In some cases there is a list of bullet points and in others more text or essay style, however they are representative of the content expected in your responses. Information given contains the main points required by the Chief Examiner.

SECTION 1 – A1 - A10 (2 mark questions)

These questions are looking for factual information and test concise and logical thinking. As a general rule, for a two mark question CTH is looking for one or two word answers or maybe a short sentence. Therefore either text or bullet points will be accepted. If two points are asked for, marks will be allocated for each point. If only one answer is asked for we would expect a short sentence.

Here we are trying to assess your knowledge of the subject and to identify if you can recall the basic principles, methods, techniques and terminology linked to the subject.

SECTION 2 – A11-A15 (4 mark questions)

These questions are looking for factual information and test concise and logical thinking. As a general rule, CTH is looking for bullet points or a short paragraph for the answer to a four mark question. If two or four points are asked for, marks will be allocated for each point. If only one answer is asked for we would expect a few sentences or a short paragraph.

Here we are trying to assess your knowledge of the subject and to identify if you understand and can demonstrate how principles, methods and techniques can be used.

SECTION 3 – B1 (20 mark questions)

These 20 mark questions are looking for factual information and how those facts can be applied to both the subject and the hospitality industry. We expect to see essay style answers to show your knowledge of the subject and its application.

From this section you need to select three questions from a choice of five. **Do not answer more than three as only the first three answers will be marked.** These are essay style questions so you should select the three that you feel you are the most prepared for. No matter how good the answer is, if it does not answer the question you will not be given any marks – marks are only allocated when the answer matches the question.

If you run out of time in the exam jot down the essential points that you intended to include; the examiner will allocate marks for any correct information given.

It is difficult to assess how much you are required to write for a 20 mark question – some people can answer in a page, other people need several pages. What is important is that you answer the question asked – it is about the quality of the answer not the quantity written.

20 mark questions

The following descriptors give you information on the CTH marking scheme and what you need to aim for at each level.

Grade	Explanation
Level 4 (15-20)	Demonstrates knowledge of analysis and evaluation of the subject
Level 3 (11-15)	Demonstrates knowledge of application of the subject
Level 2 (6-10)	Demonstrates knowledge and comprehension of the subject
Level 1 (1-5)	Does not demonstrate knowledge and understanding of the subject

Level descriptors

The following level descriptors give you information on what you need to aim for at each grade.

Grade	Explanation
Distinction	Demonstrates knowledge of analysis and evaluation of the subject
Merit	Demonstrates knowledge of application of the subject
Pass	Demonstrates knowledge and comprehension of the subject
Fail	Does not demonstrate knowledge and understanding of the subject

EXAMINATION

CTH Diploma in Hotel Management

Subject: **Front Office Operations (DHM 122)**

Series: **January 2008**

Time Allowed: **2.5 hours**

Instructions:

You are allowed **TEN MINUTES** to read through this examination paper before the commencement of the examination. Please read the questions carefully, paying particular attention to the marks allocated to each question or part of a question, and taking account of any special instructions or requirements laid down in any of the questions.

This Examination Paper contains **TWO SECTIONS**.

Answer **ALL** questions in **Section A**.

Answer any **THREE** questions in **Section B**.

Marks allocation

Section A = 40% of the module grade
Section B = 60% of the module grade

SECTION A

Answer **all** questions in this section. This section carries a total of **40** marks.

A1   What information does a density chart record?

    a)   Room allocation by guest name
    b)   Availability of each room type
    c)   Current room occupants
    d)   A specific room reservations.   **(2 marks)**

A2   What is a central reservation system?

    a)   A system which groups bookings to enable customers to get group rates.
    b)   A system which take reservations for all hotels in one city.
    c)   A system which takes reservations for all hotels in one chain.
    d)   A system which allows all of an hotel's bookings to be stored on one computer.   **(2 marks)**

A3   Front office staff prepare a document to show which customers are expected each day. What is it called?

    a)   Bed sheet
    b)   Registration card
    c)   Arrivals list
    d)   Room status report.   **(2 marks)**

A4   Explain the term walk-in.   **(2 marks)**

A5   List four different ways a guest can settle their room account on check out.   **(2 marks)**

A6   If the hotel is overbooked why would you try to relocate one-night stays first?   **(2 marks)**

A7   How would you calculate a hotel's multiple occupancy percentage?   **(2 marks)**

A8   What is a block booking?   **(2 marks)**

A9   What is the role of the Concierge in a hotel?   **(2 marks)**

A10   Define the term posting.   **(2 marks)**

A11   Explain the advantages of an express check-out service.   **(4 marks)**

A12   Give four pieces of information a guest should be given at check-in before going to their room.   **(4 marks)**

A13   State the activities that would occur during the process of accepting a guest's valuables for storage into the hotel safe deposit box.   **(4 marks)**

A14   Give two examples of the formula used to calculate occupancy status.   **(4 marks)**

A15   List eight methods of payment which are commonly handled by front office staff.   **(4 marks)**

SECTION B

Answer any **3** questions in this section. Each question carries a total of **20** marks.

B1

a) Describe the main activities carried out by the reservations department in a large hotel. **(8 marks)**

b) Why is it important for room status information to be accurate and up-to-date? **(3 marks)**

c) Describe the methods used to communicate room status information. **(3 marks)**

d) Explain the steps that should be taken when a company wishes to open an account with an hotel. **(6 marks)**

B2

a) Draw a table to show how reception and front office communicates with all other departments in a large, luxury hotel. List the reasons why each department must liaise with reception and the specific communication methods used. **(11 marks)**

b) State how a front office department would efficiently manage the following group situations in an hotel;

   i)   advanced booking for the group
   ii)   the group's arrival
   iii)   the group's check out. **(9 marks)**

B3   All customers have different requirements and it is important as hotel employees that we understand some of these to make the guests' stay more enjoyable. Below is a list of different types of guests. List five of the different services which can be provided by a city centre hotel which will meet the specific requirements of the following guests;

a) An elderly couple on a weekend away. **(5 marks)**

b) A family with two teenage children and a three year old baby. **(5 marks)**

c) A single female business traveller. **(5 marks)**

d) An American CEO who is on business but would also like to do some local sightseeing. **(5 marks)**

B4   List and describe any four management reports that would be viewed by a front office employee and explain the value of each report to the department. **(20 marks)**

B5

a) Draw a table to list the advantages and disadvantages of using a manual billing system compared to a computerised billing system. **(14 marks)**

b) Explain the role and duties of a Night Auditor in a medium sized city centre hotel. **(6 marks)**

PRACTICE EXAMINATION
ANSWERS

SECTION A

A1   b)   Availability of each room type.

A2   c)   Takes reservations for hotels in one chain.

A3   c)   The arrival list.

A4   Customer who arrives at the hotel without a booking.

A5   Cash, personal cheque, credit card, debit card, direct billing.

A6   If you are only fully booked for the one night you do not want to lose guests for more than one night of their stay.

A7   The number of rooms occupied by more than one guest divided by the number of rooms occupied by guests (on that night).

eg. 90 rooms with 2 or 3 sleepers divided by the 100 rooms occupied times 100 gives a percentage

$$= \frac{90}{100} \times \frac{100}{1} = 90\%$$

A8   The term used for a reservation for several people at the same time, normally on the same rate, eg tours, groups or conference delegates.

(Reservations department will use a separate bulk booking form to record booking details for a group. Room allocation is usually done at this time of booking so that the group will be together on one floor).

A9   Staff member who handles luggage, mail and makes reservations and arrangements on other matters for guests or visitors including luggage delivery to rooms, looking after luggage, parking, theatre tickets, restaurant reservations, taxi etc. They work closely with reception.

A10   The term used for entering charges onto a guest's account / the process of recording transactions on a folio.

A11   No queuing at reception; when the client leaves they need only deposit the card in a special box or in the key drop and the account is finalised in their absence.

A12   Room number, where the room is, where the elevators are, how keys work, offered a wake up call, any newspapers to be ordered, any dinner reservation to be made etc.

A13   Cashier and guest each have a key.

–   Both open box together and place goods inside (sealed with signature).
–   Cashier may collect a deposit for the key.
–   A receipt is issued to guest.
–   Signatures are checked (for future ID)

A14 Room occupancy $= \dfrac{\text{total rooms sold}}{\text{total rooms available}} \times \dfrac{100}{1}$

eg room occupancy $= \dfrac{85 \text{ rooms sold}}{100 \text{ rooms available}} \times \dfrac{100}{1} = 85\%$

Sleeper occupancy $= \dfrac{\text{number of sleepers}}{\text{total possible sleepers}} \times \dfrac{100}{1} \times \dfrac{100}{150} \times \dfrac{100}{1} = 67\%$

eg. sleeper occupancy $= \dfrac{\text{actual sleepers}}{\text{potential sleepers}} \times \dfrac{100}{1} \times \dfrac{135}{200} \times \dfrac{100}{1} = 67.5\%$

Income occupancy $\dfrac{\text{actual income}}{\text{total possible income}} \times \dfrac{100}{1} \times \dfrac{400}{750} \times \dfrac{100}{1} = 53\%$

A15 Cash, personal cheque, credit card, debit card, direct billing, account to company, bank transfer, travellers cheques, travel vouchers, travel agency accounts.

SECTION B

B1

a) 1 Processes reservations by mail, telephone, telex, fax, e-mail, or central reservations system referral

2 Processes reservations from the sales office, other hotel departments, and travel agents

3 Knows the types of rooms available as well as their location and layout

4 Knows the selling status, rates, and benefits of all package plans

5 Knows the credit policy of the hotel and how to code each reservation

6 Creates and maintains reservation records by date of arrival and alphabetical listing

7 Determines room rates based on the selling tactics of the hotel

8 Prepares letters of confirmation

9 Communicates reservation information to the front desk

10 Processes cancellations and modifications and promptly relays this information to the front desk

11 Understands the hotel's policy on guaranteed reservations and no-shows

12 Processes advance deposits on reservations

13 Tracks future room availabilities on the basis of reservations

14 Helps develop room revenue and occupancy forecasts

15 Prepares expected arrival lists for front office use

16 Assists in pre-registration activities when appropriate

17 Monitors advance deposit requirements

18 Handles daily correspondence

19 Makes sure that files are kept up to date

20 Maintains a clean and neat appearance

21 Promotes goodwill by being courteous, friendly, and helpful to guests, managers, and fellow employees

22 Takes note of functions, seminars, events in local areas and know when there will be busy or slow periods.

23 Negotiates with travel agents and companies on commission rates and discounts in order for the hotel to make the highest possible revenues

b)   **Room status information**

Must be able to show whether the room is let, vacant and not ready, vacant and ready, closed for repair or decoration, so that all departments know what is happening eg reception for room allocation, special requests. Room maids/attendants and housekeepers for cleaning and checking.

c)   Methods used to convey room status information: bedroom book; bed sheet; room board; room status board; computer.

d)   To check whether the customer is creditworthy, either by obtaining satisfactory references from another supplier, or from the customer's bank. The hotel has to obtain a list of authorised users, and agree a limit for individual bills and what can be posted to account eg, accommodation, meals, laundry, and telephone calls.

1   The rate is negotiated and agreed on

2   The hotel will run a credibility check with the individual / company

3   The contract is signed between the hotel and the company. The contract will have an expiration date when rates will be reviewed.

4   The reception and reservations department will be informed of the changes and also the terms of contract.

5   The hotel will also set up their terms for instance that they cannot guarantee rooms reserved less than 24 hours in advance notice.

B2

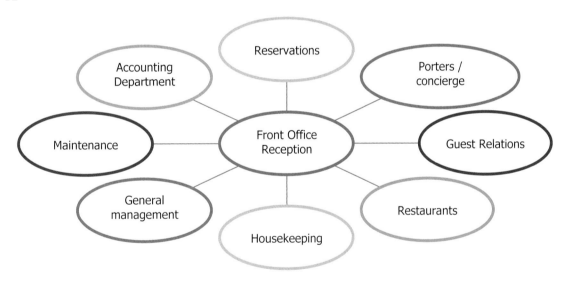

- Department name; reservation, reason; room availability arrivals list, method; arrivals and departures list.

- Department name; porters, reason; ready to carry luggage, method; arrivals and departures list.

- Department name; accounting; reason; state of business, method; guest list (memos).

- Department name; restaurant, reason; table booking, method; keep restaurant bookings diary at reception.

- Department name; housekeeping, reason; room status, method; housekeeper's report.

- Department name; general management, reason; complaints, method; telephone/memo.

- Department name; maintenance, reason; health & safety reasons, method; telephone or written report.

- Department name; guest relations, reason; VIP requests, method; in person. VIP sheet.

i) **Bookings**

- Use a bulk booking form.
- Request a rooming list later.
- Do room allocation at this time (block of rooms together).
- Collect deposits.
- Agree contract (cancellation).
- Request names, passport numbers, addresses, special requests such as dietary requests and extra beds/ cots.
- Method of payment known, if not pre-paid.
- Ask for group to have name-tags on bags.
- Meal requests / reservations

ii) **Check-in**

- Know estimated time of arrival.
- Have rooms ready.
- Have keys and packages of information ready.
- Have porters ready to carry luggage.
- Pre-registration if possible.
- Use a separate desk and senior receptionist.
- Upon arrival have the registration cards printed and ready.
- Great each group member by name, and check that registration completed correctly.
- Have porters take guests luggage to rooms and make sure that they are shown to rooms.
- Arrange for coffee, tea or welcome drinks to be available in a separate area of the reception so that the lobby is not cluttered with luggage and people during the registration process.
- Arrange for information sheets to be printed out – instead of communicating to each member individually – and place in rooms (if not already there).

iii) **Check-out**

- Give a departure time and adjust departure list.
- Check payment carefully.
- Use a separate desk.
- Collect key/return guest's valuables.
- Get questionnaires completed – a lot of feedback.
- Make sure that all extra charges have been posted to the bill such as a mini bar etc.
- Split bills as requested, and check that payments have gone through.

B3

a)   1   Easy access

2   Low floor

3   Nice quiet room with attractive view

4   Extra blankets

5   In house doctor

6   Flexible meal times

7   Low fat options in restaurant

8   Airport transfer services

9   Arranged tours

10   Discounts for over 50's in restaurants

11   Luggage carried by porters; elevators not stairs

12   Help with introduction of technological aspects in a room such as air conditioning, how to work the television

13   Provide the hotel information in bigger print that is easier to read

14   Concierge may help with reservations for shows, restaurant and local sightseeing, how to get around the city

15   Porter/ doorman to help with doors and to hail a taxi or arrange transport

b)   1   Children's TV channel
      2   Kids' menu
      3   Adjoining room
      4   Low floor
      5   Children's play area
      6   Baby food
      7   Cot
      8   Baby changing facilities
      9   Require a cot and baby chair in restaurant
      10   Room needs double/king size bed or two twin beds and a baby bed
      11   Help with luggage
      12   Baby sitting facilities
      13   Children's excursion or children's play area
      14   Family menu – more food items for children
      15   In house doctor
      16   Express check out service
      17   Elevators not stairs – easy with a pram

c)   1   Discretion when issuing keys
      2   Toiletries
      3   Ladies' magazines
      4   Business magazines
      5   Secure room away from groups of men
      6   Healthy menu in restaurant
      7   Room service female server
      8   Spa
      9   Leisure club
      10   Express check-in
      11   Business channel on TV
      12   Laundry service
      13   Security is most important, so female guests feel safe
      14   Business facilities such as an executive floor
      15   Feminine touches in room, flowers, slippers
      16   Arrange for taxi to pick up and drop off
      17   Porter to walk to room at night so as to not walk on own
      18   Internet and fax in room
      19   Express check out
      20   Spa/ gym for recreation after business

d) 1   Executive room
   2   Lap top connection
   3   Business magazines
   4   Newspaper
   5   Business channel on TV
   6   Spa
   7   Dressing gown
   8   Wake up call
   9   Concierge
   10   Business facilities, executive floor
   11   Internet/ fax in room
   12   Express checkout
   13   Concierge arranges tour/ advice on sights
   14   Car service, limousine service
   15   Gym/ spa
   16   Information package on local area

B4   Examples could include the following:

Room status report, identifies the status of all rooms in hotel and allows for staff to sell or bill accordingly. It indicates whether a room is occupied, vacant or reserved at any given time.

Departure report – enables employees to prepare bills accordingly. This list shows current expected departures. However not all guests on the list will check out, some may stay longer and others may check out earlier than expected.

Daily report – highlights previous days business levels and current daily room targets

Arrivals report – who is arriving and when – facilitates planning in relation to room planning and allocation.

Occupancy Report – room types are shown individually to show how rooms are let and which are the most popular. Discounts and complimentary rooms are listed separately so that management can ensure all reductions have been authorized and see their source and all out-of-order rooms are also shown. This assists in planning and overbooking, and shows how the hotel is progressing.

Financial reports – include sales figures and turnover which can also be presented as ratios and percentages. This form of presentation is easier to interpret than the raw figures. Reported daily to management who are practised in the assessment of financial statistics. Upper and lower limits and limits for bad debts are set by management and no action is taken unless these limits are exceeded.

Room rate discrepancy report – lists all rooms in the hotel and their current rate. Following this is the rate that was charged for the room the previous night and if there are any discrepancies, reasons for discrepancies are given. Management will review this report daily and follow up on discrepancies. By totalling the report, management is able to see better the potential revenue that was sacrificed due to these discrepancies and judge whether or not all of the reduced rates were necessary, this will help in determining future offers of these rates.

Room repairs report – informs management of any rooms that are being repaired and therefore cannot be sold. This makes the management aware of the percentage of total rooms available for sale. It also enables management to determine whether or not repairs are being completed on a timely basis.

B5

a)

Manual – Advantages	Manual – Disadvantages
▪ Basis of all systems	▪ Untidy bill (unprofessional)
▪ Easy and inexpensive	▪ Open to human error
▪ Ideal for small hotels	▪ Easy to lose vouchers
▪ It does not depend on electricity	▪ Could be messy
▪ The cost are not high	▪ The entries must be done one by one
▪ Less training time	▪ Easy to make mistakes with calculations
▪ No memory restrictions and no compatibility problems	▪ Easy to lose
▪ The 'emergency copy' is not needed	

Computers – Advantages	Computer – Disadvantages
▪ Excellent control and security	▪ Expensive (uneconomical for small hotels)
▪ Fast and efficient	▪ Time for training
▪ Can link up all management information	▪ Possible breakdown
▪ Itemised bills	▪ Noisy
▪ More secure (to see the date a password must be entered)	▪ Specialist cleaning required
▪ More accurate and less chance to make mistakes	▪ It doesn't work in case of power failure
▪ More tidy	▪ An 'emergency copy' must be done
▪ Easy to refer to	▪ It can have memory restrictions when storing all data
▪ More entries can be done at the same time	▪ It can have compatibility problems
▪ Preparing bill is quick	▪ Long training time is needed
▪ Easy to send information to different departments	▪ Initial costs are high

b) **Night Auditor**

Manages night time activities. Helps with security checks i.e.; with duty manager Checks all charges have been posted onto guest bills. Compares vouchers with tabular ledgers. Spot checks on petty cash float. Notes any unusually high bills (floor limit!) Processes early morning calls.

Night auditor is a hotel employee who typically handles both the duties of the front desk agent and some of the duties of the accounting department. This is necessitated by the fact that most fiscal days close at or around midnight, and the normal workday of the employees in the accounting department does not extend to cover this time of day.

In larger hotels, night auditors may work alongside other night-time employees, such as security officers, telephone attendants, room service attendants, and bellhops. In smaller hotels and motels, the night auditor may work alone, and may even only be 'on-call', meaning that once he or she completes running the daily reports, the auditor retires to an area away from the desk while remaining available to attend to unexpected requests from guests.

- Check that all the outstanding transactions are correct

- Check that all the bills are correct and up to date

- Check that the list of the actual guests in house is correct and up to date

- Prepare statistics and reports such as occupancy report, guest's satisfaction report and financial report

- Check that all payments are settled

- Prepare the documents and lists that would be useful the following day

- Check that wake up calls are entered in the system and that they are correct

- Take payments from early check-outs

BIBLIOGRAPHY

BIBLIOGRAPHY

The following key text books have been consulted in the preparation of this Study Guide, and referred to (where relevant) in the text.

Abbott, P & Lewry, S (2008), *Front Office: Procedures, Social Skills, Yield and Management* (second edition), Elsevier Butterworth-Heinemann.

Baker, S, Bradley, P & Huyton, J (2000), *Principles of Front Office Operations*, Cassell.

Bardi, J A (2007), *Hotel Front Office Management*, (fourth edition), John Wiley & Sons.

Baum, T (2006), *HRM for the Tourism, Hospitality and Leisure Industries,* Thomson.

BPP Learning Media (2009), *CTH Finance for Tourism and Hospitality* Study Guide, BPP Learning Media.

BPP Learning Media (2007), AAT *Health and Safety and Personal Effectiveness Combined Companion*.

Clutterbuck, D (1994), Making Customers Count: A Guide to Excellence in Customer Service, Management Books.

Dix, C & Baird, C (1998), *Front Office Operations* (fourth edition), Pearson Education.

Numerous websites have also been consulted, as cited in the text.

The author would also like to acknowledge the assistance of Ms Rachel Stockton, a hotel Front Office Manager whose experience informs the 'A Word from the FOM' features included in this Work Book.

INDEX